THE WILDERNESS YEARS

THE WILDERNESS YEARS

Newcastle United 1978–1984

Gary Sherrard

pitch

First published by Pitch Publishing, 2025
1

Pitch Publishing
9 Donnington Park,
85 Birdham Road,
Chichester, West Sussex,
PO20 7AJ

www.pitchpublishing.co.uk
info@pitchpublishing.co.uk

A CIP catalogue record is available for this book from the British Library.

ISBN 978 1 83680 145 0

Typesetting and origination by Pitch Publishing

MIX
Paper | Supporting responsible forestry
FSC® C010615

Printed and bound on FSC® certified paper in line with our continuing commitment to ethical business practices, sustainability and the environment.

Printed and bound in India by Thomson Press

Contents

To Mam and Dad, for having the good sense to have a son born in Newcastle.

Thank you to Christine and Conor, supporters as loyal as any.

To everyone at the Matt Hampson Foundation for continued inspiration.

And for heroes on the pitch and in the crowd since 1892.

Introduction:
We've Passed the Point of No Return

FEW FOOTBALL clubs have a history as full and varied as that of Newcastle United, my team by accident of breeding and birth. I was definitely born in the right place. Just not at the right time.

The Black-and-whites enjoyed a golden age in the early 20th century when they were league champions three times in five years and finished outside the top four just once in nine seasons, as well as reaching five FA Cup Finals. The next decade, too, was spent in the top half of the league, when the team's offside trap efficiency led to changes in the rules of the game to preserve it as a spectacle. The legendary Hughie Gallacher led the charge to another league title and then, in the post-war period, there were three famous Wembley wins in five years during football's most romantic era.

Those glory days, though, had long gone before I made my debut at St James' Park in the mid-70s. I just caught the end of an entertaining team created by Joe Harvey but had missed a European adventure which yielded a trophy at the first attempt. Even then, victory in the Inter-Cities Fairs Cup – a precursor of the UEFA Cup and, later, Europa League –

came off the back of an unremarkable mid-table finish in the league and was secured with three goals in the final from a player who otherwise hardly troubled opposition goalkeepers in a decade of service.

By my matchday debut, that triumph already seemed like distant history, coming at a time when my grandparents still had years of their working lives ahead of them, when my parents were still in their 20s and I needed help to get dressed in the morning.

The European conquest captivated the Geordie public like Wembley had done just over a decade earlier and we've been craving fresh glories ever since. That is the vacuum into which numerous generations have now been blooded.

My formative fan years were spent following a club which had suffered a humiliating relegation in the same year as a return to Europe and one which almost immediately appeared resigned to its new home in the wilderness with a tatty stadium and a team scratching for any sense of identity beyond wearing the famous stripes.

It would take more than mediocrity, though, to keep us on the outside. Matchday was still the highlight of the week.

There may have been more punishment than nourishment during the club's longest peacetime spell outside the top division, coinciding with an era when football in general was also short of friends, but just being there was a key part of growing up. And if you had to go through some pain in the process, well isn't that what being a teenager is all about?

What follows is the story of those six Second Division seasons from 1978 as I remember it, viewed through the lens of an impressionable young fan, with reference to diaries, scrapbooks and the shared memories. This is not a minute-by-minute match-to-match commentary – if you were there, you've suffered enough – though there is a timeline and there are facts and a few figures. Wherever possible, I have checked sources and timings but what follows remains the truth as I see it.

Chapter titles may prompt as many memories as the matchdays, as they are taken from two of the North-East's foremost cultural reference points of the 70s and early 80s, namely *Whatever Happened to the Likely Lads* and *Auf Wiedersehen Pet,* TV favourites with which we could identify emotionally, as well as regionally.

The years at the heart of the story are described in contemporary terms, when the 92 Football League teams played in Divisions One to Four with the best declared as league championship winners. They alone represented England in the European Cup while a handful of others contested the UEFA Cup and European Cup Winners' Cup tournaments. Leagues were without sponsors, television coverage was limited and stands in every ground were mainly known simply as 'New' or 'Old', 'North', 'South', 'East' or 'West'. Kick-off everywhere (except Friday night specialists Tranmere and Colchester) was at three o'clock on a Saturday, the only statistics were contained within the league tables and the list of goalscorers and the Football Pools dominated Saturday evenings in a way that even reality TV would struggle to equal.

We had no way of knowing when – or even if – our time in the wilderness would end but, from reliving the experiences in these pages, I fully understand they are part of what and where we are now, both individually and as a club. In 1978, my team descended without any idea of how deep and dark the pit would be and with no inkling that a superstar would eventually arrive to show the way back to the surface.

When visiting fans taunt with chants of 'Where were you when you were s***?' I have an answer, like all those around me on the terrace steps. I was right here, living every minute of it.

Chapter One:
Breaking Away

THE ATTRACTION of the first five steps behind the goal was always a mystery to me. From there, standing at the front of the terrace as a youngster, on those cold, bleak, concrete steps, with your feet below pitch level and chest on the perimeter boards, you literally looked up at your idols. You could see a little of everything but not much of anything in particular.

Too low to tell whether a shot at the far end of the field had flashed narrowly off target or squirted miles wide of the posts, you had to be in an eternal state of excitement because every effort on goal looked like it was going in – until it didn't.

The camber of the pitch meant you could perhaps follow the top third of a player at the other end, reduced even further occasionally as part of the portion you could see disappeared earthwards, put there by an opposition challenge or, as home fans called it, a blatant and vicious foul.

From those steps you had a close-up view of the Northumbria Constabulary and the volunteers of the St John Ambulance – or the backs of them, anyway. But you didn't hand over pocket money to watch *those* black-and-whites in action. Photographers, ballboys, programme sellers and other hawkers also got between you and the match, while stadium kiosk staff headed home that way during the second half.

So, it wasn't much of a view, which is why we ended up a few yards further back, despite a height disadvantage in comparison with many of the grown men around us.

Whatever your view, the terrace is where you *feel* matchday. You could hear it and, by God, you could smell it. The fags, the beer breath, the pies and the pee, the sweat and the sulphur. Nearer the front, there would be a one-off whiff of freshly cut grass and occasionally, if the players came close enough, you could also catch the smell of liniment as they retrieved the ball for a goal kick or a corner or when they celebrated a goal with pumping fists in front of their adoring public.

After a downpour, the fans at the front felt it from the ground up as much as head down, with water filling the void between the bottom step and the perimeter wall. If it rained on a Friday, the standing water absorbed dust and litter in a slimy film guaranteed to soak into your shoes by Saturday afternoon, too.

All the senses combined in an incident we witnessed on those front five steps in the Gallowgate End of Newcastle United's St James' Park. A pitch invader – either joining goal celebrations with the team or possibly providing entertainment for his mates with a fleeting beer-fuelled appearance on the turf – had just given the police and stewards some afternoon exercise with a runaround on the grass and then, rather than being caught and thrown out into the street, possibly via plod's charge room, he instead headed back in our direction and launched himself at full pelt from the cinder track towards the safety of numbers on the terrace.

As everyone at our end followed this action, there was a hush in full realisation of what was coming next as the fan took off from pitchside. Even the cheers which followed – you cheered anything at the expense of the local constabulary – could not fully muffle the thud of his bare feet at the conclusion of the steep drop towards sanctuary. Becher's Brook on Grand National day had a smaller fall than the plunge to the unforgiving concrete of the front five steps and a notably softer landing.

That sound was something you experienced rather than simply heard. While the escapee was swallowed up into the bosom of black-and-white kith and kin, disappearing into the mass of bodies behind the goal, I could still hear the thud echoing inside me. Concussion by proxy, it rattled my skull and I know it's still there, a pinball making regular ricochets against the other memories of afternoons spent supporting my team.

When we grew into terrace regulars with a defined place that was ours behind the Gallowgate goal, well back from the front five steps, a piece of the concrete from our perch found its way into my possession. It was a jagged fragment about an inch across and had cracked off the leading edge of a step due to wear, tear and salt tears, and I claimed it as a souvenir. It lived in a jacket pocket, taken out ceremonially and offered to the football heavens on matchdays as we reached our spot where the step continued to gently crumble under our feet.

Looking at the results, you couldn't say it was much of a lucky charm but it *was* a piece of St James' Park. And it was mine.

* * *

Perched on an abrupt hill, just a few hundred yards beyond the edge of the city centre and an easy walk from car parks, bus stops and train stations (unless you were an away fan, of course), St James' Park has always stood out as home to what one-time club chairman Sir John Hall revelled in calling the 'Geordie Nation'.

When you follow a team around the country and have had to navigate your way from transport hubs or shopping areas to another club ground before the invention of GPS and Google Maps in places like Leeds or Manchester or many of the newer venues, it makes you appreciate the location, location, location that Newcastle United possess.

We would see its concrete pillars on the approach from the north without even sitting on the top deck of the bus and St James' was just a short sprint back downhill to catch a return ride home – red buses bound for the county towns of Northumberland or yellows for the city area. It could not have been simpler.

Unlike many other league grounds which were established during Victorian times and enhanced piecemeal over the years, St James' was not hemmed in on all sides by residential rows. Unlike, say, Ewood Park in Blackburn, Coventry's old Highfield Road home or Liverpool's Anfield at the time, you didn't suddenly 'happen upon' it if you were walking. You always knew you were getting close, with clear lines of sight for its landmark stands or imposing floodlight pylons in all directions.

At Ewood Park, Highfield Road and Anfield, you could be anxiously unaware of your proximity to the stadium from even just a couple of hundred yards away, so camouflaged were they among the rhythmic brickwork of traditional local housing. Turnstiles were hidden among rows of terraced houses at places like Leicester City's Filbert Street and Luton Town's Kenilworth Road, with stadium urinals adjoining private backyards, and I remember matchday programmes being sold from a window (or maybe a coal-hole) in a brick outhouse just outside the gates of Anfield on my first visit there just as the turnstile blocks came into view at what was then the home of Europe's dominant football force.

Standing on top of a hill above a compact city centre, St James' Park is often described as a cathedral, but it is even more a medieval castle. You approach onwards and upwards right to its ramparts, with the imposing position accentuated even within its own boundaries as the original official car park behind the old West Stand during our early fan days dropped down towards the Gallowgate End like lava flow from a great volcano.

Long overdue redevelopment work has provided a rejuvenated, bustling, vibrant, energetic post-industrial modern city and the stadium has, likewise, become more impressive, its walls far higher, its approaches grander, its footprint larger and its floodlights brighter as it preserves its place as the icing on the city's cake. It is visible for miles around – across the Town Moor from the north or through Gateshead on the other side of the Tyne – keeping watch over a region which has known some tough times and whose fortunes have often been reflected in its football team.

Born in the second half of the 60s, we grew up in an unkind era for football in this country, in the middle of a 12-year drought between England appearances at a World Cup, in the days when the game put an emphasis on defensive strength over attacking skill and of some horrendous tackling to go with a thuggish, abusive and discriminatory culture on the terraces and the streets outside. But this is where we started. Even coupled with some desperate times on the field, none of it did anything to dim the lure of matchday in support of our team.

Thanks to a neighbour with a spare ticket, I first got to experience St James' Park from plastic seats in the New Stand (as it was then) on the east side of the stadium. Just a year earlier, the team had been to Wembley for the first time since the mid-century glory days and there was still a remnant of a swagger about the place. The team still fancied themselves to give anyone a game on their good days, though they finished between 7th and 12th in the league table during the opening years of the decade and the only consistency they could find was in annoyingly then finishing a remote 15th for three seasons in a row.

The last trophy had been won six years earlier during a groundbreaking journey into Europe, though even that had been born in the more regular surroundings of a mid-table finish in the league during the previous season. According to long-serving full-back Frank Clark, everyone thought it was a joke that Newcastle had even qualified for the Inter-Cities Fairs Cup. 'To be perfectly honest, we could hardly blame them,' he said. The competition's one-club-per-city rule had played into Newcastle's hands, though skipper Bobby Moncur defended the team, pointing out they had not bent any rules 'or crawled in on our bellies'.

Instead, in an age when few of the fans would have had much use for a passport, manager Joe Harvey and his team set out to enjoy to the full a first experience of Europe while also proving to doubters that they were worthy of the opportunity. They were not going to look this gift horse in the mouth. As Roger Hutchinson described it in *The Toon,* his history of the club: 'Newcastle United had traditionally fed upon a diet of passion and drama … What was needed, said the fans of the late 60s, was another burst through the pack, another full-speed chase with winners take all.'

They did it in style, too, beating some top names, starting with the elimination of a Feyenoord team that would become European Cup winners just a year later, even before their

Dutch domestic rivals at Ajax, Johan Cruyff and all, had reached that level.

Despite an inferior pedigree and a team inexperienced in the home-and-away format of the competition, not to mention the novelty of travelling abroad before foreign holidays became mainstream, Newcastle marched on. The bulk of the team, without any international football experience, had to adjust to alien conditions and diverse temperaments and would do so without any great knowledge of their opponents in an era when sport was so much more insular and short-sighted.

After beating Feyenoord, enormous crowds packed into St James' as the Geordies saw off Sporting Lisbon, Real Zaragoza, Portugal's Vitória Setubal and a Glasgow Rangers team that had already been to two European finals. The name of their last opponents, Újpest Dozsa, may not mean much now – and it would be years before I even learned which part of the name referred to their location – but the Hungarians were, at the time, embarking on a run of seven successive league titles and were described by legendary Leeds United manager Don Revie as the best team in Europe when they eliminated his side at the quarter-final stage. That attractive but ruthless Leeds team were partway through a spell in which they finished in the top two places in the Football League seven times in ten years and also had the more than adequate consolation of winning it for the first time in their history in that 1968/69 campaign, so Revie knew a good team when he saw one.

Newcastle scored three times in each of the home and away legs of the final, with skipper Moncur remarkably contributing half of the total. The Scot had played all over the field in his early days with the Magpies after turning down both Manchester United and Wolves to take the train to Tyneside and join the youth ranks. He eventually settled into a sweeper role in defence and made such a good job of it that he became a senior international and captained Scotland in just his sixth appearance.

But before the European final, Moncur had never scored for United. After it, he added just seven more to total ten in 350 games with the club.

Moncur was among five of the European heroes who stayed around long enough to play in a run to the FA Cup Final in 1974, though the appearance at Wembley would be his last before a shock free transfer (and an even more shocking switch to Wearside). Full-backs Frank Clark and David Craig, goalkeeper Iam McFaul and midfielder Tommy Gibb, who had just arrived from Partick Thistle in 1969, were the other survivors of those two campaigns. Only Craig would remain by the time Newcastle returned to Wembley in 1976, though injury unluckily kept him on the sidelines once again.

The trophy which closed the 60s provided a wave of optimism just four years after United had come out of a spell in the Second Division. They had dropped out of the top flight after conceding more than 100 goals in the 1960/61 season but the anguish was mostly forgotten thanks to those new challenges abroad, not just in 1969 but also a strong run in defence of the silverware a year later. Defeat eventually came on away goals in the quarter-final when Belgian outfit Anderlecht supplied the killer blow in the final minute when some fans were already celebrating their team's progress.

The European experience captivated Tyneside and provided Harvey with some decent cash to attract new talent. A sizeable chunk of it was used to make Scottish midfielder Jimmy Smith the club's first £100,000 signing, brought in from Aberdeen, and another part of the pot was earmarked for development of the stadium in a rare example of long-term planning.

* * *

The Leazes End terrace, to the right of where I sat for my debut, traditionally housed the hardest and hardiest of the hardcore support, as well as the noisiest and most partisan. Unchanged since the addition of a roof in the 1930s, this is where the masses roared on the cup kings, the European winners and everything in between. It was where Milburn, Mitchell and Macdonald were worshipped; where Brennan and Moncur were backed in defensive resistance; where toasts had been made recently to Bryan 'Pop' Robson and Wyn 'The Leap' Davies as it rocked during the Fairs Cup runs and where favourites like 'Jinky' Jimmy Smith and 'Terry, Terry, Terry Hibbitt on the wing' had their public.

From here, the rattles and rosettes of the flat-capped 40s and 50s had given way to the singing and swaying of the 60s, to those floodlit Fairs Cup nights when more than 50,000 Geordie voices filled the air, where the rounds of 'Blaydon Races' and the chants of 'Supermac, Supermac' were captured by television cameras, though many of its residents were shrouded in the gloom under the roof during the depths of winter.

By the time I started attending regularly a few years later, the roof had come off in more ways than one and ambition had crumbled like the old beams.

The Leazes was cut off at the knees at the exact same time that the team slumped, suffering a humiliating relegation from the top division in 1977/78. That end of the ground was unceremoniously torn down, originally as part of a redevelopment programme, but instead was left, uninspiring and forgotten, mirroring the status of the team.

There were reports and artists' impressions published in the local newspapers of what the stadium could look like by an undetermined date in the future but only a blank, bleached concrete stump of a wall remained, marking a boundary at the back of a short set of grey steps which formed a truncated terrace. With no Liverpool or Manchester United in the second tier of the league, a single corner of this ramshackle remnant was sufficient to house away fans most weeks. With an extra length of fence added a short distance away to serve as segregation before the black-and-white pen directly behind the goal. Occasionally, too, the club had to find a more fluid solution in line with the numbers of travelling fans, increasing their accommodation to include the centre, while also pinning Magpies fans into a smaller area in the other corner, outnumbered in their own home.

The state of our stadium uncannily echoed the club's declining fortunes and it was both humiliating and embarrassing that this backdrop remained for so many years. Even the fabled Keegan-Waddle-Beardsley line-up went to work in front of a terrace which would have done a disservice to a lower league club as the redevelopment took not so much a backseat as a place in a flatbed trailer behind it.

My first experience in the Leazes End was shared with a friend's family for a midweek win in the First Division over a Leeds side who had already started their own transition. They had left their greatest era behind, though they had still been good enough to reach the European Cup Final just a couple of years earlier, with Jimmy Armfield doing the rebuilding job as manager after the bruising arrival and swift departure of Brian Clough once Don Revie had taken the England post.

Their team for the trip to Tyneside featured a selection of heyday survivors including the evergreen Peter Lorimer,

Scotland international goalkeeper David Harvey and defenders Paul Reaney and Paul Madeley, while big blond centre-back Gordon McQueen led a younger generation at a club so many football fans loved to hate. Growing up, all I ever heard about them was 'Dirty Leeds' and opinions on how they had bottled it at various points under Revie but it was only after revisiting highlights of their better days in later years that I could properly appreciate just how good players like Bremner, Giles, Clarke, Gray, Madeley, Jones, Reaney, Cooper and Hunter had all actually been.

On the night we went to watch them against Newcastle, the team list in the programme must have been put together by Eric Morecambe – with all of the correct numbers and all of the correct names but just not necessarily in the right order – and the maze of arrows I drew to the correct spots made the back page look like the *Dad's Army* map rather than a precious souvenir of a Leazes debut.

We stood near the front of the big, dark, roofed terrace, to the right of goal as the players looked from the pitch. An oddity of the original stand was that, as well as running behind the goal, it also took in one corner before giving way to the New (East) Stand, built as a replacement in the early 70s for what in previous generations had been known as the Popular Side terrace.

We were, of course, blissfully unaware that we would watch that traditional home of black-and-white support reduced to a blank concrete wall which would remain through year after year of my youth. Almost everyone I have met subsequently who visited as an away fan or even viewed television highlights at the time has asked what the club planned to do there. They'd expected to see it once but then roll up for a return and enjoy new facilities in a new stand. But this was Newcastle United and that was not how the club worked.

* * *

Ground development has regularly been a hot potato in the history of Newcastle United, most notably when the club missed out on the status of a World Cup host in what turned out to be the glorious summer of 1966.

There was a fallout with the city council, which held the lease on the stadium and insisted on seeing a reshaped management structure at the club before providing further commitment. A standoff with the elder statesmen who comprised the United board followed and there was even talk of the club having to find a new site to call home.

In the end, the World Cup went ahead without Newcastle and, instead, the spotlight switched to the neighbours. Roker Park welcomed Italy, Chile and the USSR to Wearside, while an Ayresome Park stadium which was home to a Middlesbrough team freshly relegated to the Third Division enjoyed an unexpected share of global headlines when North Korea – who played all three of their group games there – sensationally beat two-time world champions Italy. Newcastle United, on the outside of the party, could only watch jealously through the steamy windows.

Ayresome, surrounded by the terraced rows of local housing, had been built at the turn of the century, with its last major improvements in the 1930s, but they still managed to beat the clock in replacing the East Stand roof and adding more than 7,500 seats before the tournament kicked off. At Roker, with its pre-war main stand designed by the renowned Archibald Leitch, they lengthened the pitch, while also adding extra seats and a roof to the Fulwell End. The reward was to join Wembley, Goodison Park and Hillsborough as a World Cup quarter-final venue, with the USSR beating Hungary there ten years after Soviet communist authorities had crushed an uprising on the streets of their Eastern Bloc neighbours.

The annexation of St James' must have hit a nerve because Newcastle City Council suddenly produced plans to involve the club, the community and the university in proposals to build a sports complex based on a redeveloped 60,000-capacity stadium. Multi-use proposals of this type are common in the 21st century but were almost unheard of back then.

Newcastle United and the city that the club represents would have been pioneers of public planning, joining forces to put sport at the very heart of the community during the redevelopment of a modern city. Obviously, though, the proposals got no further. Simon Inglis wrote in his original guide to the nation's football grounds that 'United's willingness to enter such a scheme was not the major barrier. Money was. The scheme never left the drawing board.'

The consequence was that, not only was the carpet pulled from under these ambitious plans, but also that any future development would be done without input from the council or any other major organisations and at the club's exclusive expense. They were on to another loser.

For much of the 70s and 80s, beauty at St James' was only ever in the eye of the beholder. Even then, you still had to turn a blind one to blot out the more basic elements.

As I walked up to those seats for my debut, the statement concrete construction of the unimaginatively named New Stand was just three years old. The pillars on its outside included large chipped corners as a design feature, though they looked more like they'd been modelled on careless car parking, and the stadium's most striking feature was not this new cantilever roof but, instead, the floor-to-ceiling letters which ran along the full length of the brooding Old Stand opposite.

Looking down the hill from Barrack Road, the back of the stand spelled out the name of the club and simultaneously provided a giant and obvious link to its glorious past.

In his guide to the football grounds of England and Wales, Inglis compared this façade with the side of a battleship. Forty years later, best-selling author and travel writer Bill Bryson echoed this view in the pages (and website) of the *New Yorker.* Bryson was born in Des Moines, Iowa, and followed a different ballgame as he accompanied his journalist father on the baseball circuit but when he wrote that 'the stadiums I spent my childhood in seemed to be built of iron and girders and outsized rivets, as if from old battleships', any Newcastle fan would know exactly where he was coming from, even from a spot thousands of miles east of the pitcher's arm.

The Old Stand dated from 1906, from a time when Newcastle had just become league champions for the first time and were quickly on the way to doing it again. By the years of my first appearance, it came in two shades of corrugated grey on the outside, while the seating deck was wooden and dark, very dark. 'Surely there are no stands so dark, so grey, so brooding,' Inglis commented. 'Gritty' is a word frequently used to describe the overall ambience of St James', though a rhyming alternative would be more descriptive. And accurate.

On the roof of the Old Stand was the precipitous press box, which by then had been given a grey paint job but was highlighted in white in older images. Jackie Milburn, Len Shackleton, Ivor Broadis and Dave Hilley were some of the past players who moved to this lofty perch as members of the press once they'd hung up their boots. They must have had a good head for heights and some serious stamina.

On a stadium tour with a school group in the early 80s, we climbed up to sample its rows of stacked seats and wooden window frames and it felt like the way up went on forever. The bird's-eye view was accentuated by the way the whole structure seemed to lean forward over the crowd below. In the days when just about every media man was a serious smoker, though, they were probably lucky if they could see through its windows at all.

My memories of our tour through the bowels of the stand below are of grimy corridors, dulled and flaking paint on old wooden panels, an associated smell of damp and of one lad helping himself to a pair of shorts he found stuffed behind a heating pipe in the narrow corridor. Thereafter, he strutted around in his player-issue cotton kit while the rest of us could buy only the nylon replicas. It didn't make him any better on the pitch though.

The dressing rooms felt as ancient as the rest of the stand. I think there were white wooden lockers where the players could hang up their flares, though they would not have been wide enough for the jacket lapels worn by Malcolm Macdonald and his mates.

To be able to go behind the scenes was much more unusual then than now and it was only a basic walk-through compared with the sensory overload experiences marketed today. We didn't even get to sit on the benches where Milburn, Mitchell, Macdonald, Moncur and Mick Martin had prepared for a game or celebrated a win with bottled beer in the communal bath, let alone walk on to the pitch. I don't think we even got as far as the tatty little wooden dugouts either side of the tunnel.

My entire experience of the Old Stand seats amounted to just a couple of games, including a mid-season friendly against Eastern Bloc heavyweights Dynamo Kiev, but any visit there or in the paddocks below did inspire feelings of travel through time. It looked like Edwardian Newcastle because most of it *was* Edwardian Newcastle. The only things missing were woolly moustaches, suffragettes and a Liberal government.

You could almost feel a presence of earlier times when you took your place in those tip-down wooden seats, burnished by backsides over the generations. The stand had been built shortly after Edward, playboy heir to the throne for the best part of 60 years, finally got a chance to reign over us following the death of Queen Victoria. By the time he died in 1910, Newcastle had already won the league title three times. If he'd lived for another hundred years, he would have seen them win just twice more.

When construction finished in the early years of the 20th century, with the Magpies chasing league and cup glory (in finals played mostly at Crystal Palace before the birth of Wembley Stadium), St James' Park could hold 60,000 supporters. Even 70 years later, only 4,600 of them could claim a seat, all in the upper half of this stand. When the New Stand was added shortly before I started out, there was still seating for only 8,000 fans in the whole ground.

So, the stadium of my formative years would win no awards for appearance but I did claim one for myself as 'First Fan in the Ground' and made the most of it, basking in the glow as thousands of others followed me in.

It was season 1980/81, when Newcastle, going nowhere fast in mid-table of the Second Division, suddenly found themselves just 90 minutes away from the FA Cup quarter-finals and with even lower league opposition standing in the way.

After regular failure to get beyond the opening rounds, this time the Magpies beat Sheffield Wednesday and Luton Town by matching 2-1 scorelines to reach the fifth round, where we had been drawn to face Exeter City of the Third Division.

While no one was being fitted for their Wembley suit or booking Inter-City train tickets just yet, such a plum draw had fans starting to ponder the possibilities. So much had changed – not least the standards and expectations – during the five years since the team had last made it this far that it seemed like a dream to those of us experiencing it from the terraces for the first time.

It was a curious year, with Barnsley, Bristol City, Peterborough and Wrexham – more of them to come – also among the competition's last 16 teams. There was no Manchester United, no Liverpool and no Arsenal. There was no Aston Villa, who were on their way to a first league title since World War One and no West Ham, winners at Wembley a year earlier thanks to the only header of Trevor Brooking's long career (TV commentary on one channel initially credited it to Stuart Pearson on the grounds that Brooking would not have put his head in the way, though it was edited later).

With a group of my usual mates, plus a few extras now that interest had risen with the cup run, we queued from mid-morning at the gates to the 'E' Wing paddock in the Old Stand. Crisps eaten, can of pop gone and that perforated piece of pink paper which served as a match ticket thumbed a hundred times, we eventually heard the rattle of chains and locks from behind the metal doors and, as the turnstiles finally clicked open, I was right at the front. I immediately realised what this meant and, with the entrance block located at a 90-degree angle to the terrace, as soon as it released me, I raced like a dog out of the Brough Park traps, turned right and dashed across the terrace to the fence separating us from the Centre Paddock. I stopped and looked around all four sides of the ground and for a second or two I could not see another soul. I had a claim to fame to take home.

I miss the excitement of that run from turnstiles to terrace. You don't do that as an adult or when you're in charge of your own kids. And you don't have to be so zealous in orderly, allocated, numbered seats. But that run was a part of matchday on the terrace and if you had an innocent face and didn't get body-searched on the way in, you were already jumping the queue ahead of the adults who had been stopped by stewards or police.

When the turnstile clicked, the charge was like news footage from the January sales before the days of Black Friday or the race to get up close to the stage when a major rock band comes to town. Getting to the front of the queue and hearing the mechanical click constituted the first thrill of matchday, with the emergence of the players for a warm-up and then the whistle to get the game started still to come. It's completely different when you're told where to sit on tip-up plastic perches, where there are access aisles and a constant bobbing up and down of fans in their seats.

The camaraderie is different when you're all moving together, too, holding up or clambering over each other, craning to get a better view of the pitch and your one chance to see a goal which is not going to be caught on TV cameras from any angle, let alone multiple vantage points in high-definition super-slow motion. Terraces are more spontaneous, free flowing and, in their own way, welcoming. Also, it was easier to move away if you didn't like the company you were keeping and you can't do that in a stadium of taken seats.

Another 37,000 fans followed me in for that tie against Exeter, sharing the return of cup fever for one afternoon. Pity then that we could only manage a 1-1 draw and the team had to take on the long midweek trip down to another St James Park (the one without an apostrophe) in Devon for a replay a few days later. Cup holders Tottenham were waiting after the sixth-round draw had been performed in its usual Monday lunchtime slot but a tantalising glimpse of the big time died in embarrassing style as United were beaten 4-0 in the rematch. One of the goals was scored while midfielder Kenny Wharton played the opposition attack onside by virtue of being stretched out cold on the turf closer to our goalline than they were but it was still over for another year.

* * *

As young fans, we served our apprenticeship chiefly in the paddock (is that word even used any more in all-seater stadiums?) known as 'E' Wing. At the front of the Old Stand, it was on the same corner as the away enclosure in what was left of the Leazes, so some of the likely lads liked to gather closest to the fence on that side to share their animosity. Otherwise, nothing much happened other than the enterprising few who waited for a steward to turn their back so they could go over or round the fence to access the more expensive Centre Paddock. When one of our crew did it, he ended up standing right next to us and remained part of our conversation, separated only by our black-and-white 'Berlin Wall'.

Two good friends were already season ticket holders with dads and grandads in the seats above us, which may have been one reason why we started on that side of the ground. The main consideration, though, was deciding this was probably our best chance to get in as cheaply as possible and actually see the pitch while also being away from the intimidating terraces behind the goal. I don't know now why we selected 'E' Wing rather than the identical 'A' Wing at the other end of the same stand, which we actually had to walk past to get to our entrance, though perhaps the reason was as simple as shorter queues the first time we tried because 'E' Wing was further away from the city centre. Also, the ticket office was closer to our end. So that was it, decision made and the habit formed.

I don't know who decided we should go to games unaccompanied by parents or if we even asked permission; it was probably just a decision taken as a group and our folks would have been satisfied that we were safer travelling in numbers. Going in the paddock was also an easier sell to telling them we'd be mixing it in the mayhem elsewhere.

Most weeks, there would be up to half a dozen of us, some who met at our house in time for *Football Focus* on BBC One and then *On the Ball* on ITV before going to catch the bus, and others who we met on the way. Then, as we moved on to senior school, we grew brave enough to graduate to the Gallowgate End, which had become host to home fans by default after the sacrilegious demolition of the Leazes.

The Gallowgate, in front of land which would become St James' Metro Station and now the fanzone on matchdays, was a completely spartan terrace. It had never had a roof. Like many things down St James' way, apparently there had been proposals but they'd never got off the ground after the builders put in their estimate.

Therefore, by the late 70s, our ground was without cover at both ends. It not only left the majority of supporters at the mercy of the elements in the English game's most north-easterly outpost but also allowed some of the noise to escape into the city skies rather than bounce round the rafters. It did, though, mean that the terrace crowd remained entirely visible in natural light. Kevin Keegan's memorable debut goal in 1982 and the Peter Beardsley beauty in the final game of the promotion campaign a season later would have looked very different against the backdrop of a hooded terrace, even in the bright afternoons of early and late season.

The Gallowgate End was described by Simon Inglis as dour, 'bordered by thick concrete walls like a huge open bunker'. He was not wrong. In rain, hail and snow, you could walk back towards town and spot anyone who had been at the game, not by their striped scarves but rather on the evidence of a wet head and shoulders above dry legs and feet where the huddled masses had provided partial mutual shelter on the terrace.

If you looked at the Gallowgate from anywhere else in the stadium or through the television cameras, you could observe the seething masses, watch the clapping hands and constant cigarette smoke and see the scarves, denim and donkey jackets long before replica kit took over. You could also observe the surge of bodies from back to front and the swaying from side to side and the heads and limbs when a goal was scored or a chance went begging in the goalmouth. You'd see momentary pockets of space quickly filled by staggering and bouncing groups followed by a shuffling retreat to restore some kind of equilibrium. It looked great from elsewhere in the ground, though not so good to your mam when you pointed out your position during the TV highlights the following afternoon.

But that swaying mass was what you went to the game for and what you talked about afterwards, especially if you ended up miles away from where you started, carried away from your mates on a tide of bodies. A crowd surge was like a mosh pit at a rock festival but more unpredictable and on a sloping, unforgiving, stepped concrete floor. You were pushed ten yards down the steps by blokes twice your size, copped an occasional elbow in the ribs or a hand in the face and neither you nor anyone else batted an eyelid. The lads who instigated the surge and everyone else just picked their way backwards and upwards again, then you waited for the next one. You moved as one mass and you either edged a way back to your spot or you made do with where you ended up. Either way, your eyes rarely left the action on the grass.

Sometimes in the early days, we got a good view by sitting on the concrete barriers before being catapulted off. You didn't climb back on; you'd had your warning. Safety considerations never really came into it, which made the tragic terrace events of later years even tougher to contemplate.

The mutual movements had a tribal hold and the adrenalin just heightened the excitement, with the air filled by nervous laughter as you moved one way and then the other. If a shot hit a post or a goalkeeper parried the ball in making a save, you were neither quite up nor down when another player followed up to hammer it into the net and there was a split-second where you almost recovered equilibrium before bouncing again in celebration.

It wasn't just the terrace that neglected to have a roof. The toilets at the back of the Gallowgate were open to the elements through all weathers, too, though the access to fresh air was actually among their few plus-points.

These small red-brick enclosures within the banked steps up from the turnstiles featured a wall painted black from chest height down and a shallow concrete gutter overflowing below. They wouldn't have been out of place in a zoo but they catered for thousands on the terrace, many of them straight out of the pub. I've no idea what the arrangements were if you wanted or needed to use a proper toilet; I was never brave enough to find out. There would be no toilet paper, that's for sure, because that had been lobbed across the terrace at the start of the game.

Where did the toilet roll throwers come from and why did it become such a thing? How many schools and factories experienced an embarrassing shortage on Friday afternoon and Monday morning? I can't imagine the circumstances where I would get ready to go to a game, picking up my match ticket and scarf while ensuring I also had a bog roll on my person. The rolls of paper always found a way to either tangle in the net, where they might be removed by the linesman, or land at the side of the posts, where they inconvenienced goal kicks or necessitated collection by the goalkeeper when the ball went out of play. No wonder they started wearing gloves.

The solidity of the St James' Park brickwork, the concrete and the crash barriers provided the backdrop to where we grew up as diehard fans, where going to the game and talking about it meant almost as much as the result itself.

The stadium did look down on its luck but we hadn't lived through its glory days and its appearance somehow strengthened our identity with it – 'you don't like it, we don't care' – because this was home and these were our people, the people we wanted to grow up to be and to be around. It was ours, for good or for bad.

There was nothing we could do about the timing of our introduction or the results which followed, but it was still our home in one of football's traditional hotbeds and it was still our team. As a fan, there are no transfer windows, no negotiations over terms – when you're in, you're in to stay. Welcome aboard.

Chapter Two:

The Only Thing to Look Forward to, the Past

MALCOLM MACDONALD was my first football hero. This does not make me unique. Supermac had it all – the goals, the ferocious shooting and impressive pace. He also had bandy legs, mutton chops, missing teeth and a big mouth. He was a full-blown cartoon superhero, just without the tights.

His two goals against Burnley in the 1974 FA Cup semi-final at Hillsborough epitomised what he was all about – pace, power, strength and ruthless finishing. 'Never afraid to miss,' said Supermac, the most popular southerner on Tyneside.

My dad's generation liked him because there was sense of throwback to the era of Jackie Milburn's pace, coupled with the physical threat of forwards who could freely shoulder charge goalkeepers in those days, like the challenge which broke the cheekbone of Ray Wood – who turned out to be the uncle of my primary school teacher – playing for Manchester United in the 1957 FA Cup Final.

I learned the meaning of the words arrogant and brash because of Supermac. He looked like he owned the pitch when he was on one of his days and he intimidated defenders by lurking on their shoulder, waiting for his moment in on goal.

When he was terrorising defences, no one talked about what detractors would later describe as a perceived lack of workrate on behalf of the team. Macdonald did his work around the penalty area and his team-mates supplied the ammunition; that was the deal as far as supporters were concerned. As a young fan, teamwork has nothing to do with selection and tactics; what you wanted was a chance to worship your heroes. All that really mattered was watching Supermac or hearing his name on *Final Score* every Saturday and seeing it in headlines on a Sunday morning. We wanted to see his name in the match reports for scoring goals, not for chasing back and closing down or making lay-offs for others. If he was so selfish, how did John Tudor and Alan Gowling get so many goals playing alongside him?

Macdonald's pace allowed him to chase a through ball or go for goal himself in possession from deep. He played like he spoke – flamboyant and direct. There was no need for plan B. He took the shortest route towards the opposition net and hammered the ball goalwards. Even when he rounded the last line of defence, as in the opening goal of his pair in that semi-final against Burnley, it was because the goalkeeper was still picking himself up off the floor, winded and looking for his false teeth in the dirt after getting in the way of Mac's first effort.

Just to add to the legend, comic strip hero Roy of the Rovers named Malcolm as his favourite player and he was a superstar of *Superstars,* taking top billing in the BBC multi-event sports programme which attracted audiences of ten million and more. Seasoned commentators Ron Pickering and David Vine positively drooled after watching Mac set a series record for the 100m, stopping the clock at something around 10.9 seconds despite the handicap of having his knees lining up in two not necessarily adjoining lanes. I think the record was eventually broken by Des Drummond, the rugby league winger, but Macdonald's prowess was remembered just as much as Kevin Keegan's bike fall or the startling style of judo champion Brian Jacks in the gym tests.

Macdonald also had two of the best left feet in the country, the one on the end of his own left leg and the one which otherwise belonged to Terry Hibbitt, whose defence-splitting passes provided much of the ammunition, just as Joe Harvey had predicted when he first brought them together in 1971.

Harvey spent big on Macdonald when other clubs hesitated but he also got away with daylight robbery when he simultaneously took Hibbitt from the fringes of Don Revie's successful Leeds team and into black-and-white stripes. The short and spiky Hibbitt was already a league championship and Fairs Cup winner without ever being a regular first choice at Elland Road, though that was no sign of limitation on his part, with the quality of internationals Billy Bremner, Peter Lorimer, Eddie Gray and Johnny Giles the main obstacles to his progress. Harvey could hardly believe his luck when a £30,000 fee was agreed to take him to Gallowgate.

* * *

Everyone wanted to be Supermac. We all longed to be the next Newcastle United No.9, no matter how far short we fell in terms of stature or ability. A chosen few had the single digit on the back of their replica shirts in the days when you could do this only by buying a red cloth number and asking your mam to sew it on. There were no printed replicas, no squad numbers, no names, no pack-drill. We didn't need the names, though, because everyone knew that the '9' was Macdonald's for as long as he wanted it. I'm not even sure I saw an alternative number on sale anywhere.

Macdonald was a larger-than-life legend at St James' Park but he was pretty well thought of elsewhere in the game, too, at least when it came to goalscoring. There were a number of deadly strikers around at the same time, with John Richards (Wolves), Kevin Hector (Derby), Bob Latchford (Everton), 'Pop' Robson (West Ham), Frank Worthington (Leicester) and John Radford (Arsenal) regularly among the leaders in the goals charts, while the English game also boasted the maverick skills of forwards such as Charlie George, Rodney Marsh, Peter Osgood and Stan Bowles. But Supermac won more international caps than any of them under Sir Alf Ramsey, Joe Mercer and Revie.

He was listed third in the era's best forwards in the *Football In the Seventies* book published under Kevin Keegan's name a couple of decades later, behind only the double European Footballer of the Year author and his successor at Liverpool, Kenny Dalglish. For context, third place in the 60s equivalent behind Jimmy Greaves and Denis Law was Geoff Hurst, hero of the World Cup win.

'Supermac, Supermac' was the soundtrack of the terraces during the first half of the 70s, a war cry while our hero punched the air or strutted, both arms aloft with a wide, toothless grin after another net-buster. There was also the offering of 'Supermac Superstar, how many goals has he got so far?' to the tune of 'Jesus Christ Superstar', but the shorter chant was more popular and infinitely louder, with an added touch of menace. 'Supermac's back, Supermac's back' also rang out whenever he returned from injury or ended a drought with another goal. He loved every minute of the adulation, too.

Where Alan Shearer was intimidation and inspiration, Macdonald was pace and power with an extra bit of mouth thrown in. The eve-of-FA-Cup-Final 'I'll thump Liverpool' quotes, though, will not be recalled among his finest moments. Apparently, the words were pinned on the dressing room wall of Wembley rivals Liverpool and manager Bill Shankly's pre-match motivational talk was almost done for him.

Photos in the build-up had Supermac with champagne glass (or Babycham bowl) in one hand and a juicy cigar in the other but a lacklustre display in the final, despite having scored in every round on the way there, was followed by another in the colours of a different team in 1978 (more about that to come) and gave rise to a tongue-in-cheek answer to the age-old pub quiz question: What is taken to Wembley on cup final day and never used? The answer to some critics became 'Malcolm Macdonald', where the correct response was 'the losing team's ribbons'. Still, live by the sword and die by the sword.

Malcolm also had massive credit in the bank. He scored a hat-trick against Liverpool on his Magpies home debut, before being carried off concussed and minus some teeth after a collision with goalkeeper Ray Clemence, and he'd crashed in those two magnificent goals against Burnley to get to Wembley, as well as scoring many others in between, mainly with his left foot or from a large number of headers for a not particularly tall centre-forward. A right-foot swinger, on the pivot direct from a throw-in during a cup tie away to Bolton Wanderers, was another memorable contribution to the legend. In the away-day yellow shirt and blue shorts, it was, indeed, just like watching Brazil.

Malcolm used his right foot at least once more, to create a goal in a Wembley final as Alan Gowling turned his cross past Joe Corrigan for an equaliser in the 1976 League Cup defeat by Manchester City.

There was also the time I was allowed to get up out of bed to watch *Sportsnight* – on a school night, too – when Macdonald was in the England team. These were the days before frequent live television coverage of the national team or video recorders and Dad had listened to the radio report before revealing only that 'Supermac scored', which earned me the promise of being able to see the highlights if I went to bed at the usual time and got some sleep first.

Supermac did, indeed, score. Five times. A national newspaper headline screamed 'Supermac 5 Cyprus 0', though having watched the goals on numerous occasions since, none would count as a classic against a lightweight Cyprus who were out of their depth at Wembley.

Newcastle's favourite adopted son, Mac made his England debut as a 22-year-old just a year after arriving in the North-East and had netted his first international goal in a more memorable win over world champions West Germany, but the Cyprus haul didn't count for much more than an entry in the record books as England finished second in the pool and failed to reach the European Championship finals. Instead, Czechoslovakia not only topped the group but then went all the way to lift the trophy with a deciding penalty in the shoot-out against West Germany taken by Anton Panenka, who cunningly chipped the ball over the conned goalkeeper and thereafter had a style of penalty kick named in his honour.

Macdonald's domination of the limelight at St James' was so strong that you need a double-check of the record books to confirm he donned black-and-white for just five years. I got to see him on a limited number of occasions, as I went to my first games towards the end of his goalscoring reign, but I still carry the hurt from his shock departure, feeling unwanted by a new manager and, so the stories say, wearing the patience of fellow players a bit thin, too. His legend on Tyneside, though, remains along with memories of the excitement and expectation, the rampaging runs, the goals and the arms-aloft celebrations.

* * *

Like first-team players Alan Gowling, Mick Mahoney, Tommy Craig and Geoff Nulty, I made my first appearance at St James' Park in 1975 when Malcolm Macdonald was still at the height of his powers and, thanks to a neighbour, we had seats near the front of the New Stand to take it all in.

It was also the year that I collected football stickers for the first time, so I already knew all of the names. I eventually got the full set and still have it – *Soccer Stars '75 '76* with its bright yellow cover showing a clash between Leeds striker Allan Clarke and a Manchester United defender, who I think is Steve James.

You had to glue in each entry yourself and have the patience to wait long enough for each one to dry before turning the page to paste in the next, being careful to only gum up the top edge because there were biographic details of each player printed on the page underneath.

With only 14 players per club, you didn't learn much about the depth of any squad, though that didn't seem to be a priority to managers in those days, and I do remember having swap after swap of defender David Crosson, who I otherwise never encountered in his United career. His biography correctly stated that 'opportunities had been restricted' and he made just six appearances before heading down the A1 to join lower league Darlington.

The other names on the Newcastle page that we all raced to complete were the ones on which my support was built – Macdonald, Jimmy Smith, Irving Nattrass and Alan Kennedy; Hibbitt, John Tudor, Stewart Barrowclough and Pat Howard; Frank Clark and David Craig; Tommy Gibb, Glen Keeley and Iam McFaul, who is there despite having already played his last game for the club. A 5ft 10in goalkeeper with six caps for Northern Ireland, McFaul was registered for that season as emergency cover for his successor, Mahoney, but did stay with the Magpies for many more years as a coach and then as a manager known best for bringing in Mirandinha from Brazil and Dave Beasant from Wimbledon.

In the same album, the Manchester United page includes Mick Martin, a young Irishman playing for an ailing giant but later to become Newcastle club captain and colleague of Kevin Keegan who, in turn, is bang in the middle of the Liverpool collective next to Terry McDermott and the Northumberland-born Ray Kennedy.

That season marked Manchester United's return to the top division after the wake-up call of relegation. They had predictably topped the second flight on the way back, just half a dozen years after being crowned champions of Europe, but they hadn't run away with it, which illustrates just how far they had fallen as Tommy Docherty continued his rebuild without the talismanic trio of Charlton, Best and Law, who, for different reasons, had all moved on or out.

Flicking through those pages, it was a shock for this nine-year-old football nut to comprehend that 'the Famous Man United' had ever been in the Second Division. Armed with just a couple of years of football knowledge and some late-night extensions to watch *Match of the Day*, I was aware of what that club stood for and of how many great names had worn their red shirt. At the same time, I didn't realise that my own team had been at the same second-tier level just before I was born. It was shocking to learn that Newcastle United had been among anything but elite company at all, let alone in such recent memory. At least with Macdonald on song in front of goal it was unlikely to happen again.

Already a big football fan and a young bookworm, I was given some annuals from the mid-60s by family friends – *Charles Buchan's Soccer Gift Book* and *All Stars Football Book* mostly – whose pages talked about how our sleeping giants were plotting a return to the top flight. When I checked, I found that the Magpies had also had another spell in the Second Division either side of the war, a lean period which was mentioned a lot less frequently than the six FA Cup wins and a record 11 cup final appearances.

Perhaps if the club had taken the opportunity to learn from the fate of Manchester United in 1974, Chelsea in '75 or Tottenham, who were relegated two years later, we might have escaped a few tumbles of our own.

* * *

Stepping over a game of Striker – an entry-level drug before my addiction to Subbuteo – and the Action Man and Matchbox cars, the Lego, Frustration and Buckaroo, the cowboys and commandos, I managed to make my St James' Park debut at a win over Arsenal while still in primary school.

The game featured a thumping 20-yard goal from full-back Irving Nattrass and an opener not from Macdonald but his strike partner Gowling in a season which would also feature two good cup runs and a final fling in black-and-white for our hero in the No.9 shirt.

Just a week ahead of my return for the December draw with Ipswich Town, their midfielder John Peddelty hit a sublime volleyed goal to claim a place among the goal of the month contenders on *Match of the Day* but he failed to find a repeat in the North-East, with Geoff Nulty providing one of his season's tally of nine goals to ensure us the two points.

The team selfishly played seven times without me between those two visits and, remarkably, had kept an unchanged team to start all of them. It was a trait of the season, with Gordon Lee, having become manager in succession to Harvey, keeping faith with his core squad.

His team started with 'Mick Mahoney, super goalie, la-la-la-la-la', who had taken over from the long-serving McFaul and missed just a handful of matches. One of the last of the bare-handed keepers, satisfied that the 'spit only' solution to shot-stopping would keep out the best strikers of the day, the ginger Mahoney had to be patient in his professional career, leaving Bristol City to find regular football with Torquay United before becoming Newcastle's No.1 in the same season I became a matchday fan.

Selected ahead of Roger Jones, who had been signed by Lee on the back of 400 appearances with Bournemouth and Blackburn, Mahoney was also part of the gang who commonly wore a pair of white sweatbands, joined most notably by Alan Kennedy, Micky Burns and Gowling plus, of course, Supermac, who was regularly spotted by television cameras using one wrist to mop his fevered brow and the other to address a snotty nose.

Just a touch taller than his immediate predecessor, Mahoney was still under 6ft, a full 6in shorter than the going rate for top-flight goalkeepers in the Premier League. But he was still able to make the *Match of the Day* save of the season during 1975, his agility and reflexes no doubt improved by having Glen Keeley line up in front of him on a regular basis.

The tough and unfussy Pat Howard, a veteran of both recent Wembley appearances, joined regular full-backs

Nattrass and Kennedy in defence, with John Bird or the versatile David Craig completing a back four. In midfield, Stewart Barrowclough provided another link to the 70s cup finals, while Nulty came in from Burnley as a leader alongside the creative Tommy Craig, who was there as a supply line to Macdonald and Gowling up front. Micky Burns supplied energy and goals from a variety of roles. 'He's here, he's there, he's every-effin-where, Micky Burns, Micky Burns', said the crowd and the homemade pin badges enterprisingly sold outside the ground. It was not the kind of chant we'd used for Supermac, though the pair did feature in the same team with some success before our legendary centre-forward moved on and Burns flourished again in a more advanced role.

Ray Hudson, a talented youngster from Dunston on the south banks of the Tyne, got a run of games towards the end of that campaign as injuries mounted among senior alternatives, and utility player Graham Oates, a favourite of Lee's but of few in the stands, filled in when Howard was ruled out for the whole of April, during which the Magpies had to fit in seven league games as a consequence of a fixture pile-up after long runs in both cup competitions.

The late changes mattered little as Lee's men spent the entire season in mid-table, eventually finishing 15th, with a frustrating inconsistency illustrated by outscoring every other team at home – the haul of 51 was even ten more than champions Liverpool – but winning just four times away, including an opening-day trip to Bobby Robson's Ipswich and a last-day victory at Tottenham's White Hart Lane as Macdonald bookended his campaign with a pair of goals in each.

Supermac saved his best moment, though, for the FA Cup and a fifth-round game at Bolton when his goal following a throw-in had eloquent and educated commentator Barry Davies searching for superlatives.

Sam Allardyce had headed Bolton in front before Macdonald scored twice. The first was reminiscent of his famous semi-final strikes two years earlier, latching on to a pass which Tommy Cassidy had cannily floated over both the defence and the mud to put his centre-forward through on the left of the penalty area, and there was no doubt he was going to make it count. His next goal was a one-off, converting a throw-in with a first-time volley despite facing away from goal and having to trust his unfavoured right foot. 'What a goal … what a BRILLIANT GOAL … magnificent,' spluttered BBC man Davies. 'And with the right foot, too. Superbly hit, that leaves [goalkeeper] Siddall wondering where it came from.'

United were in their away kit of yellow shirts and blue shorts, which may have looked like Brazil, though completing this ensemble with orange socks could not have happened in any other era than the multi-coloured 70s.

A defensive mix-up between Mahoney and the lanky Keeley, who made only a handful of appearances that season, gave Bolton an equaliser before Cassidy sent Gowling in to put United ahead again. It was a lead they held until an 84th-minute leveller. With nothing to separate the teams in a goalless replay, the Magpies eventually made progress with victory in a third meeting hosted at Elland Road, Leeds, with strikes from Burns and Gowling, who ended the campaign outscoring Macdonald with 30 goals thanks to a remarkable haul of 14 in the two cup runs.

In the opening months of the following season, Hibbitt made a sentimental return as a Birmingham City player, though Dad and I missed his warm welcome. After being given tickets at short notice, we had not even reached our seats until about 20 minutes in, with both sides already on the scoresheet, but at least we cheered the rest of a 3-2 win, with Burns scoring twice in the new minus-Macdonald era. We had no way of knowing, also, that Hibbitt would soon be back for a second spell in Newcastle colours.

The busy Burns was a big favourite with supporters; a vertically challenged livewire with a battery that would put a Duracell Bunny to shame. Originally an amateur footballer, first as a student and then as he began a teaching career, Burns was a tip-toes player who nudged the ball this way and that, picking his passes and linking play all over the field. He liked the give-and-go and running at defences and his workrate was a feature whether he lined up in midfield, wide on the right, up front or just behind the main strikers. He had followed the legendary Tony Green in taking the road from Blackpool to Tyneside and, with his influence, adaptability and likelihood of getting an important goal, he was a kind of prototype Robert Lee. It was a shame, therefore, that he would have only another 12 months at the club after enjoying his best-ever season in 1976/77.

The Birmingham result lifted the Magpies from ninth place to sixth in the table and, other than during a brief lull in February, they continued to improve, eventually finishing fifth to claim a place in Europe. With just one year to go before my teens, it was the perfect time to be part of the Black-and-White Army (I was unaware of a Toon Army until the Keegan years).

The new boss had eradicated a lot of the team's inconsistencies in the league but they did return for one miserable night of cup football which still gets a mention at St James' Park. Just four days after I'd cheered the victory over Hibbitt's Birmingham, an unchanged line-up went to Old Trafford in the fourth round of the League Cup. The outcome created the terrace rendition of 'We hate Man U, cos they beat us 7-2', though the lyricists could have also searched for something to rhyme with Walsall, Chester, Exeter, Wrexham and Bury to commemorate further cup embarrassments during the years afterwards, not to mention earlier catastrophes against Hereford and Bedford. Who would have thought we'd still be singing about one defeat five decades on? I never did learn where the second line of 'go left go left, go left right left' came from though.

Checking the records, a single goal separated the teams as they headed back to the dressing rooms at half-time, with the hosts 3-2 ahead and a chunk of black-and-whites in the 52,000 midweek crowd starting to think this could be their night. It wasn't, as Gordon Hill hit three of the seven for a Red Devils team under the management of Dave Sexton. They were, though, beaten at home in the next round by Everton, who then met Aston Villa in a final which needed three games before an extra-time strike from Brian Little decided the trophy's destiny and launched a thousand lookalike haircuts.

* * *

When Gordon Lee moved in as manager, he said he considered Newcastle United to be 'the best club in the world'. It was a useful line for journalists and to get fans on his side from the outset, though, if it had been meant literally, you do wonder why the man chosen to take over had only a promotion from the Fourth Division with Port Vale and a Third Division title at Blackburn Rovers on his CV. It's not where Barcelona, Real Madrid or other clubs with pretensions of being the world's best would start looking for a new man in charge.

Lee got his crack at the job based on work in the nether regions of the Football League following an unheralded playing career as a right-back at Aston Villa and then Shrewsbury Town, where he also began coaching. Lee looked like an authoritarian and was a big believer in teamwork. He commented that there were 'no stars' at St James' Park and, within two years in charge, sadly he would be proved right.

Initially, though, he took United towards the top of the First Division table for the first time in decades and the team he built went on to qualify for Europe for the only time between the Fairs Cup years and the arrival of Kevin Keegan's 'Entertainers' more than two decades later. He also managed to do it without Macdonald. Whatever results his team produced, Lee will always be remembered as 'The Man Who Sold Supermac'.

Tyneside was in thrall to Macdonald, his goals and his personality. His sideburns, barrel chest and bandy legs were as much a part of Newcastle United as the black-and-white stripes or the Hereford United highlights. He was larger than life – he had arrived in a Rolls-Royce on the day he signed from Luton Town – and he wasn't afraid to speak his mind, which made him popular with the press. Usually, though, he walked the bandy-legged walk as well as he talked the brash talk.

On-song, there was no doubting his star quality in the No.9 shirt. Macdonald was the spearhead of a team that could thrill and frustrate in almost equal measure, with the creativity of Terry Hibbitt and then Tommy Craig, the individual talents of Tony Green (all too briefly) and Jimmy Smith, and the energy of Terry McDermott, Stewart Barrowclough and Micky Burns.

He formed feared goalscoring partnerships with John Tudor and Alan Gowling along the way, too. But there was only ever one Supermac.

Rumours circulated during the 1975/76 season that Mac's days as the darling of Tyneside were numbered, though he played at Wembley in the League Cup Final and ended the campaign with two memorable goals in a win at Tottenham, missing just three league games to shush speculation about issues with his troublesome knees. But for the first time, I had to contemplate seeing my hero playing for someone else, like seeing a new *Blue Peter* presenter in place of John Noakes, a new incarnation of *Dr Who* or your favourite band unveiling a new lead singer.

Before the summer was out, the breakdown of relations with boss Lee reached a peak. Neither man spoke fondly of the other, with Macdonald referring to his early years at the club as a honeymoon which was well and truly over. After 138 goals in 257 appearances, a deal was done in August to take the swashbuckling centre-forward back south with Arsenal for the curiously accurate transfer fee of £333,333.33. It made Macdonald both United's record signing and record sale, a distinction he would retain until the departure of Peter Withe. The outlay to bring him in the first place would stand until the arrival of midfielder John Trewick.

At the age of 26, Macdonald was in his prime as a professional footballer, although he had already accomplished so much as a player who had started out as a full-back at non-league Tonbridge Town. As well as his United record, he had been capped 14 times by England, including three times in the previous season.

Forget about Manchester United selling 'Goldenballs' Beckham. Letting go of Supermac was an apocalyptic moment on Tyneside, where we did not have Cristiano Ronaldo, Paul Scholes, Ryan Giggs and Roy Keane to take on the mantel once the crowd hero had been sold off, and we didn't have Alex Ferguson in charge, either.

The fans would, of course, get used to seeing the club sell off more of our favourites over following years but the storm over this departure was comparable only with Andy Cole's sale while in record-breaking form in the 90s, though at least the manager fronted up to explain that one and remained a fan of the player he had traded to title rivals. Kevin Keegan went out on to the steps of the main entrance at St James' Park to plead with the Toon Army to trust him, and the Cole-shaped hole was filled in due course by 'Sir' Les Ferdinand and then local hero Alan Shearer, both added for record sums. Lee did not have that rapport or cash and he would also soon be on his own way, stirring up another popular revolt, this time among the players.

If Supermac's exit was difficult to contemplate, the sight of him in Arsenal's red-and-white round-necked cotton shirt brought me close to tears, especially the night I stayed up after the watershed to watch his hat-trick on *Match of the Day* in a Highbury thumping of his former team-mates.

Macdonald loved the limelight; he had a boutique carrying his own name – 'For the Exclusive Fan' as it said in a 70s typeface above the door – and he was as much a part of the North-East as any born Geordie, while still finding time to associate with the great and the good around his old manor in London. His goals and his relationship with the fans justified everything.

There were countless highlights and when Macdonald received the ball, fans expected something to happen. Sadly, his immediate successors at No.9 – a shirt so famous it had a bar named in its honour across Barrack Road – did as well as expected, though by then we didn't expect much.

Sadly, seeing stars head over the horizon was an experience we would come to know only too well, with future heroes Waddle, Beardsley and Gascoigne reaching their playing peaks after leaving Gallowgate. He may not have matched their achievements on big stages but Andy Carroll also threatened to when Liverpool provided a £30m windfall for another young player who had made the grade first on Tyneside.

The Supermac departure was bigger than the disappointment of losing two Wembley finals because it was difficult for a hero-worshipping pre-teen to understand. It hadn't dawned on me that, if we weren't winning trophies, a player would want to leave our club. There didn't seem to be any mention of earning more money, of seeking a fresh challenge or furthering claims to an England shirt but it was obvious to Lee and to Macdonald that the time had come.

The League Cup Final was Macdonald's last big day out as a Tyneside talisman and, by the end of the season, he said that, with Lee and coach Richard Dinnis in charge, 'the fight' had gone out of him. Supermac wanted out but it wasn't to prove that simple.

First, although his contract had expired in the red-hot summer of '76 while I was playing on Seaton Sluice beach, the club held an option for another year. The player made a legal challenge, refused to train when everyone reported back for pre-season and then saw a transfer saga develop over the proposed move to Arsenal, during which their rivals Tottenham also expressed an interest, though not at the quoted fee, which was then £275,000. The deal with the Gunners was finally done just in time for the new season, though Macdonald later admitted he also had a difficult relationship there with his new boss, Terry Neill.

The departing hero believed the team he played in had 'barely touched the potential lying dormant at St James' Park' when it started to fall apart, though he would have been hard-pressed to predict the crest of a slump which would soon see the club back in the Second Division with a tattered, unlovable team playing in a tatty, unloved stadium.

* * *

Macdonald identified the day that full-back Frank Clark was told he could leave as the catalyst for what followed. Joe Harvey was a manager with passion for the club and the game but he was not a coach, relying on Keith Burkinshaw to work with the players. But as Clark departed after more than 400 appearances, Burkinshaw also moved out.

Clark became a league championship and European Cup winner under Brian Clough at Nottingham Forest after being jettisoned, while Burkinshaw won the FA Cup and UEFA Cup when he stepped up to the manager's job at Spurs.

During the tricky transfer, Malcolm said he would have gone abroad if the switch to Arsenal had not been completed and there were plenty of Geordies wishing he'd done exactly that as he netted a hat-trick in the first meeting with his former club after finally completing the move. To make matters worse, the BBC cameras, so often the harbingers of doom when they crossed paths with the Magpies, were there to record it and I can still remember the horrible, hollow feeling of watching Supermac, forever *our* Supermac, racking up the goals against his old team.

Incredibly, a win at Highbury that afternoon could have taken United to the top of the table, which shows how well Lee and his team coped without him. No wonder Jimmy Hill and company were there.

Instead, though, Supermac struck three times on an emotional afternoon in a 5-3 win for his new employers. He described the treble as among the most satisfying goals of the 200 and more he struck in professional football, despite admitting to nerves before the game, no doubt fuelled by a determination to show Lee who was top dog. Below his headline grabbers, Trevor Ross and Frank Stapleton got the other goals for the Londoners, with Micky Burns (two) and Alan Gowling, now combined as a front pairing and doing very well thank you very much, on the mark for the outgunned visitors.

Considering how well Newcastle had played in the rest of the campaign, it was almost as if the BBC had something against us. I looked it up a few years later – not being one to harbour a grudge unless I had to – and found the Highbury hammering came during a period when successive *Match of the Day* appearances (when the programme featured 20 minutes of action from just two chosen fixtures) featured a 4-2 defeat to Derby in the FA Cup quarter-final, a 5-0 cuffing by Wolves and defeat at Norwich early in the 1976/77 season (courtesy of goals from World Cup winner Martin Peters, and Viv Busby, a man with the dubious double of playing for Newcastle on that infamous afternoon in Hereford and then coaching Sunderland) as well as Supermac's Arsenal hat-trick, a loss at Liverpool, a goalless home draw with Leicester, defeat at home to Derby, for whom former Roker hero Billy Hughes scored, a draw at home to little Wrexham in the FA Cup (before defeat in the replay) and a loss at Nottingham Forest.

I'd almost got into the habit of begging to go to bed *before* it started. Later, in the Mike Ashley years, I didn't need to beg; as a grown-up bad loser, I just sloped off quietly upstairs after the headline game most weeks because I couldn't stand the pain of watching another struggling team rattling around the lower reaches of the Premier League table after already absorbing reports of their inadequacy throughout the afternoon.

Finally, there was a 3-1 win at Fulham to end that dismal televised run. The month was December 1978, a full two and a half years after the quarter-final at Derby's Baseball Ground which had kicked off such a depressing TV sequence. And we'd had to drop into the Second Division to do it! It's a wonder anyone in the North-East stumped up the licence fee.

But, true to form, there were further crashes in front of the cameras to come, including a 4-0 and a 6-0 double at Stamford Bridge – the latter in black-and-white shirts with white shorts, a combination which continues to make me nervous, though the hoodoo did not prevent a hiding handed out to Paris Saint-Germain at St James' in 2023 and another 4-0 at Swansea in December 1980 before Supermac did the business against us again.

It is easy to forget that Macdonald continued to score goals for the Gunners. He was the First Division's top scorer in his debut season there in 1976/77, finishing level with Aston Villa's Andy Gray on 25 league goals but gathering another four in the cups. One of his tally came at St James' in the return fixture during the closing weeks of the campaign. I still have the picture of him hugging conquered keeper Mahoney at the final whistle. For such a brash, barnstorming goal-getter, he looks almost apologetic.

A season later, Macdonald struck another 15 league goals – matched by Micky Burns on Tyneside – but Bob Latchford scooped a national newspaper bounty of (pause for effect ...) £10,000 for hitting the 30 mark. Supermac added 11 in the cups, including seven in a run which took him to another FA Cup Final. Sadly, he felt the bitterness of defeat again as Ipswich upset the formbook at Wembley. He missed a possible return in 1979 when Alan Sunderland hit the decider in a thriller against Manchester United and, with his left knee giving up on him, Macdonald was forced into retirement at the age of just 29 with a record of a goal every other game and legions of fans at both ends of the country.

Just a year or so later, he surprisingly returned to his first professional club, Fulham, as manager and in 1982, he led them out of the Third Division. The following season, they attracted all sorts of attention for an attractive playing style which pushed them towards a second successive promotion.

The national news angle was obvious when he returned to Tyneside for the first time as a manager against a Magpies team which included Kevin Keegan, the only man who could rival Macdonald's popularity in the region. I never thought I'd see Supermac back where he belonged but he came out to give a wave and then sat back in the wooden dugout as his crisp-passing side destroyed the Mags.

His team were fantastic, weaving intricate patterns across the pitch as Gordon Davies, Dean Coney, Ray Houghton and the rest ran rings round us. It was caught on BBC cameras (of course it was) and I found a half-second of 'fame' as their fourth goal went in right in front of us. I could even see myself clapping on the highlights! To be fair, I was not alone, as it featured a superb move full of first-time passing and a final looping shot over goalkeeper Kevin Carr into the Gallowgate goal, but I was still worried I'd be recognised on my next visit as the lad who clapped the away team.

That win moved Fulham up to third in the table and they stayed in the promotion spots until, agonisingly, they were beaten four times in their last five games to finish a point short of a place in the top division. Their final game, a single-goal defeat at Derby, ended 78 seconds early due to crowd encroachment, scenes which were captured on the evening news. Fulham's appeal for a replay was rejected by the Football League and promotion, instead, went to Leicester behind Queens Park Rangers and Wolves. It was a dramatic day elsewhere, too, most famously at Maine Road, where a late goal by Yugoslav substitute Radi Antić not only saved

Luton's place in the First Division at the expense of hosts Manchester City but also inspired manager David Pleat's soft-shoe shuffle in beige suit and pale slip-ons at the final whistle.

The BBC, though, had still not done with us. They would have to take at least some of the blame for Keegan's decision to retire after just two seasons as a player in black-and-white. The corporation revelled in the romance of the FA Cup and had the cameras there when the draw sent the former 'King of the Kop' back to Anfield. When Keegan later announced that enough was enough and he would walk away from the game at the age of 33, he highlighted an incident during the meeting as one of the reasons behind his decision.

The pundits picked up on it, a seemingly minor moment in a 4-0 routine win for the Reds when the No.7 took possession somewhere in the attacking half of the field but was chased down and dispossessed. Kevin identified that as the moment which triggered feelings within him that he could no longer meet his own exacting standards at the highest level.

The player who caught him was Mark Lawrenson, widely acknowledged among the quickest and canniest defenders in the game, but it still hurt Keegan that he could not dominate as he had once done.

* * *

I don't remember whether my idolising eyes had already moved on from Supermac by the time of his controversial exit but I do remember a workmate of my dad talking to me about the quality of two young full-backs who had replaced stalwarts David Craig and Frank Clark in the Newcastle defence.

The veteran duo – one brought over from Northern Ireland as a youth-teamer, the other a grammar school boy with hopes of going to university after a couple of false starts in the professional game at Sunderland and Preston – managed 700 games between them for the Magpies across the 60s and 70s. Finally, though, their days were numbered.

Craig, described at one stage as the best right-back in Britain, started to struggle with injury, which would eventually finish his career, while Clark had already been told he was no longer required, manager Joe Harvey breaking the news in the dressing room after learning he, too, was being axed.

In their place, Irving Nattrass and Alan Kennedy, graduates from the youth and reserve teams, became first choices, a full-back pairing totally in keeping with the standards set by their immediate predecessors.

Nattrass was equal parts leggy and elegant, defensively strong but also capable of lining up in midfield. At his Newcastle peak, he established himself as a stylish right-back with good pace and confidence on the ball. My own opinion of him was boosted by his thumping 20-yarder in a win over Arsenal during my matchday debut. Alan Gowling scored the other goal past Jimmy Rimmer and I have no recollection of how but I know it wasn't a patch on the full-back's. If I'd had my way, he would have made an England shirt his own and everyone outside of Liverpool would have remained blissfully unaware of Phil Neal and his chin.

But on the other flank, Kennedy became my new football hero. I was convinced our left-back would be an international star and was not alone as the chant of 'Alan, Alan Kennedy … England' regularly rang around the stadium after a characteristic charge down the wing or a thumping tackle near the touchline.

Being born in Sunderland was unfortunate but not as unlucky as having to wait a decade before finally claiming a measly two England caps as Kennedy patiently joined the queue in an era when Kenny Sansom took possession of the white shirt 86 times.

Kennedy had pace and power to go with a hammer-strength left foot and he loved to bomb forward as full-backs started to become more adventurous than being satisfied merely with catapulting wingers into the paddock enclosure. He wasn't afraid to have a shot, either, as he ran on to the ball at the edge of a rival penalty area – sometimes they even went in.

He got a leg-up when, as a 19-year-old with barely 20 first-team games under his belt, he received a call to start the 1974 FA Cup Final in the absence of the unlucky Craig, with Clark switching across to the right-back slot. Kennedy had to wait for another run of games but, when he did get in, he settled into it and became a big favourite with an even bigger future.

At the end of the relegation season in 1977/78, Liverpool boss Bob Paisley pounced, handing over a fee comparable with the amount received for star centre-forward Macdonald and, although he took a while to find his feet among the serial winners of Anfield, Kennedy was eventually adopted as a cult hero there, replacing the popular Joey Jones in the No.3 shirt and becoming a firm fixture on the left of defence. He also remarkably claimed the winner in two European Cup Finals – running into the box to drive in the only goal against Real Madrid in 1981 and adding the decisive penalty in a shoot-out against Roma three years later when his celebrations could have got him medicated before he'd even reached the dressing room.

When he finally left Liverpool, some 350 games and a sideboard full of silverware later, the man known among fellow players as 'Barney Rubble' after the *Flintstones* character was set for a return to Newcastle. The Evertonian John Bailey, nicknamed 'Gnasher' because of his likeness to the Dennis the Menace dog, was the incumbent when talk surfaced that five-time league championship winner Kennedy would be on his way back. But then, at the 11th hour, he instead opted to sign for his hometown team down the road.

After watching his breakthrough at Newcastle and his glory days at Liverpool closely, I forgave him this mortal sin on account of an almost understandable loyalty to his birthplace and to his family but I shed no tears when his colleagues suffered relegation to the Third Division for the first time despite the funds provided for big-time manager Lawrie McMenemy's squad building.

Even without knowing that he would become a legend on Tyneside, I grew up as a fan of Kevin Keegan – a little man overcoming the doubters was a narrative I believed in – though I did first have to get over the heartache of his cup final double against us in 1974. There was also a brief pause when he missed a penalty for England – I think it was against Austria – which us kids spent a full week recreating in our kickabouts at the Welfare with a mixture of cuffed and wrong-foot shots to emphasise our disproval at his technique.

As well as his up-and-at-them, all-action playing style, as I got older I admired that Keegan had been brave enough to try something different in his career, winning everything he could with one dominant club and then rejecting a move to global icons Real Madrid to try his luck with SV Hamburger in West Germany instead. He also moved into marketing Patrick boots when he could have taken Adidas or Puma, and when he became a magazine columnist, he got on board with the newcomer *Match Weekly* rather than the older *Shoot*. He was his own man, all right.

Around the same time, I also loved Peter Barnes and Dave Thomas, the best performers in the left-wing position I filled in my earliest school teams.

Barnes was blond, direct and totally one-footed, giving perhaps the best performance of his career when he surprised Brazil at Wembley, where had also claimed a goal against Newcastle in the League Cup Final. It was a shock when he left Manchester City to go to West Brom, though not as big a jolt as his next transfer, to Leeds, where my fandom completely cooled. He did, though, win England caps with all three clubs.

By the time I completed my first football sticker collection, Thomas had already left Burnley to join QPR, playing alongside England captain Gerry Francis, Stan Bowles and Don Givens in an entertaining, attacking team. The page in my book described him as 'a winger who can also scheme', using a phrase borrowed from the 50s which meant he could play a bit in midfield or the old 'inside-forward' space. I followed his progress closely in London and then with Everton – where Gordon Lee signed him for £225,000 – and also with England.

Thomas had real pace, a steely commitment and a good goalscoring record. He seemed to have an in-built ready-reckoner to calculate angles from his part of the pitch and, to me, he looked like the best crosser of the ball in the country. Hugging the touchline to receive possession, he could deliver towards his strikers at top speed just ahead of a full-back's lunging attempt at a block. He could do it from either side, with either foot, too.

Even better, Thomas took on full-backs with his socks rolled down around his ankles, trusting his footwork and pace to avoid injury or just running off the inevitable knocks. The socks were properly folded over the top of his boots, too, rather than just falling down Nora Batty-style in an age when everyone else had socks uniformly up to the knees rather than the modern style, precipitously poised halfway down the shins or, much worse, stretched towards the thighs.

I had previously only seen his style of bared shins in clips of pre-season workouts on hot summer days or among the fancy-pants Brazilians, but that did not prevent me from slavishly copying it – despite pale Northumbrian skin – in kickabouts and then in my first school team before being told to wear shinpads. Made with thin metal rods wrapped in man-made fibre which made your legs itch, those pads resembled cut-offs from cricket and were uncomfortable and uncool but their purpose was more prosaic and, even in arguing that it was okay for Dave Thomas to go without, I didn't have a leg to stand on.

In later years, Thomas championed the national charity for the blind after losing his sight, including donating the proceeds of his autobiography, and he has always been warmly welcomed during his matchday appearances at former clubs.

Many of the influential players in Burnley's most successful period of the 60s, when the Lancashire town boasted an unlikely league title win, and into the following decade came from the North-East and, despite being born in Nottinghamshire, Thomas firmly identifies as a son of the region, too. His family moved to County Durham when he was just a few weeks old and, although he was past his peak as a player when it was first shown on television, he was related to the 'Ticer' Thomas featured in *The World Cup: A Captain's Tale,* which recounted the tale of the West Auckland pitmen who won what was billed as the World Cup in the early years of the 20th century. Starring Dennis Waterman, a legend of the small screen in *The Sweeney* and *Minder*, it also provided a stepping stone for Tim Healy as Dirty Hoggy en route to becoming the donkey-jacketed Dennis Patterson in *Auf Wiedersehen Pet*.

I recorded that film (on a VHS C90 tape) and watched it maybe 30 times in the space of a couple of years, getting to know the dialogue from beginning to end. 'Could I have a small sherry perhaps?' 'Er, you're not in Darlington now,' is just one exchange which became a family standard. 'Allow me to lace your boots madam,' as a way of offering an explanation is another. Or the scene when a visiting team departs West Auckland with a win thanks to a late penalty given against Hoggy, who looks at their transport and exclaims, 'They've got a bloody charabanc,' to which skipper Bob, played by Waterman, responds, 'Aye and thanks to you, they've got two bloody points an aal.'

In the 90s, when I visited a lot of Northern League venues before the clubs started to move around the non-league pyramid, I did make a point of a pilgrimage to West Auckland, only to find their game postponed by the time I got there. At a second attempt, I saw them at their Darlington Road home with Eric Gates, formerly of Ipswich and England, playing sweeper (with his socks round his ankles). I think his brother was assistant manager. That trip coincided with the offer of a £3,000 reward for the return of the small town's most precious possession, the Sir Thomas Lipton World Trophy, subject of the Waterman film, which had been stolen. Sadly, it was never recovered, though a replica now stands in its place and the design of the football club's badge celebrates their unlikely success.

Those Northern League trips took me to many places where time, if not standing still, seemed to tick by very slowly, including Crook Town with its impressive main stand, or where the names nodded to different days (Norton & Stockton Ancients and a number of Colliery Welfares) or genuine exclusivity – Bedlington Terriers, Billingham Synthonia, Shotton Comrades and Darlington Cleveland Bridge are not the kind of names you encounter if you limit your matchday experience to the 92 Football League clubs.

* * *

For the start of the Macdonald-less era of 1976/77, Newcastle leapt into the future with an eye-catching new kit supplied by Bukta. A brave new era had been born and we were exactly the right age to get involved in it.

I'd had the previous kit, the round-necked 1974 cup final one with hooped cuffs, but I don't recall wearing it much. The new one, though, I wore to death.

In the commercial era of the Premier League, with changes to kits and at least three alternatives every season, it is hard to relate now just how much of an impact this Bukta kit made in more innocent days when a kit launch was what happened in the dressing room after a home defeat. This was a revolution in 100 per cent polyester.

It was the first regular kit to adopt any kind of manufacturer signature, with Bukta's whatever-they-were swooshes completely replacing stripes on the sleeves. Out, too, went the city coat of arms badge and in came a simplified version with a magpie in front of a castle, next to a river. Genius.

The back of the players' shirt was given over to a large rectangular white patch to include a red digit in a computer-age font (even if we still didn't know about computers), helpfully making it easier for commentators, journalists and fans to identify on-field culprits after trying to pick out red against the stripes for years before.

Traditionalists made a big fuss but the shirt remains my all-time favourite. Not just because 'things were better in my day' but because it is actually a stunning, gorgeous kit with wide, striking stripes and the Bukta ribbon down the sleeves. I got the full black-and-white replica version for my birthday while best friend Alan had the yellow-and-green away option, and we posed for commemorative photos at my front door hoping they'd be used on BBC's *Look North* when we eventually signed for Newcastle (as a lethal strikeforce with 'an almost telepathic understanding born in the back streets and park pitches of their home town' as the media were bound to report).

Although branding and marketing were in their infancy in football, the three stripes of Adidas had been highly visible at the World Cup and there was quite a stir when Admiral created England's new red, white and blue kit. We also knew all about Puma boots and had seen the Umbro diamond. But the Bukta look was completely revolutionary.

As a family company dating back to the 19th century, Bukta had actually been active in football throughout their history, from early links with Nottingham Forest to reportedly supplying more league kits than any of their competitors during the 60s, but it had all been done without fanfare. Shirts generally did not carry a maker's mark – many were only just starting to incorporate club badges – until the 70s. The only giveaway was the tag in the collar.

The Magpies had been longstanding customers, wearing unmarked Bukta shirts in the Fairs Cup years and in the FA Cup Final of 1974 when their little 'buck' did appear on the chest, though the team's regular kit that season came from rivals Admiral. Bukta reverted to being anonymous suppliers again afterwards, then United wore Umbro – with their diamond logo – before the buck returned in spectacular style.

Gavin Haigh, a shirt collector, tells the stories behind his favourites in a book called *Black-and-white Stripes* and, with his whole collection to choose from, he has the 1976/77 shirt on its front cover. Just flicking through the early pages takes me back to that photo in our hallway. That shirt also still stands out against the tech fabrics and computer designs of recent years. A pity, then, that it is associated with a grim period in the club's history.

Even more gorgeous than the strip was the tracksuit, with its black bottoms and bright white top, complete with contrasting logo ribbon down arms and legs. I'm not sure getting a white manmade-fabric football top was as popular with mams on washday but proof, if needed, of its great appeal came with the decision from new kit suppliers Castore to produce a copycat retro version in 2022.

The new magpie-and-castle badge was already attached to this tracksuit, which was an upgrade on the old style I'd had sewn on to my generic all-black, thick cotton version of previous years, and I felt like a first-teamer already when I put on my Bukta ensemble for the short walk to where we played on the Welfare, especially on the occasions when twinning shorts with that tracksuit top. It was like cup final day. There were times when we even paused at the edge of the field, side by side like real teams, before walking down the short bank on to the grass. There was no marching band and no national anthem, but we still looked smarter than the club's infamous 1974 Wembley effort.

The only flaw was that manufacturers had not yet learned that the inside ankle was not a great location for a zip. They did help you get the tracksuit bottoms on or off over your boots, but also inflicted a sharp stabbing pain if the ball made contact with the zip on your ankle bone when you tried to control it or made a tackle.

The new yellow-and-green away strip replaced the yellow-and-blue version and at least looked like it had been designed by an individual rather than by committee, though I was never a true fan of any 'second strip' as we called it until the silver-grey of the 80s and then the incredible maroon and blue hoops of the David Ginola years, which made a reappearance in 2024. We also seemed to lose on telly whenever we wore any of them. Away colours were not as cursed as wearing stripes with white shorts but they were jinxed all the same (Exhibit A: Derby County, 1976 FA Cup quarter-final, with Bruce Rioch blasting holes in a flu-hit team that had been dreaming of a Wembley double).

The Bukta outbreak spread to Sheffield Wednesday, Brighton and Hibernian – with their new star signing George Best – among the trendsetters to join us in those tell-tale patterned sleeves. Blyth Spartans even wore a green-and-white version during the later stages of their epic FA Cup run.

Later, Bukta gave us an away kit featuring a blue shirt and white shorts. Another mate, Kevin, had that one. Within another few seasons, though, their logo had all but disappeared, swamped by Adidas stripes and Umbro diamonds. They did produce a series of inventive looks for Crystal Palace and had the thrill of seeing Diego Maradona in their brand during a spell with Sevilla in the 90s but then the brand disappeared before returning at Motherwell, of all places, in the new century.

In full Bukta, Newcastle's 3-2 win over Aston Villa in May 1977 secured a place in Europe for the following season and qualification for the UEFA Cup for the first time. It had been six seasons since the end of the team's initial adventures abroad, the exact length of time a generational star had spent at the club. Malcolm Macdonald missed out on both eras.

Even the new US president, Jimmy Carter, wanted to be in on the moment. Arriving in the North-East on a state visit during the same month, he received the Freedom of the City and opened his address at the Civic Centre not with a stuffy, formal thank you but with 'howay the lads' and a characteristic toothy grin. It was more Georgia than Geordie but the crowd cheered like he'd netted in front of the Leazes End. It was his first foreign trip in office and the peanut farmer from the Deep South told the crowd: 'I am very grateful to be a Geordie now.'

The stars had aligned, as a couple of months later we also welcomed the Queen and Duke of Edinburgh to officially open our Concordia Leisure Centre in Cramlington as part of their Silver Jubilee tour. I was there, representing my cub scout pack, which meant having to wear shorts for the day, just about the worst thing you could do during your first year in middle school. I don't recall their majesties commenting on our favourite football team, though even they must have known fifth place in the Football League was a huge achievement and to do so without Supermac an almost unthinkable one.

Club historian Paul Joannou recounts that local bookmakers slashed the odds of relegation from 25/1 to just 4/1 when Macdonald's departure was confirmed. It may have been born in a purely emotive response to the news but the bookies don't make many mistakes when it comes to money. And I still wonder what the consensus would have been if we had been given the choice between still having him and finishing lower or letting him go and playing in Europe.

The season's outcome could be seen as justification for Gordon Lee's management style but by the time European qualification was confirmed, he had already headed for the exit, too, kickstarting another turbulent period for the club, its players and the supporters.

With Newcastle genuinely in the fight to win a league title for the first time in half a century, Lee suddenly packed his bags and was gone, despite having 18 months left on his contract. He joined Everton, saying he wanted to be closer to his children, who were at school in Lancashire. The Merseysiders had already reached the League Cup semi-finals but they were down in 18th place in the league table when they showed the door to Billy Bingham who would, of course, recover sufficiently from that indignity to take Northern Ireland to successive World Cup tournaments and earn hero status.

Back on Tyneside, fans started to speculate on which big-name manager would come in to finish the job of guiding the title challenge. Envious eyes were cast on World Cup winner Jack Charlton and the work he was doing with Middlesbrough, as well as towards any possible unrest at Nottingham Forest, where Derby were apparently trying to lure the Brian Clough-Peter Taylor combination back to the Baseball Ground. There were other managers with North-East connections doing well in the game, too, including Lawrie McMenemy, who had taken Southampton to a surprise FA Cup win from the Second Division, and Bobby Robson, who was about to become another Wembley winner with Ipswich.

Ian Greaves, a Busby Babe as a player with Manchester United in the 50s, was approached on the strength of a reputation built in charge of Huddersfield and Bolton. The players, though, believed coach Richard Dinnis should be allowed to carry on the good work he had performed at Lee's side.

Lines were drawn and stories of infighting dominated Tyneside, played out through the local back pages as much as within the corridors of power. There was even talk of the squad contemplating industrial action, with a strident senior group at the forefront before Newcastle's board of directors reached something of a compromise. They decided to hand the reins to Dinnis, a 35-year-old former schoolteacher who'd never had a playing career in professional football, but only on a short-term basis. As caretaker-manager, he would have a chance to state his case *in situ* for a longer-term appointment.

Against this background, the team still managed to finish in fifth place, though they would have done even better if not for four defeats in the last five games of the campaign, including the loss to Arsenal when Macdonald inevitably added a goal on his return to Tyneside. After defeats against Leicester and Ipswich, there was relief all round when victory over Villa secured a European place, though the team then promptly lost to Lee's Everton on the final day at Goodison Park. Worryingly, depressingly so with the added benefit of hindsight, Dinnis had seen his team fail to score a single goal in those four defeats.

Qualification for the UEFA Cup should have been cause for celebration throughout the summer. Instead, there were still issues to address, despite the board and Dinnis reaching agreement on his terms in charge. Contract matters simmered and had not been resolved when time came for players to set off on the pre-season tour.

'How on earth can we try out new ideas on the field when half of us won't be here to see them carried through?' midfielder Tommy Craig asked through the back pages of the *Evening Chronicle*. There were reports of 11 rebels getting ready to walk out amid 'Newcastle Dis-United' headlines and Dinnis, contemplating having to rebuild a squad that had just enjoyed its best season in a generation, commented: 'It could take me the rest of my two years here – at least.' As the situation escalated, the manager tellingly informed the media: 'I thought I was going to prepare a team that was going to be capable of fighting for the championship. Now it would seem I am trying to get one together that can fight off relegation.'

Gowling, Nulty and Burns attracted interest from rival clubs, there were reports that Craig would soon start looking for a new employer and speculation that Dinnis might even quit the job he had just inherited if four key men were lost. Another story claimed a reduced offer had been made to midfielder Cassidy, while Stewart Barrowclough, also yet to agree, described himself as 'shattered and bewildered' by the whole thing.

When a breakthrough was finally made, in typical Newcastle style, it came with a sense of drama. 'Peace in our time' screamed the headlines, echoing Neville Chamberlain on his return from Germany in 1938, and, spoiler alert, we all know how well that worked out.

Nulty, Burns and Gowling – a trio seen as the manager's senior lieutenants – were first to reach agreement with the club. David Craig, Alan Kennedy, Irving Nattrass and striker Paul Cannell committed, too, though during the dispute the latter had said: 'When I scored two goals to help us beat Aston Villa and qualify for Europe, I felt on top of the world. Now I'm flat.' Mahoney, a goalkeeper in the best form of his career, had previously admitted he could be on his way out but, instead, signed a new two-year deal.

Progress had finally been made and chairman Lord Westwood declared that the wages and loyalty bonus structure meant the club could now compete with the best around in attracting players. But just as Prime Minister Chamberlain found out decades earlier after his misguided announcement, peace was not a state of permanence.

Whatever had come together to make the Magpies the fifth-best team in the country – behind Liverpool, Manchester City, Ipswich and Aston Villa but above Manchester United, Arsenal and Gordon Lee – came apart completely in the early weeks of the new season and it would be years before it was rediscovered.

Victory at Leeds on the opening day of 1977/78 proved to be a false dawn and the team slumped to rock bottom of the table without a win in the next ten attempts. Incredibly, the seeds of a demoralising future had been sown in a season which had marked European football's return to St James' Park.

They had already lost at Liverpool and Middlesbrough, as well as at home to Millwall in the League Cup, before I got to check them out against West Ham. 'I'd hoped for four points from those three opening games, so I'm two down,' said the manager in his programme notes, still in the days of two points for a win. 'We got some praise from those who saw us at Anfield and I thought were worth a point at Ayresome,' he added. As a former teacher, he had transcribed a 'could do better' straight from a report card.

For the Hammers game, we had a birthday treat of seats for me and some friends in the five-year-old New Stand, an impressive facility for its time which would remain the club's most significant ground development for another two decades. Checking out the new strip as part of a 27,000 crowd, we lost 3-2 and my main memory is of a thumping volleyed goal from Cassidy, a Northern Ireland international who had his critics, largely due to a heavy build and a lack of pace, but who performed a steady job over a decent length of service, neatly using his short passing game and also looking for telling through balls to the forwards. Of course, 'Pop' Robson, who played more than 200 times for Newcastle before bouncing between West Ham and Sunderland for the majority of what was left of a lengthy career, got the winner for the visitors.

It may have been the day when the stadium announcer asked for 'the owner of the blue Ford, registration number …' to go back to their car and move it urgently. The owner obviously didn't fancy giving up their place because the music was interrupted again a few minutes later to repeat the message. After another few minutes, the tone turned into a plea rather than a request, which piqued the interest of a few more thousand around the ground. Another few minutes, another go, then finally, with the announcer almost begging, we were given a little more in terms of relevant information: 'Please move your car, it is parked over a gas leak,' which brought a cheer as big as any other during the afternoon.

Another favourite from the man on the matchday microphone which stayed with me was partway through the usual rundown of the 'happy birthdays' during which the announcer casually dropped in: 'A message for Terry Black (or whatever the name was) from his wife … It's a boy.'

* * *

Richard Dinnis had already been forced into changes, with early season injuries to skipper Nulty and the reliable Nattrass, while Steve Hardwick was called in to deputise for Mahoney in the two away defeats. Hardwick became an England Under-21 cap (as understudy to Blackburn's Paul Bradshaw in a squad which also included Glenn Hoddle, Peter Reid and Laurie Cunningham) and stayed around long enough to play in the same team as Kevin Keegan. He continued his career as part of Oxford United's rise through the divisions, though he had never been very highly rated by fans in the North-East.

The midfield in the West Ham game included young David McLean, making a first senior appearance in more than a year, and the squad had its largest number of local players for many seasons, though that was nothing to be proud of once you knew how the season would eventually unfold. Club secretary Russell Cushing pointed out in an early season match programme that 20 of the 50 playing staff had been born in Northumberland or Durham (using the traditional county boundaries) and Dinnis seemed keen to give them a chance, though seeing the reserves concede seven at home to Wolves before the West Ham game would have done little for confidence or any claims on a senior call-up.

McLean added only a handful of appearances before departure from his hometown club but he remained a professional player – and a highly valued one at that – when he joined Darlington and played more than 300 times in the lower divisions.

* * *

Defeat at West Bromwich Albion followed the West Ham disappointment and the Magpies, therefore, would make a return to European football on the back of five successive losses and sitting at the foot of the First Division table.

Time matters most when you're young – in the period when you still count birthdays, know the exact number of days until Christmas and the weeks until the next school holiday. For a youngster, there is a massive difference between being aged 'eight and a half' and 'eight and three-quarters'. So, when Newcastle United earned the right to play in Europe in 1977/78, it seemed like a lifetime had passed since the Fairs Cup win of 1969. In that intervening period, as a family we had moved house, installed a first telephone (with a four-digit number) and switched on our first colour television, while I had both started and left primary school.

After the glory of 1969, there had been further Fairs Cup runs in 1970 and '71 and a win in the exotic-sounding but meaningless Anglo-Italian Cup in 1973 but they all felt like a different age. Therefore, it was a landmark day in our short lives in May 1977 when United guaranteed a place in the following season's UEFA Cup. It was six seasons since the end of the initial adventures on the continent but there were many more contrasts than similarities.

After the win over Villa which secured the points to book that European place, the *Sunday Sun* celebrated with the headline 'We want Dinnis' and a picture of the acting manager being carried shoulder-high off the pitch by fans and players. 'This is my greatest moment in football,' he told the region's Sunday newspaper. 'Better than when we won the Third Division with Blackburn.' Even in my pre-teen years, my reaction would have been a whispered 'well, I bloody well hope so, Richard' but let's not detract from the achievement. Not yet, anyway.

During that landmark afternoon, Villa went ahead in the opening minute of the game thanks to Durham-born Brian Little. Cannell and Graham Oates, though, provided the response against a team who would finish the campaign as the division's top scorers. There was still time for Villa to leapfrog into fourth place before their season's end but the Magpies stayed ahead of Manchester United to seal a place in Europe as Liverpool celebrated another title victory.

For those of us who were too young to recall the Fairs Cup, just having a team at that level again was massive. Having seen goals from all over Europe on BBC's *Football Focus* – including ones still filmed in black-and-white in Portugal, where you also occasionally saw painted hoops on the goalposts – being in the UEFA Cup was next-level exciting. There would be new opponents, new names on the radio commentary, flashy continental kits and a hexagonal-panel black-and-white matchball to go with the trumpets, drums and savage tackles we associated with foreign football.

There wasn't much spectacle to accompany the opening-round meeting with Irish side Bohemians but United made up for it in the next stage by being paired with the exotic SC Bastia from Corsica, a place that not even *Holiday* programme hosts Judith Chalmers or Cliff Michelmore had visited regularly in the 70s.

This was the true appeal of the competition. Bastia were pretty much unknown outside French football, while Corsica had a mysticism of its own, with its rebellious spirit, independent nature and a unique heritage shared periodically by both France and Italy.

We might not have known much more about Corsica, but Bastia possessed one of the Dutch masters of the era in striker Johnny Rep.

The 1974 World Cup was the first tournament I followed as a football-obsessed youngster, and Johan Cruyff, *the* Dutch Master, had already become a personal hero. He remains my all-time favourite footballer based almost entirely on what he showed the world that summer.

The legendary Pelé had come and gone, Brazil without him weren't great, while finding a West German player to follow (or East German, as they uniquely both qualified for the finals in '74) felt like treason. Argentina had an impressive all-action attacker in Rene Houseman and the Scots made the trip with a good squad, too. Denis Law was enjoying a swansong on the biggest stage 15 years after his international debut and there was plenty of quality around him, with Billy

Bremner, Peter Lorimer and Joe Jordan from Leeds, plus Willie Morgan, Martin Buchan, Jimmy Johnstone and Danny McGrain. While the English representation was limited to referee Jack Taylor, the butcher from Wolverhampton who took charge of the final, debutants from Zaire and Haiti provided the curiosity.

But it was the Dutch that lit up the summer, especially their captain, Cruyff. He was at the peak of his international powers and it seemed impossible to believe that the domestic league in which he made his debut as a teenager had only been professional since the 50s. After Feyenoord won the country's first European Cup in 1970, big rivals Ajax completed a hat-trick of wins, with Cruyff as their catalyst. He unquestionably had his diva moments and exerted too much influence on and off the field for one man, but his individual skills and his value to the team cannot be overstated.

Perfect balance, a balletic poise on the ball and a superb turn of pace combined to make him a devil for defenders. Just ask West Germany's Uli Hoeneß, whose desperate lunge as Cruyff surged away from his marker, Berti Vogts, and into the box presented the Dutch with a penalty in the opening minute of the final in Munich. Such was the electric start by the men in orange that his illegal outstretched foot was the closest any German had got to actually touching the ball in that opening phase of the match.

The fact that Cruyff was totally one-footed – while I was responding to advice by spending hours at a time kicking against the garage wall with right and left in turn – did not diminish his powers by a single percentage point. One of the iconic moments of the tournament was what became known as the 'Cruyff Turn' when he wrong-footed a Sweden defender on the wing by shaping to cross the ball but, instead, doubling back on himself to leave the opponent grasping at thin air. Let the tape run a few more seconds and you'll notice that Cruyff, despite being on the left flank and heading towards the goalline, still attempts to whip the ball across the face of goal with a flick of his right foot.

His one foot was as magical as others who followed him as the world's best, Diego Maradona and Michel Platini, neither of whom seemed to have done much with a ball against their garage wall but still managed to weave magical images on a football field.

Cruyff was the icing on the cake of the Netherlands' first great line-up. The names of Neeskens, Rensenbrink, Van Hanegem, Suurbier and Krol gave them quality in every department of the pitch as the 'Total Football' pioneered at Ajax took on the world. In their bright orange shirts – equally classy with white or black shiny shorts – they became my team. My grandad had no interest in their football but he told tales of patrolling the dykes there during the war so I, too, would always defend the Dutch, even though they eventually went home empty-handed, not just in 1974 but four years later in Argentina, too.

Throw in the black-and-white ball – which looked like it was spinning backwards across the turf – the team's portion of petulance, a goalkeeper who wore white kneepads and the novelty of seeing squad numbers rather than just one to 11 like we were used to at home and the Dutch had everything we considered 'continental' in that squad.

So, the blond-haired Rep was not their main man but he was one of the undoubted up-and-coming stars in the team. There were also reports of a rebellious nature in him, to such an extent that, at times, he alone apparently dared to stand up to Cruyff. He added to his appeal when he came up against Newcastle in the colours of a French island club we knew so little about.

The exoticism of Corsica could not have been in more stark contrast to the opening tie against Bohemians, played at Dalymount Park in Dublin and featuring barbed wire, brick-hurling and other unruly behaviour during tense times in the relationship between Brits and the Irish.

Manchester United's Ashley Grimes and future Magpies captain Mick Martin were previous Bohs players but Gerry Ryan, who went on to enjoy a long spell at Derby and a cup final with Brighton, was the best-known figure in that 1977/78 squad. The name of team-mate Turlough O'Connor stayed with me, too, though I've still not encountered a single Turlough in South Northumberland.

After a goalless draw in Ireland, marred by rioting in the crowd, Newcastle hit four without reply in the return to make safe progress. Barcelona were among the other big winners, putting eight past Steaua Bucharest of Romania over two legs, while AZ67 Alkmaar hit an aggregate 16 past Red Boys Differdange, who nevertheless secured a league and cup double in Luxembourg a year later.

For the trip to the Mediterranean, Newcastle-born striker Cannell justified his selection with a seventh-minute goal for a dream start. For the hosts, it wasn't Rep or François Félix, scorer of a hat-trick in the previous round, nor the mercurial Yugoslav wing Dragan Džajić, apparently described by Pelé as the most natural footballer he had come across, who replied, but their No.10, Claude Papi. I listened to radio commentary at home, lying on the floor in the living room to get closer to the speakers of our stereo and hearing about Hardwick's string of saves and Nattrass surviving a shout for a penalty. Like the rest of the Geordie fans, I looked forward to bringing them back to St James' level, so I was distraught when Papi added another goal in the closing seconds of a game played in front of a crowd recorded at just 8,000 but no less fervent or passionate than bigger arenas around the continent.

In the cold light of day, perhaps a 2-1 defeat away from home for an inexperienced team should not be considered the end of the world with a return leg to come. The faces of the players across the back pages of the newspapers a day later, though, betrayed exactly how much of a hammer blow that late goal had delivered to a team on the back of such a wretched run of domestic form since the second week of the season.

The crowd figure quadrupled to 34,850 at Gallowgate but they had little to cheer over the 90 minutes as Rep justified his top billing by scoring twice in a 3-1 win, including one long-ranger which instantly earned a place in St James' folklore. There are many around who still describe it, struck from anything between the edge of the penalty area and up to 40 yards, depending on the angle of their view on the day and the haziness of recollection.

It provides some consolation to know that Newcastle were not alone in being on the receiving end of the mystery men from the Mediterranean. Bastia had announced their qualities by beating Sporting Lisbon twice in the opening round, scoring two goals in the last five minutes away from home, with Rep on the mark in front of a 60,000 crowd in Portugal. After ending Newcastle's dreams (and season), they also overcame Torino home and away in the third round (where Barcelona put out Bobby Robson's Ipswich on penalties) and carved a way past Carl Zeiss Jena of East Germany in the quarter-finals, winning 7-2 at home before a 4-2 defeat behind the Iron Curtain. The two away goals in the first leg of their semi-final against Grasshoppers of Zürich proved invaluable as Bastia reached their first and only European final. There, they met PSV Eindhoven of the Netherlands. A goalless draw in front of a 15,000 crowd in Corsica provided their warning and, sure enough, Willy van der Kerkhoff, one of the twins who played in two World Cups with the Dutch, broke the deadlock in the return as PSV eventually triumphed 3-0. But it had been quite a ride, one which is still celebrated in this football outpost.

Although our European dream was over and I hadn't been able to see any of it live, as I listened I became entranced by the names and the descriptions of Bastia's play. I picked up a copy of the programme for the home leg on my next visit to the supporters' club shop in The Haymarket and learning about a team that had come from so far away lit a spark within me. Such was this infatuation with the island that years later it would be the venue of our honeymoon and we also returned for our first holiday as a family. I even got to experience a matchday at Bastia during the 2001/02 season when a Monaco side which included Germany's Euro 96 hero Oliver Bierhoff were the visitors. I continued to follow their fortunes, especially when Ajaccio won promotion to set up a top-flight island derby, though Bastia have been nowhere near major honours since.

They even had the indignity of having to start again after financial issues led to relegation to the third tier of their league and their yo-yo history makes the 1977/78 season assume even more mythical proportions for their supporters, as well as at least one impressionable Northumbrian. From a black-and-white perspective, it was not long before we traded Europe for league games against the likes of Shrewsbury, Cambridge and Orient (while only just missing brief Second Division days of micro-minnows Hereford, York and Mansfield).

Between Newcastle's two memorable meetings with Bastia, Brazilian superstar Pelé played his last match for

New York Cosmos, lining up ceremonially against Santos, the club where he had spent the bulk of his illustrious career. At the same time, a controversial penalty followed by a brilliant headed goal from Kenny Dalglish secured victory over Wales at Anfield to book Scotland's place at a second successive World Cup. Meanwhile, John Neal took charge of Middlesbrough on the back of his work with Wrexham, and his predecessor, Jack Charlton, joined Sheffield Wednesday in the Third Division. Former Torquay striker Colin Lee enjoyed a fairytale debut for Tottenham, scoring four times in a 9-0 win over Bristol Rovers and the *Match of the Day* cameras captured it all as the BBC got lucky with a rare dip into the Second Division.

Even more dramatically, Newcastle finally ended a run of ten consecutive league defeats with a single-goal win over Chelsea. But less than three weeks later, Richard Dinnis was sacked. Magpies chairman Lord Westwood said change was unavoidable, though blame for the club's circumstances rested at numerous doors. The board were inevitably in the firing line and the players were obviously culpable, not just for results and performances but also for their determination in talking their bosses into giving Dinnis the job in the first place. Westwood, in the statement announcing the manager's dismissal, took the opportunity to continue the cold war with Gordon Lee by referencing his 'defection' to Everton the previous season.

Speculation about the next move swung into overdrive again and it was reported that former Leicester and Manchester United boss Frank O'Farrell had been offered the job but turned it down. Instead, Bill McGarry was announced as the new man in the hotseat at Newcastle.

From the inexperience of Dinnis, the board had taken on a steady hand and a tough one at that. McGarry had been capped by England as a no-nonsense wing-half before management roles with four clubs in the Football League and two national teams in the Middle East. He had been angling for a return after a stint in Saudi Arabia and accepted the United job two days after declining an opportunity with Port Vale, who were at the foot of the Third Division.

Taking over in November, he had six months to inspire some upward movement in his charges at St James' Park and made an instant impact with three successive wins in December and the completion of a seasonal double over Leeds, which initiated a lift from the foot of the table. But then, just as hopes started to rise, the team imploded again.

They won only once in the next four months to confirm relegation, and a crowd of less than 8,000 turned up for the last home game of the season. The Magpies still somehow finished off the foot of the table, though only on goal difference over Leicester. Both won only four home games, though Leicester's Filbert Street goal tally of 16 in 21 games was ten fewer than Newcastle's. The Foxes managed only ten away, too, half a dozen less than their relegated rivals.

Burns top-scored for Newcastle with a respectable 15 but Gowling added just three in his 15 games and Mark McGhee the same from 18 to match the contribution of full-backs Kennedy and Nattrass. Leicester's top scorers were Geoff Salmons and former Derby man Roger Davies with four, including one each in a 3-0 win over Newcastle on the last day of a wretched campaign. Significantly, Leicester had lost Frank Worthington to Bolton, where he hit 11 goals on the way to a Second Division title. The Foxes of Filbert Street probably thought they were doing smart business with the £90,000 income for a player in his 30th year and who had won the last of his eight England caps a few seasons earlier but they could not have known, especially considering his lifestyle, that he would continue to play for another decade at nine more league clubs and then into his 40s at lower levels. At Bolton, he was joined in attack by Gowling who, having been signed for a club record £120,000 in Bolton's push towards promotion, exchanged divisions with his previous employers.

The Magpies were doomed long before the end of the season and were 11 points – or six wins to be sure – short of safety in the final reckoning. The unthinkable had happened. After a traumatic nine months, Newcastle United were heading down to the Second Division.

The benefit of the European experience and a new-look squad could have been the platform the club had been looking for since lifting a trophy in 1969. Instead, it would signal the start of one of the blackest periods in the black-and-white story. A rich history counted for nothing as Newcastle plummeted.

Such was the malaise, the Magpies did not even play a part in St James' Park's biggest night of the season; the six-time FA Cup winners were upstaged by a team of local part-timers who borrowed the stadium for one night of pure romance and momentarily lifted a sense of doom and despondency in the region.

Predictably, in such a desperate season, Newcastle fluffed their lines in the fourth round of the FA Cup with a 4-1 defeat by Wrexham but the Welshmen were then paired with Blyth Spartans from the Northern League, who had incredibly made it all the way to the fifth round, potentially just three more games from running out at Wembley.

After a draw in the original tie, the replay was switched to St James' in response to the level of interest and a crowd of 42,000 – several thousand more than the town's total population – gathered to share an historic moment in the world's oldest knockout competition.

Already winners at Stoke City during a long and demanding run which had started in the qualifying rounds, Blyth were close to not needing the replay at all, having been in front at Wrexham's Racecourse Ground thanks to a goal from Terry Johnson, a former reserve-team striker at Newcastle who had played league football at lower levels. With players from both sides spending 90 minutes slipping and sliding their way through a raucous cup tie on an unforgiving frozen and bald pitch, the visitors retained that advantage until the closing minutes.

Then referee Alf Grey (of Great Yarmouth … officials always had their home town listed in the match programme) awarded the hosts a corner even though Blyth defender Dave Waterson had clearly played the ball out via Wrexham striker Bobby Shinton (yes, that Bobby Shinton, but more of that for another day). Grey meddled theatrically with the corner flag as it struggled to gain a hold in the bone-hard ground before finally the kick was taken. With the Welshmen in search of a late lifeline, goalkeeper Dave Clarke reached through a crowd of bodies to punch the ball back from whence it came and Blyth braced for a second set piece. This time, Clarke, who had been in Newcastle's Fairs Cup squad in 1969 as understudy to Iam McFaul but never made a first-team appearance for the club, made a clean catch, to the delight of the green-and-white fans on the frozen terrace just a few yards behind him and to all the football romantics at home.

Grey, though, insisted on a retake because the corner flag had been lying flat on the ground when the kick was taken, contrary to the laws of the game (Law XVII, if anyone actually cares). With the flag back in place, Les Cartwright somehow stayed upright in his smooth-soled Adidas trainers and took the kick again, and this time, rather than Clarke's hands, the cross was met by home centre-forward Dixie McNeill, who scored with a far-post header.

McNeill was one of those lower league marksmen who waded in with goals wherever he went throughout the 70s, including one for Northampton on the day that George Best returned from suspension to hit six in reply for Manchester United in an FA Cup meeting in 1970. It was obviously the day's headline-grabbing game and the man marking Best was Ray Fairfax, who reflected: 'Why, oh why, did it have to happen to me? The only time I got close to him was when we went off at half-time and full time. On top of his baffling skill, Best had all the pent-up energy and frustration of four weeks out of football. And he unloaded the lot on to poor me.' Still, it is better to be known for something than not known at all.

To repeat the words of BBC commentator Barry Davies, thanks to McNeill 'the engineers, the fitters, the sales representatives and the policemen of Blyth Spartans' had to try again, having already played ten games to get this far in the competition.

A huge crowd gathered all around St James' waiting to get in for the replay and, in the days before mobile communications, we somehow managed to locate my dad's mate and his son in the street behind the New Stand to collect our tickets and the four of us made our way into the paddock on that side, the only time I ever went in there before the benches were added in the 80s. Inside, the football experience of the immediate post-war years was being recreated by a new generation. We were shoe-horned in and, as youngsters, shepherded towards the front while the grown-ups remained further back.

A row of kids perched on the edge of the cinder track and we were among the first few stood just behind them, almost high enough on the steps to see past the police in their macs and on their three-legged stools. It wasn't quite like being passed over the heads of grown men in flat caps and mufflers in a thick fog of Woodbine cigarette smoke, as our predecessors recalled of their youth, but it was as close as we would ever get. It also belted down with rain, which, following the ice and snow of just a few days earlier, made a complete mess of the pitch.

Blyth's odds on lifting the trophy at Wembley had been cut from 200,000/1 to 500/1 during their giantkilling run and they gave it everything one more time. Wrexham, though, held their nerve, with McNeill inevitably scoring again in a 2-1 win, which earned a home game against Arsenal in the quarter-finals.

Spartans were out but they had gone further than big brothers Newcastle. They had also gone further than Sunderland, knocked out at the first hurdle by a Bobby Gould goal for Bristol Rovers at Roker Park. Everton, Liverpool, Aston Villa, Wolves, Leeds, Tottenham, West Ham, Manchester City and holders Manchester United were also eliminated earlier than the mighty men of Blyth. And, even in their absence, the giantkilling continued, with Orient reaching the semi-finals after overcoming Norwich, Blackburn, Chelsea and Middlesbrough on the way and then Ipswich defeated Arsenal at Wembley with a goal from the unsung Roger Osborne to lift their first and only FA Cup.

Two days after that cup final, we were back at St James' for Jimmy Smith's testimonial match. I'd seen the clips, heard the stories about his individual skills and we had friends who were related to him but I hadn't witnessed 'Jinky' in the flesh before injury had cut short his career. The Scot was your throwback to the 'tanner ball player', as they called them, with superb close control, an eye for a telling pass and a liking for mazy dribbling. As Newcastle's first £100,000 signing, his place in history is assured, though there were also critics of his overall effectiveness and a frustrating inconsistency. After retirement, he remained within range of a badly hit shot, running a trophy business next to the ground – the irony not being lost over the years as his old club continued to go empty-handed.

On the evening of his testimonial, we had seats in the New Stand again as Newcastle were beaten 6-3 by Smith's Select XI. The plan had been to see Malcolm Macdonald again – alongside a promised reappearance of Tony Green – but an announcement to a crowd of around 17,000 said the centre-forward would unfortunately be absent after playing in the FA Cup Final, his third Wembley disappointment in four years.

There was, though, still an opportunity to see Blyth and Wrexham go at it again, this time in the Debenhams Cup Final, a fixture featuring the two teams from outside the top divisions who had progressed furthest in the FA Cup.

Wrexham had finished the league season as Third Division champions, with Shinton scoring 16 times and McNeill 13 in support of top scorer Alan Whittle's 18, but they were beaten 2-1 by their part-time visitors in the first leg of the final. The return at Croft Park in Blyth attracted a crowd of more than 5,000, including us, standing tight up against the picket fence in line with the right-hand penalty area.

I've seen a report which identified Dave Varty's goal as Blyth's 153rd of that momentous season and, despite an equaliser in the second half, it was enough to seal a 3-2 aggregate win. My own recollection, though, was of the acrobatic performance by visiting goalkeeper Eddie Niedzwiecki, later of Chelsea but then just making his way as a young deputy for Wales international Dai Davies, so Spartans must have done a lot more than just hang on to their lead.

That was the last we heard about the Debenhams Cup for four decades until Graham Usher, a Blyth fan researching football history, followed a trail which eventually led to the club being reunited with the silverware. Apparently, it had been returned by the club during the 80s at the request of its sponsors, who intended to recycle it for use in a golf tournament. But Usher's interest spiked the power of social media and led him to someone who knew where the trophy had been stored following the company's change of head office. The trail took him to the top ranks at Debenhams, who agreed the cup should be kept by its last outright winners and, in 2019, it was returned to Blyth.

'We couldn't be happier reuniting the cup with its rightful owner, where it can be shown and admired by the faithful supporters of Blyth Spartans,' said their spokesman as national football silverware made a rare trip to the North-East.

Chapter Three:
Until the Good Times Come Around Again

AS ENGLISH football hit its peak with three different clubs lifting the European Cup over a run of six consecutive seasons, Newcastle United headed towards one of the worst sequences in their history.

Terry McDermott, signed from the Magpies in November 1974, launched this continental conquest, marauding forward from midfield to score the opening goal – thereby equalling his league tally for the whole campaign – in the 1977 European Cup Final win over Borussia Mönchengladbach in Rome on the same evening that Kevin Keegan played in red for the last time. As he did so, Newcastle's players were on the beaches of the Mediterranean toasting a fifth-place finish in the First Division and their own return ticket to European football. It looked like a new dawn. Instead, it was the kick-off to one of the darkest periods of the club's existence.

Just a year later, as the Magpies were relegated, finishing 11 points short of safety in the days of two points for a win, McDermott was part of a Liverpool team that retained their European crown with Scotsman Kenny Dalglish, given the task of replacing Keegan in the No.7

shirt, scoring the only goal in a Wembley win over Belgian outfit Club Brugge.

The holders were dumped out in the opening round of their title defence by Brian Clough's Nottingham Forest, who went all the way to win it with million-pound man Trevor Francis landing on the shot putt circle of Munich's Olympic stadium as he nodded the only goal of the final. Forest's former centre-forward Peter Withe had been sold to Newcastle for £200,000 and he finished the season with 16 goals in an eighth-place finish in the Second Division.

Forest retained their trophy in 1980 against Keegan's SV Hamburger – the era becoming a high-water mark in the history of both finalists – as the Magpies still sat in second-class seats, with former non-league striker Alan Shoulder outscoring Withe.

Alan Kennedy, whose stock remained high enough with Geordies to be forgiven for his exit at the start of the doomed battle against relegation, drilled in the only goal of the 1981 final to make Liverpool three-time European champions and stretch English football's record to five in a row. As he did so, his former club finished 11th in the Second Division, having spent the whole winter in the bottom half of the table.

Another 12 months on, a journeyman centre-forward who had played a handful of games for Southport and Barrow before they were both voted out of the Football League altogether – who also had a spell playing in South Africa before finally establishing himself at a higher level – was the scorer of the winning goal as Aston Villa, a Third Division club less than a decade earlier, were crowned champions of Europe. The marksman's name? Peter Withe.

Ipswich in the UEFA Cup and Aberdeen in the Cup Winners' Cup also lifted European silverware during this period of Newcastle's increasingly anxious exile from the top flight. Arsenal, Tottenham and the Manchester duo also experienced big nights under floodlights in continental competition. Everton, Wolves, West Brom and West Ham, too. Celtic and Rangers, Hibernian, St Mirren and Dundee United, Wrexham and Newport County, Glentoran, Ballymena and Linfield all did likewise.

But the closest Newcastle United fans got was the TV highlights late on a Wednesday night and the bonus of live coverage if any British team actually reached a final. From supporters of a team stuck in the middle of the Second Division, these games at least provided some light relief but little relevance.

* * *

Awareness of football beyond our own shores had increased exponentially during the summer of 1978 thanks to the sights and sounds of a World Cup in Argentina which did feature live on television's two main channels. We got used to the manic tickertape welcomes and the incredible spectacle of high-banked stadiums as we learned dozens of new names and faces from the pages of our World Cup sticker books, which was just as well, for there were no album pages to fill from the Second Division.

I got the Argentina 78 album free with *Scoop*, a weekly comic based on sporting characters including Jonny Stark, the match-winning striker for hire who joined anyone in need of goals, a sort of Darren Bent in pen and ink. It also featured plenty of photos, skills tips and behind-the-scenes stuff with big-name players, as well as straying into sports beyond football. *Scoop* also featured a prototype fantasy league page, with regional teams playing against each other 'virtually' in its pages. This was where I always turned first, finding out how many Newcastle players had pushed their way into the North-East selection from week to week and the identities of players from other represented clubs. I don't remember our region ever being a title contender, though, having to compete with combines from the North-West or London, with at least one of our lot in the Second Division and the likes of Hartlepool and Darlington offering precious little further down.

Albums in this period still required manual labour, though at least it was reduced to a simple lick and stick rather than having to find a gunked-up bottle of Gloy from previous years to put the player stickers firmly in place.

Osvaldo Ardiles – looking like a high school swot who had his dinner money regularly requisitioned by others – had the distinction of appearing in the opening space in the album in a summer which earned him a headline move to England. A creative midfielder, he wore a No.2 shirt in the tournament before uniquely wearing No.1 in Spain four years later, as Argentina adopted alphabetical order in listing their squad.

Flicking through the album's pages, Zbigniew Boniek, a rising star with Poland, is wrongly captioned as 'Bonier' but more curious is the presence of Belgium, Denmark, Wales, Northern Ireland and England, none of whom even qualified for the finals. They did, though, presumably boast large enough markets to sell stickers in decent numbers regardless. The England selection features a picture of Emlyn Hughes wearing out-of-date team kit and, sadly, the space reserved for Johnny Rep on my Netherlands page remains empty.

Absorbing the action from Argentina, or the parts that we could on school nights with respect to the time differences in South America, was a massively exotic summer bonus but the part of the close season which occupied our thoughts and opinions most was based much closer to home and that was trying to get our heads around what the transferred players would look like in new colours.

In the days before social media channels and its influencers, and when public appearances outside of opening supermarkets and boutiques in wide-collared shirts were a relative rarity, we only ever saw these stars on the football field. And that meant we only ever identified footballers by what they looked like in a match strip.

Newspapers were printed in black-and-white, with even glossy magazines limited to a few pages of full colour. Few of them would have something as specialised as a photo of Kop icon Kevin Keegan in the kit of his new German club SV Hamburger – the editors usually opting for England action images instead – and, even if they did, you would have to imagine its lilac tint because matchday photography was almost exclusively monochrome, too.

So, there was a genuine excitement and real anticipation when *Football Focus* or television news used photos and footage of players in fresh colours during the early part of the season or when *Match of the Day* highlights featured a first look at anyone in a new club kit. It was hard to absorb the sight of Trevor Francis in red after Birmingham blue, Mick Channon in the sky blue of Manchester City after so long in stripes or Dalglish in all red after being a hero in hoops.

When players were linked with a move away from Newcastle, my first thought was always about what they would look like in other colours, not about how they would fit into a new team's dynamic or formation. It was an effort to process the image of them wearing any other strip – Malcolm Macdonald or Alan Kennedy in red, Tommy Craig in claret or Geoff Nulty in the blue of Gordon Lee's Everton.

An editor I worked with during my magazine days said he personally disliked writers using possessive description along the lines of 'Newcastle's Alan Kennedy' or 'England's Trevor Francis'. He would have had a field day with my grandad, speaker of broad Northumbrian pitmatic, who would describe people as 'belangin' a-Bedlington' in referencing where they either came from originally or lived at the time. 'Aye, he used to belang ower Bebside but nuw he's a-Blyth.' But, in football fan terms, that was also how we viewed the players.

Their identities were linked completely with the colour of the shirt (the home shirt, obviously) and there were major mental and visual adjustments required after any transfer. It took a good while longer than it would today, too, because their images were not available on demand at your fingertips every hour of every day and you'd have to wait until a weekend for them to pop up on screen.

Clubs did not routinely make sweeping changes in their squads, though Birmingham, Derby and Stoke seemed to make a good go at it from time to time, and most moves were conducted in the summer, well before the start of the season, unlike now when it appears most managers talk a good game throughout June and July, go on their global pre-season tours in August without any new faces, then suddenly join the Back to School sales and spend some serious money with the season ready to kick off.

* * *

After following the fortunes of Brazil, Argentina, West Germany and the Netherlands at a World Cup staged in a country run by a ruthless military government and hearing the names of Kempes 'One-Nil', Zico, Krankl and Zoff through the summer, it was a devastating blow when the domestic fixture list was unveiled. As I scanned my list, I could find no Liverpool, no Manchester United, Everton or Arsenal. Sadly, in the First Division there was no Newcastle United.

Bolton, Southampton and Tottenham had all been promoted as we went down, meaning Newcastle would now have to share the pitch, the terraces and the revenues at St James' with visitors from Cambridge, Oldham, Charlton, Bristol Rovers, Wrexham, Notts County and Sunderland. It was all so sadly wrong, disorientating even.

This was the club's fourth spell in its history outside the top division but the first for anyone attending their first matchdays after the Swinging 60s. Yet there we were.

Bill McGarry's grin on the front cover of the matchday programme at the start of the season did not look half as scary as his reputation led us to believe. Maybe the pure white tracksuit top helped to soften the edges of the 51-year-old with comb-over hair who had revelled in his image as a hardman wing-half before setting out on a career in football management.

He had been a key player in a Huddersfield Town team managed by Andy Beattie and Bill Shankly, where team-mates included raw teenager Denis Law and future World Cup winner Ray Wilson. The club's status has changed over the years but Beattie took over in the early 50s when the Yorkshiremen were about to drop out of the top flight for the first time in their history and just as Newcastle were launching their era of post-war success in the FA Cup.

After retirement as a player, McGarry set out on the managerial trail at Bournemouth and Watford. He then led Ipswich to promotion back to the top division and provided a link between two North-East football legends. It was McGarry who replaced Jackie Milburn in charge at the Suffolk club and then, when he left for a bigger challenge and an historically bigger club at Wolverhampton Wanderers, his seat was taken by Bobby Robson, who would remain in charge at Portman Road for 13 years with notable success. Under McGarry, Wolves won the League Cup and reached a UEFA Cup Final (losing to Tottenham) before he took a different fork in the road and decided to move abroad.

In terms of style, he was among the last generation of sheepskin coat bosses (Richard Dinnis was another) before that style went the same way as bare-handed goalkeepers and referees with white bootlaces. But he knew his way around the game, for sure, and it was accepted that the new man would need all that experience and nous to take on a club in a state of shock and general disarray.

Home crowds averaged around 20,000 immediately after relegation, the lowest on post-war record, despite the presence of me and my mates in the 'E' Wing paddock, including for the opening home game when West Ham improved on their 3-2 win a year earlier with another three goals but this time without reply on their return. 'Pop' Robson, who would pass the landmark of 200 career goals during the season, was on the mark again against his old club and, for good measure, he added another in the reverse fixture, which the Hammers won 5-0 back at Upton Park. Born in Sunderland, it's almost as if he had something against us. See also under 'Mick Harford'.

This was a landmark season for us youngsters, too, as the one in which our school team graduated from rubber-soled boots to screw-in studs. This was a man's world, a landmark event even bigger than going to the barber without adult supervision for the first time or gaining entry to a film certified at the time as 'AA' (14s and over).

My first boots were a pair of Golas bought locally from Cram Sports at what was then known as 'the shops' but has since been reinvented as the Manor Walks mall. I remember the orange box they came in more clearly than the colour of the stripes on the boots but I do recall vividly the feeling of moving into my first pair of screw-ins, to which I soon added aluminium studs and I stuck with them as my weapon of choice in every subsequent boot until my 30s, when most of my football was transferred to artificial turf or council-run sports halls.

Other than the superstars who wore Puma, and the Gola range modelled by recent England captain Gerry Francis, it seemed every professional wore boots with the tell-tale Adidas three stripes. The Stylo style advertised by George Best and the pioneering white efforts boasted by Alan Ball and Alan Hinton were already out of fashion and we were yet to hear of Nike, Mizuno, Le Coq Sportif, Patrick, Reebok and the rest. The best young players I knew had Adidas Beckenbauer Supers with the bright yellow stripes and, if you couldn't afford the genuine version, the Woolworths own-brand lookalikes were known as Winfield Supers or, even cheaper, there were Ballmasters, which boasted a passing resemblance from a distance but featured a big, rounded, hard toe apparently left over from either a bygone era or a factory floor.

Having new screw-ins did necessitate an extra element of preparation for a kickabout on the Welfare because the studs were too precious to wear down on the pavement – it was banned, like bouncing a leather 'caser' on the path or kicking it against a wall until at least some of the top coating had worn away. So, you had to walk there in trainers and change before they got muddy. But there is nothing so evocative of nearly being a footballer than the clatter of screw-in studs on hard ground. It still gets to me when I hear it now, whether that's from footage of the players' tunnel in elite professional environments or from park pitch players heading back to their cars for fags and a lighter.

At this point, I was also still hanging on to the belief that I would have all the answers to Newcastle's questions, even if I was a bit afraid of Mr McGarry. It was just a case of someone spotting talent and then nurturing it and waiting long enough for me to grow into it.

We played football every day, in the street, on the playground, in the park or at the Welfare, so surely someone would notice where the club's next big thing was going to come from? If it meant giving up the concrete steps of the terracing for a place in the team, that was a sacrifice I was prepared to make. I was even prepared to relinquish the No.9 shirt if the club brought in another Supermac to wear it. I would expect the crowd to chant my name, obviously, even if it didn't seem to scan well in anything when I added my own commentary over Subbuteo matchplay. But, such was my humility at the thought of playing for the Magpies, I promised myself I'd still be a man of the people. I might even still take the X25 Blyth-Newcastle bus for home games like the heroes of earlier eras, though without the Woodbines and Gabardine mac.

My grandparents had been raised in the mining communities of the North-East and I had already bullishly promised that I would buy a bungalow for them to retire to once I'd become the local hero. One grandad worked as a colliery blacksmith – 'I'm not gannin' doon the pit till the' put windaes in it,' he vowed – while the other had been a collier, hewing for long shifts in tiny, black seams to power the Empire, motivated by the simple, singular ambition that he would never allow a son to follow in his footsteps underground.

Also, I knew that being in the Second Division would provide an easier route into the team, though, as I was still only 12, time was on my side and, anyway, we wouldn't be there for long, so I wouldn't have to worry about lowering my standards.

Curtains twitched in the adjacent streets and old men walking dogs often stopped to see what was happening on the Welfare pitches but somehow my call from the scouts sadly never came. Perhaps if I'd managed some games with Cramlington Juniors rather than just training there during the summer, that may have worked out differently. A significant increase in talent, height, weight, application and aggression might also have helped.

* * *

Chances to watch a team from outside the First Division on *Match of the Day* were few and far between as the BBC featured highlights from just two games each Saturday night. These were the days before the programme added a goals round-up from the other nine fixtures in the top flight or even truncated clips of a third match, so the only way to see something new or expand your knowledge beyond the top 22 teams in the country was on a Sunday afternoon when the regional commercial stations screened their own shows.

Being regionalised, we at least had a reasonable chance to see our team alongside coverage of our closest geographic rivals, while occasionally (I'm told when the area's outside broadcast unit was otherwise engaged at horseracing) there would be *The Big Match* from London instead, where games always seemed to be played in perpetual sunshine and had Brian Moore as their peerless commentator, or occasionally from other regional broadcasters, including Granada, Yorkshire and Anglia.

The Tyne-Tees version was called *Shoot* and was shown at two o'clock on Sunday afternoons, straight after families finished their tinned peaches and cream, though the show eventually found another slot a couple of hours later when absolutely nothing else happened. The shows did a great job, even if everyone felt their club had a bigger and better game than the one chosen for broadcast.

The television deal included a requirement to visit the region's lower league clubs from time to time, too, which meant an occasional venture to Feethams at Darlington and Victoria Ground at Hartlepool in the Fourth Division, as well as the more regular trips to Ayresome, Roker and St James'. We joked that Tyne-Tees always managed to send their cameras (one on halfway and one behind each goal) to the wrong place at the wrong time. In later years, recalling these with colleagues on a North-East newspaper, we all would roll out impersonations of anchorman George Taylor, saying: 'It's been some weekend for our clubs with Newcastle winning at Anfield, Jack Charlton's Middlesbrough going top of the table and Sunderland creeping into the top half … while we were behind the floodlight pylon at Feethams to enjoy Darlington against Rochdale.' There were also sweepstakes on whether George's false teeth would get through the full hour intact.

Newcastle did, at least, supply the perfect footage in one of the title sequences, showing midfielder Tommy Craig beating two opponents (from Middlesbrough, if I recall rightly) without actually touching the ball. Craig was one of those perfectly poised left-footed midfielders, a precision passer with a great delivery into the penalty area, despite swinging his leg slowly enough to look like an action replay. In this clip, he has the ball on his left foot, fools one opponent by dummying a pass inside and sends another rival back to the dressing room as he dummies to run to his right, all the while with the ball stationary. The clip was shown every Sunday afternoon and was exactly the kind that would make him an internet sensation in the modern era, though I doubt anyone outside the Tyne-Tees region ever saw it. We attempted to copy with varying degrees of slapstick during our games played under lamp-posts as makeshift floodlights to eke out a few extra minutes of play in the evenings.

All alternative title sequences on *Shoot* would look incredibly outdated now, including the theme tune of a crowd chanting and clapping 'Shoot ch-ch ch-ch, Shoot ch-ch ch-ch'. It sounded great when your team lined up a free kick on the edge of the penalty area but it wasn't the kind of earworm that had you whistling the tune for the rest of the afternoon.

We were honoured in that our regional commentator was Kenneth Wolstenholme, he of 'they think it's all over … it is now' fame from the last seconds of the 1966 World Cup. In later years, the microphone was handed on to the channel's sports reporter, presenter, commentator and Arsenal supporter Roger Tames, who looked like Roger de Courcey, the TV ventriloquist partner of a bear by the name of Nookie. It could only have happened in the 70s.

With the advent of live broadcasts of top-flight football, these regional shows were consigned to history, though we did have a special edition to celebrate another promotion in 1993 when an agreement was made to show the entire second half of Newcastle's home game against Leicester City, followed by the presentations of the old trophy, which went to the winners of the former Second Division, now reborn as the Championship. Best-laid plans of mice and men and all that, the first half gave us incredible viewing of text updates exclusively on Ceefax as Newcastle scored six times. The second half, live on camera, included an anti-climactic one goal each. Kevin Keegan, by then manager and messiah, tried to tell everyone afterwards that there were bigger fish to fry than lifting a second-tier trophy – and he was right – but it's not as if the club's captains had strained themselves lifting silverware in the preceding half a century.

Shoot and the other Sunday shows were great if you could wait 24 hours to see the action but, if you didn't go to a game, the only way to keep up 'live' was via local radio commentary. With a team in the Second Division, there was no point in listening to national programmes before the *Sports Report* round-up at five o'clock. But we did have *It's a Goal* on BBC Radio Newcastle or reports from the independent Metro Radio station. I re-tuned constantly between the two, a task made easier with little sticky labels to help locate each channel as I rotated the dial.

The Radio Newcastle team nipped in and out of reports around the grounds, including some in the local non-league scene. Dad's gardening and DIY projects were regularly interrupted by the pre-recorded shout of catchphrase: 'It's a goal!' from a transistor radio, followed by a few anxious seconds patching through to the reporter while you wondered which game they were going to and which end of the pitch had hosted the important action. Many afternoons of my Subbuteo fantasies were played out to this backdrop, though the broadcast also provided a chance to record snippets of crowd noise or commentary to play over the plastic action.

The busiest days for the radio teams were the Saturdays during the early rounds of the FA Cup, with reports from the top divisions of the league alongside updates from the region's representatives in the lower divisions and non-leaguers like Blyth or North Shields, often with the reporter shouting to be heard above the locals on a landline somewhere in the ground but not necessarily with a clear view of the pitch. I know, I've been there and done it myself.

But it didn't matter what was being said or by whom, if a ball went into the net during a featured match, there was an immediate 'it's a goal' and a breathless bulletin from a reporter on the spot. Sky Sports and talkSPORT may believe they invented helium-driven live football updates but our interruptions could come in the middle of the weather forecast, travel news or the international headlines. If it had happened on a Saturday afternoon, even Neville Chamberlain would have had to wait with his 'no such undertaking has been received' announcement if Albert Stubbins had buried a shot past a flat-capped custodian in the opening weeks of the 1939/40 season.

* * *

Terry Hibbitt, who at times could provide a decent match for Bill McGarry's apparent grumpiness, had been an influential part of an attractive Newcastle team earlier in the decade and he returned to the club after a spell at Birmingham to compensate for injury to Tommy Craig. John Connolly and Jim Pearson also arrived on Tyneside from Everton.

The striking Bukta kit survived from the relegation season and, now installed as captain, Hibbitt said: 'I've always wanted to be skipper of the Black-and-whites. I would have liked it last time but Bobby Moncur was a great captain. I've learned a lot being captain at Birmingham, like controlling my temper for one thing. Everyone here wants success. I've met a lot of fans and they want that success as much as me. If we all work for each other, we could do well. I am very optimistic.' Success by this time, of course, meant getting into the promotion places, out of the Second Division and back among the best 22 teams in the country.

During his first spell with the club, when he exhibited a prodigious talent for finding Malcolm Macdonald with raking left-footed passes, Hibbitt had been mentioned alongside many of the top midfielders in the country but, tasked with providing ammunition for the frontrunners on his return, it was not Macdonald and Tudor in his rangefinder but the homegrown Kenny Mitchell, who started the new season in the fabled No.9 shirt, and young left-winger Stuart Robinson, as well as the more experienced Scottish new arrivals, Pearson and Connolly.

For the best part of a century, Scots had been central to any success at Newcastle. It was a trail blazed by Andy Aitken and Peter McWilliam and followed by the likes of legends Hughie Gallacher, Bobby Mitchell, Frank Brennan and Ronnie Simpson, then Bob Moncur, Jimmy Smith and Tommy Craig. The group which followed relegation included Mike Larnach, Mark McGhee, Brian Ferguson and Ralph Callachan, who were nowhere near in terms of impact.

Connolly and Pearson had at least previously played in the First Division. After a quick check in my football stickers from a previous year, I found them in the Goodison squad alongside the likes of Bob Latchford, Mick Lyons and Martin Dobson. Both had started out playing at St Johnstone and were described as 'Under-23 international', though they were well over-age by the time they docked on Tyneside. The Under-23 system was the precursor to Under-21 level of international representation and a mention next to a player's name typically meant they had already passed the peak of their potential, as in 'did well early in his career but has now found his level'. It may have been accurate in many cases but also seemed unfair to use a representative honour the rest of us would have given our front teeth for as a barbed character reference.

Neither Pearson nor Connolly made much of a career with the Magpies, though injury played its unfortunate part and, to their credit, they remained in the region afterwards and played a prominent role in its non-league scene, particularly with Blyth and Gateshead.

Winner of a single senior cap in 1973, when he replaced George Graham in the line-up, Connolly was a left-sided striker who enjoyed running at defenders out wide or through the middle and spent two full seasons at Gallowgate. Pearson, though, made just 11 appearances in 18 months before being forced into retirement. One of those games was a League Cup tie against Sunderland when he etched his name into North-East football folklore by missing the crucial kick in a penalty shoot-out. The young Robinson from Teesside, incidentally, matched that number of games before slipping into lower league football with Aldershot, while the manager quickly identified that Mitchell was not the answer in attack, though he did become more of a regular in the team after moving to left-back or central defence.

* * *

During the 1977/78 campaign, the principle of freedom of contract had been agreed by the chairmen of the league clubs, providing another step forward for players following abolition of the maximum wage and outlawing of the retain-and-transfer system a decade and a half earlier when George Eastham's struggles with the Newcastle board went all the way to the High Court. The players' union (Professional Footballers' Association) was still not totally happy, though, believing that an unequal share of power remained with employers.

Under the new regulations, players would be able to choose their club (which seems a pretty basic requirement) in return for a transfer fee being agreed. A tribunal system was put in place if agreement could not be reached and I remember a newspaper cutting in my scrapbook revealing its work in the £350,000-plus transfer of Kevin Hird from Blackburn to Leeds, a record fee for a full-back, as the first of its kind.

McGarry, meanwhile, still had some star material in his squad which could attract attention from elsewhere but he also needed to strengthen his own options in the rebuilding of Newcastle United, especially in attack, and this is where he did the best work of his time in charge.

First, he managed to secure the signature of Peter Withe, a centre-forward he had previously bought and sold while in charge at Wolves, to operate as his traditional targetman, and then he made a surprise move for Alan Shoulder, one of Blyth's FA Cup heroes of the previous campaign and who had juggled playing non-league football with his commitment to work with the National Coal Board.

Mickey Walsh, the Blackpool striker who had the decency to score *Match of the Day*'s goal of the season with a 30-yarder against Sunderland on a rare occasion when the cameras visited a Second Division ground, had been targeted as a £200,000 recruit during the spell of unrest the previous year but nothing happened and it got me thinking about the transfer stories which appeared on the back pages of *The Journal* and the *Evening Chronicle* but never came to pass.

In Withe's centre-forward role, there were several mentions of Coventry's Wallsend-born centre-forward Mick Ferguson. Later, it was Trevor Christie, another Tyneside discovery who was doing a decent job outside the top flight, and West Ham's David Cross, with his big broken nose. Later, under Arthur Cox, there was a big push to sign Andy Ritchie, who had cost Brighton a pretty penny but instead chose Leeds, which was a big call for a graduate of Manchester United's youth teams. Wearside-born midfielder Micky Hazard, Barnsley centre-half Mick McCarthy and his club colleague Ronnie Glavin, Wales midfielder Peter Nicholas and the battling Danny Wilson – one of the few *not* to play for both the Magpies *and* Sheffield Wednesday in this period – were all mentioned more than once.

But the best of all was speculation of a potential move for Brazil's majestic captain Sócrates after the 1982 World Cup because he was apparently going to continue his medical studies at Newcastle University. An international captain with a global profile to join our down-on-their-luck outfit; that would never happen, would it?

Back in the real world, by the end of the opening month of the 1978/79 season, as Tyneside settled into Second Division football, Micky Burns was gone. We all thought he could have done better than signing for Cardiff City and, as it turned out, he played just six times there before joining Middlesbrough where, picking up where he had left off in the North-East, he averaged a goal every other game.

Even more sadly, Alan Kennedy left, too, though who could begrudge a transfer to Liverpool for the exciting young left-back? Aiden McCaffrey, who had been highly rated as an England Youth international defender on his way to first-team action, left to join a Derby County defence which had lost the classy Colin Todd.

The unloved Callachan predictably returned to Scotland. What had once been such a happy hunting ground for Newcastle managers had turned into a parched wasteland, with the midfielder gone after just nine appearances. It was reported that he had been signed by the directors and had never even been watched by the manager, which illustrated again the depth of the issues afflicting our club. Regardless of whether he had the necessary ability or not, Callachan can count himself unlucky, as his name will continue to be mentioned in any list of transfer miss-hits during this period.

* * *

The arrival of Peter Withe gave the fans their first real successor to Malcolm Macdonald in the No.9 shirt which had been worn by so many favourites over the years.

Liverpool-born and with a ready smile and easy-going manner off the field, he was already 27 years old when McGarry brought him up to Tyneside. He had taken a while to make his mark in the game as an unremarkable targetman with numerous stops on the journey before maturing into a decent centre-forward with Birmingham and then Nottingham Forest, where he top-scored in their promotion season and then in a surprise league championship win at the first attempt. It was undoubtedly a shrewd piece of work by McGarry to bring him in as the team's attacking focus when he surely could have gone elsewhere in the top division instead.

Since Supermac's departure two years earlier, there had been no big-name signing as a direct replacement, with the effervescent Micky Burns initially moved further forward to play alongside Alan Gowling, with some success, too, especially in front of goal.

The gangling Gowling was not your typical centre-forward and was a textbook player only in the sense that he was a university student while registered as an amateur with Manchester United. He came out with a degree but was also pigeon-holed by many in the game, still suspicious of education or perceived entitlement.

None of us in the playground ever shouted, 'I'm Alan Gowling,' as we lined up to mimic our heroes and he would not have shifted many replica shirts in the modern era, but he had a very decent goalscoring record for Newcastle, despite the shadow cast by Macdonald. He was also valued as a more rounded team player but the former England Under-23 cap did not even see out the entirety of the 1977/78 season, which brought both UEFA Cup football and relegation, leaving to join Bolton Wanderers in March as their record £120,000 signing.

Bolton boss Ian Greaves had previously taken Gowling from Old Trafford to Huddersfield, so he knew what he was getting for his money. Wanderers were already on their way to promotion when the signing was completed and the following season Gowling again played a perfect supporting role to a charismatic star, scoring the team's first goal back in the First Division while strike partner Frank Worthington hogged the headlines. He still had time, too, to add further strings to his bow, alternating his future appearances between attack and the centre of defence while being elected chairman of the Professional Footballers' Association in 1980.

McGarry needed to address the turnover of striking options. He had already lost Cannell, a local prospect who had not been totally overawed by bigger personalities during his rise through the ranks. From an initial role as back-up to the senior strikers, he earned a run in the team and totalled more than 50 first-team appearances, including the UEFA Cup adventure, and making more of a fist of the No.9 challenge than any other pretenders before taking his talents to the United States.

The other contenders were either not ready or not up to it, though it did not help that the team was being rebuilt around them and that they were having to learn to sink or swim in the goldfish bowl that was a struggling Newcastle United.

Among those quickly deemed to be surplus to requirements, Mark McGhee and Mick Harford, in particular, would come to be seen as victims of poor timing.

United lost money on the £150,000 signing of McGhee from Morton, where he'd had a strike rate of two goals in every three games while playing outside the Scottish

Premier League. But then we could only watch as his star began to shine brightly when he was sold to Aberdeen. He later courageously tried again south of the border and made up for lost time with a much more impressive second spell on Tyneside towards the end of his career, establishing an irresistible strike partnership with the equally experienced and even more prolific Micky Quinn.

Harford, meanwhile, left and established himself as a menacing centre-forward feared by defenders all over the country, which was exactly what Newcastle had been looking for when initially taking him from Lincoln City. As a reward for his persistence, Harford earned an England debut after his 30th birthday and is revered as an all-time great by Luton Town supporters. Derby and Chelsea also paid good money for him later in his career and Sir Alex Ferguson is on record as regretting that he never added the big man to his squad at Old Trafford. After a short spell at his hometown club on Wearside (you know the one), Harford scored the winner *against* Newcastle in his only game for Coventry and he was into his 39th year when he finally hung up his boots as a professional. Newcastle were not alone in celebrating finally seeing the back of him.

Mike Larnach, signed for £100,000 with a decent goalscoring record at Clydebank but little experience of anything else, was thrown straight into a relegation fight when previously he would have expected to earn his spurs in the reserves and he was on his way back north within a year without a United goal to his name.

We also had a fleeting look at the gangly South African striker Andy Parkinson and the homegrown Mitchell, before he was converted to play in defence as a prototype Steve Howey, giving up his attacking ambitions for a lower number, though without the England caps to go with it.

There was even a 2-0 win at Leicester with utility player Graham Oates in the club's most famous shirt (though that was usurped by seeing expensive centre-back Andy Thorn following Mirandinha as the 'nine' during the last few weeks of another relegation season in 1989) and the search for a talismanic centre-forward saw both Harford and Ray Clarke come and go in the space of one season.

After the departure of Withe, the experienced options of Billy Rafferty and Bobby Shinton led the line as we waited for the next man to earn a place among heroes in the Number Nine Bar.

I was there for Withe's debut in the third game of the 1978/79 season, against an enterprising Luton team fancied to go well under manager David Pleat. But it was Jim Pearson who got the goal which provided the opening points of what we hoped would be just a brief taste of Second Division football.

Without the injured Nattrass and the departed Kennedy, McGarry promoted from within, as former apprentices Peter Kelly and Micky Barker started as his full-backs. The young Alan Guy was drafted in, too, as attacking cover for McGhee, who would return to Scotland by Christmas to kickstart a glittering career there. In theory, their introduction at this level should have been valuable for their development away from the pressure of the top division but that also depended on joining a settled and harmonious team with senior players able to assist in improving their craft.

John Blackley had provided a rare chink of light in the relegation year as supporters' player of the season but the freckled central defender with the baggy shorts missed the opening game in the Second Division before partnering John Bird in an experienced pairing at the back.

The season opener was, however, the last time we saw super goalie Mick Mahoney. As he set off for a new career in the States, Steve Hardwick became Newcastle No.1 with back-up from Kevin Carr, who had first tasted senior action a year earlier, a reward for the Morpeth-born youngster who had come through a trial period to earn his first professional contract after failing to make the grade at Burnley, that well-known poacher in the North-East talent pool.

The hangover from the wretched form of a relegation season carried into kick-off for a new campaign, with Newcastle apparently disorientated by their surroundings in defeat at Millwall and at home to West Ham before the players cleared their heads to go on an eight-match unbeaten run. Connolly and Withe provided the spearhead, prompted by Hibbitt and the equally experienced Colin Suggett, while the defence kept out allcomers, conceding just three goals in that sequence, including one from Roy Greenwood in a draw at Roker Park before he was sold to Derby in mid-season.

With unemployment figures at a 40-year high of around 1.5 million and newspapers referring to a 'Winter of Discontent' among what remained of the nation's workforce, there was something of a break in the clouds as a trio of wins took McGarry's team up to fifth in the table during December, with Shoulder now settled at Withe's side in a useful little-and-large combo up front. Hopes were raised of an instant return to elite company, with Shoulder hardly able to believe how far he had come from the northern coalfields in such a short time.

Every home game in the first half of the season attracted a gate of at least 20,000 and several above 23,000 before an enforced month off after Christmas during one of the worst winters in living memory. Schools closed and many roads were rendered impassable as the North-East braved weeks of freezing temperatures and deep snow. By the end of February, that icy blast had also reached the Magpies, who dropped 11 places with a wretched run of seven defeats in eight games, including a 4-1 loss at home to the Rokermen when Gary Rowell netted a hat-trick in front of a 35,000 derby crowd.

There was almost a third of the season's fixtures remaining to be played, due to all the postponements and rearrangements, but already the dream of an immediate bounce-back was waning. Like the team's fortunes, crowds dipped, too, with gates failing to reach 20,000 again until one final hurrah in May, by which time promotion was but a distant dream.

The frequency of my own visits was just about the only matchday stat going upwards, though I did choose to miss a couple of games early in the New Year to stay home and watch the Five Nations, our only chance to see any rugby live on the telly. England's meeting with Scotland was always crucial because we had a mix of both camps at our school and in our streets, while England against Wales was almost as important for different reasons. This was just after their Grand Slam days of Gareth Edwards, Phil Bennett and J.P.R. Williams but it was still a massive occasion between hot rivals and we had a vested interest, with Gosforth players including Malcolm Young, Roger Utley and prop Colin White (minus a few fingers lost in his work for the Forestry Commission) representing the North-East in a white shirt.

The national rivalry extended to the football and this was the year I put on a homemade knitted England jumper, waved a national flag and scarf, and, at the final whistle of victory over the Scots in the Home Internationals, jumped on my bike to ride past the window of a good friend who hailed from Aberdeen. When I turned around at the top of his street ready for a second 'ride-by' gloating, I saw not just him but also his brother and his dad waiting for me! Thankfully they were the non-fighting type from north of the border and also keen cyclists, so neither me nor my mount came to any harm.

* * *

The last four months of Newcastle's season were spent treading water in mid-table, though, after somehow fitting in nine league games during April, McGarry's team did eventually climb from 11th to finish in 8th place with a last-day revenge win over Wrexham. Pearson, fit again in time for the final day of the season and making his first appearance in six months, scored one of the goals as Shoulder ended his eye-catching campaign by hitting the back of the net for a third successive game.

At least this time the Welsh visitors were welcomed on a dry pitch after the quagmire of the previous year. The world has come a long way since the 70s, when local radio appeals would be made for fans in the winter to bring a spade and a broom to help clear snow in exchange for a match ticket and there was no such thing as what is now called 'pitch technology'. Pitches were pretty much universally rubbish.

St James' Park was not Derby's Baseball Ground, where the pitch was bald of grass for the whole year, under water for some of it and constantly sanded to the depth of a Wellington boot. And there are startling *Match of the Day* memories from mudbaths at Upton Park or Forest's City Ground among many others. Newcastle's pitch also had its days.

It was heavy in the years of Macdonald and Tudor, Moncur and Green. Also, for a city built on the slopes above a river, it is no surprise to learn the playing surface was not entirely flat and there was a noticeable hollow in front of 'A' Wing, the paddock in the Old Stand closest to the Gallowgate End. That was unfair on Kenny Wharton, who spent 50 per cent of his home matchdays standing on lower ground than his team-mates and may explain why every television clip I see now of Alan Kennedy rampaging forward from left-back is with the team kicking in the opposite direction, downhill towards the Gallowgate End goal.

* * *

Despite a dispiriting run-in, the Magpies did have a part to play in the outcome of the promotion race, hosting Brighton in the final home game when a win for the south coast side would take them into the First Division for the first time in their history. There was a score to settle, too, after defeat at the Goldstone Ground in December during the run of five successive losses which ended our own promotion hopes.

Hibbitt, Withe, Nattrass, Bird and Connolly provided some experienced ballast for the youngsters led by Carr (selected ahead of Hardwick during the closing weeks), Mitchell (now at left-back), David Barton and Peter Manners, but Newcastle still lost 3-2 against a composed opposition who were under the management of former England midfielder Alan Mullery in his trendy tinted specs.

Brighton's support took up the whole of the Leazes End for an historic occasion in seasonal sunshine and they enjoyed their afternoon as the club confirmed a second-placed finish in the table, one point behind a Crystal Palace side whose potential was being overblown in the (southern) media as the 'Team of the 80s' under Terry Venables. In an extra storyline, Sunderland missed out on promotion by a single point as Stoke City secured third place. Shame.

Looking back, of all the players McGarry selected in an ultimately disappointing campaign, only Hibbitt, Withe and Connolly (who statistically had a decent season but I have to admit made absolutely no impression on me) consistently held their places from start to finish. Everywhere else, the revolving door to the first team worked overtime.

During the previous season, when McGarry took over a sinking ship before Christmas, 35 players wore the club's famous colours and then 29 as everyone came to terms with life in the Second Division. In contrast, Arthur Cox used just 18 when he finally found the way to earn promotion a few years later.

Colin Suggett was unlucky, picking up an ankle injury in a 3-0 win over Bristol Rovers during the latter part of the season and it ended his career after just 23 appearances for the club. He had been noted as a teenage talent at Roker during his early steps in the game and was well regarded as he matured in spells with West Brom and Norwich. After the injury, he became a familiar figure on the Magpies staff for another decade until finally making his exit after a disagreement on policy under Kevin Keegan.

Former Scotland international Blackley had also played his final game for the club, moving to Preston on a free transfer just two seasons after his £100,000 arrival and 12 months on from being named player of the year.

With money tight and a number of bridges burned, a string of young players were handed an opportunity in senior football but few of them made a lasting impression. How could they in the circumstances? As a result, they were recognisable for many fans only through the use of their portraits on a prize panel on the front of the match programme rather than for what they produced on the pitch.

Jamie Scott, a midfielder born in Newcastle, had made his breakthrough the previous season, fulfilling the dream of every boy on Tyneside when called into the senior squad and handed a run of games. He joined a team sitting second-from-bottom in the First Division and with an ever-changing selection of colleagues everywhere he looked. A gritty player maybe and undoubtedly grateful for his opportunity, but equipped to drag a team away from the lower reaches of the top flight in his first taste of senior football? Unlikely.

There were numerous others who had an even briefer sample of life at first-team level only to find themselves jettisoned, though Scott at least played in eight of the next ten games from his debut at Chelsea in March 1978 before stepping aside for the final three weeks of a disastrous campaign. He could have been forgiven for thinking this breakthrough constituted a successful audition but, instead, he was given just two starts by McGarry – four months apart – the following season, despite the team playing in a division lower, and before long was on his way out. Scott went to Carlisle, did not play a game there and then, after a short spell at Berwick Rangers in 1980, moved into non-league football.

Martin Gorry made a single senior appearance in 1977, a mark equalled by another full-back, Keith Mulgrove, during 1978/79 (judging by his photo, he may have got the gig because management thought he was Alan Kennedy), while midfielder Manners and hotly tipped defender Tony Smith played twice in that period and Parkinson three times (all from the bench). Alan Guy managed seven games in three seasons and Stuart Robinson reached a dozen games.

For a while, it looked like Gary Nicholson would be the one to crack the code. As an exciting goalscorer playing on the wing in reserve-team football, he earned a few opportunities but, like a batsman making a solid start only to struggle in converting his innings into big runs, Nicholson was out the door before his 21st birthday. He made 17 appearances in black-and-white before building a respectable career with

200 games in the colours of Mansfield, York and Halifax in the bottom division, then returning to the North-East in non-league.

The club's reputation as a graveyard for young players continued into the early 80s, with defender Phil Leaver and striker Kevin Pugh each called up to make a solitary first-team appearance. There cannot be many other clubs where so many played so few.

Other than the youth-team graduates who had started out in regional boys' clubs and schools football, Gorry and midfielder Brian Ferguson – signed from Mansfield before making a first-team appearance – were among a group who had been brought in from lower levels with an eye to the future, enticed by the opportunity at a club with a big history and equally impressive fanbase, only to find out harshly that they would have to try again elsewhere.

Some of this cohort could put it down to bad timing, though none subsequently made a big name for themselves at an equivalent or higher level. Terry McDermott, Stewart Barrowclough and Pat Howard had previously been signed from clubs outside the top division and developed into first-teamers but Joe Harvey had spent money on them knowing he had the class and experience around his squad to help them along until they could make a shirt their own property. They were qualities in short supply, even by the first year of the stay in the Second Division.

A handful of young players did manage to get their heads above the swirling waters to breath freely and come through to make a name for themselves and a select few would be around long enough to move up with the club when the time came. One of them, miraculously given the situation he came into as a youngster, would even top 300 appearances for his hometown team.

One afternoon years later, I sprawled a load of *Rothman's Yearbooks* and papers and notes and programmes across the carpet in an attempt to catalogue the Newcastle United games I had attended as a fan, complete with line-ups and scorers. Still in the days before laptops and spreadsheets, this was worked out on an A3 sketchpad, drawing lines across the page to record the necessary details of each game. From my calculations, it emerged that I had seen Kenny Wharton in action in the flesh more times than any other player. More than my heroes Macdonald, Kennedy, Carney and McCreery; more than the *galacticos* Keegan, Beardsley, Waddle and Gascoigne; more times than many of Wharton's contemporaries had pulled on a Newcastle shirt.

He made his debut late in the 1978/79 Second Division season as a substitute and stayed in the first-team frame for a decade. I even got his autograph once when he reported for duty on a matchday, catching him on the slope within the walls behind the Old Stand where bunches of kids used to hang around waiting to see the players and their cars. I think his was a Ford Escort.

Wharton's is among only a handful of Magpies signatures I have collected over the years. I queued for hours at one of Keegan's early public appearances – at the opening of Monument Sports near Grey's Monument – and went home with a postcard and a poster signed by the great man. Otherwise, I think there is a John Trewick signature somewhere, Alan Shoulder's handwriting on a page torn from a notebook when my dad's band played at a function he attended and an Alan Kennedy autograph given to me by a schoolmate who bumped into him on a stadium tour. I recall Mick Martin's handwriting on the back of a programme somewhere, a signed copy of Terry McDermott's book and Joe Harvey's autograph on his testimonial brochure, which is a fine and fitting souvenir of the man. And there's also Bobby Shinton's signature in the England Football-branded notebook I took to a premiere of Michael Caine's *Escape to Victory* at the Odeon on Pilgrim Street, though I had been hoping to stop guest of honour Jackie Milburn instead!

After making his breakthrough, teenager Wharton was seen just once in his second season, playing at left-back at home to Swansea in the penultimate home game, a full 12 months after his previous outing, and he could have gone the way of so many others before him. Instead, he stuck at it and finally established himself from the start of 1980/81 under Arthur Cox, first on the left side of midfield and then switching between there and full-back, despite a physique which earned him the descriptive nickname of 'Bones'.

Working under six managers in his 11 seasons at the club, Wharton was always what you could call 'a bit different'. Other than weighing in at about eight and a half stone, he came into the set-up via Grainger Park Boys' Club while anybody who was anybody on Tyneside seemed to have been with Wallsend's equivalent. He tackled above his weight with a fierce and occasionally fiery competitive edge while he was also able to prompt and play from wherever he was stationed on the pitch. He would do whatever his role entailed, so long as it could be done with a left foot.

In April 1988, Wharton also famously sat on the ball during a four-goal win over Luton as the team showboated their way towards the final whistle. As he stood up again, he backheeled possession to a team-mate who continued in similar style, adding to the raised hackles of the visitors' bench, who stormed on to the pitch at the end to make their point. I don't suppose Kenny cared what they thought. Less well known, I recall clearly a moment (though not the opposition) in another game when, playing at left-back in that 'hollow' part of the pitch in front of 'A' Wing, he took a pass from the goalkeeper and, just as two opposing players came flying in to clatter their stick-thin rival, he tapped the ball forward, watched the two assailants collide like cartoon characters and went on his merry way with the home support in raptures. It happened every week in comics but this was real life.

Wharton's career was eventually ended by injury, though he had numerous attempts to convince other clubs – and probably himself – that he could still do the business before finally calling time. He moved into coaching and gained some notoriety when apparently recommending his son, Paul, to join Leeds rather than the youth ranks at Newcastle. Like I said, he was a bit different.

He was, though, one of the players that the fans identified with easily, a local lad who had made the grade with their team and made himself a key part of it. If he hadn't received the call, he'd probably be standing next to us on the terraces in jumper, jeans and trainers.

After all the chopping and changing of my early years in the crowd, I also remember the excitement of seeing Wharton close in on an appearance landmark. Frank Clark, David Craig, Nattrass, McFaul and Moncur from the not-too-distant past had all played for Newcastle for a decade or more in the seasons just before I became a regular. So, in among the chopping and changing under successive managers and the failed promotion hopes, I was thrilled to eventually see Kenny hit 200 first-team games and put a new name among the club's top appearance-makers. It was a significant moment (John Anderson followed as the only other man in that era with anything resembling a landmark number in appearance terms).

In collecting football stickers or reading biographies in my match programmes, other clubs all seemed to have players with much longer careers than ours. I had yearned to see someone clock up a high number of games for my club.

Billy Bonds, Frank Lampard (senior), Trevor Brooking and Pat Holland did it at West Ham, followed by Phil Parkes, Alvin Martin and Alan Devonshire; Steve Perryman and Pat Jennings at Spurs; George Armstrong, Pat Rice and David O'Leary went on forever at Arsenal; Ian Callaghan and Tommy Smith were followed by Phil Neal, Emlyn Hughes, Ray Clemence and others with Liverpool; Mick Lyons at Everton; Mick Coop and Tommy Hutchison at Coventry; goalkeeper Mark Wallington with Leicester; every club had players who clocked up year after year of service while the doors continued to spin off their hinges at St James'. It was odd that such a hotbed of the sport failed to find and keep someone who would stick around long enough. Was it down to the management turnaround, the money, the isolation of the far north, a lack of success or ambitions bigger than the club's?

In the days when I kept records of our players in an exercise book at home, I started to rub out Kenny's total week to week, longing to see it reach 200. It seemed an incredible number compared with everyone else around him. Being a bit different, of course, he not only got to 200 but then marched past 250 and on to 300 (including 268 league games) before cartilage trouble ended it.

I do hope, though, that Kenny forgives me for remembering a fanzine letter written at the height of fury around United being a 'selling club', fuelled by an overwhelming feeling that crowd hero Peter Beardsley had been transferred purely to finance the first phase of a not-before-time stadium redevelopment. The letter said something along the lines of: 'Now that the Beardsley Stand is sorted, why not go the whole way and sell Kenny so we can add the Wharton Hot Dog Hut too?'

A fairer indicator of the warmth for Wharton was the attendance of more than 20,000 – a figure comparable with many of his league appearances – for his testimonial fixture in 1989 when Kevin Keegan, Chris Waddle and Paul Gascoigne lined up alongside fellow England internationals Peter Shilton and Gary Pallister in an all-star team. Keegan, at that point retired and distant from the game, added his considerable influence to the uneasiness around the selling of star players, telling Tyne-Tees TV as he headed back to the dressing room: 'This club should be buying players like Gascoigne and Beardsley, not selling them. If you sell class players like that, you cannot keep producing them out of the bushes, great area that it is and the great scouting system they have.

'Great players do not come along very often. They have been privileged here with four or five of those in the last five years but they've sold them all. A [new] stand does not win you football matches, does not score goals, does not pull people in.

'If the lads think it is hard to stay in the First Division then they are going to be in for a shock next year, if they go down, to see how hard it is to get out of the Second Division.'

Sure enough, Newcastle were relegated that year but if John Hall (Sir John from 1991) was watching the local news that tea-time, he could have decided there and then on the identity of the only other man who could lead the club out of the doldrums.

Chapter Four:

Got to Find a Better Way

THERE IS a feeling that we in the north are 'hard'. Particularly in the North-East. As 'Dirty' Charlie Hogg (played by Tim Healy) put it in *A Captain's Tale*: 'We're hard men, we lead hard lives ... we don't breed weeping willows. Iron, that's what we're made of, that's what we're going to show, bloody iron.'

'Coal' would have been more appropriate for us Northumberland schoolboys but, bowing to Charlie's aggressive nature, let's agree on iron. And we felt that iron was cast even tougher on Tyneside and we were well aware of it whenever we had to face football teams from schools and boys' clubs in the more urban areas. I can't recall anything actually happening when we did play against them but most of us definitely felt an element of intimidation beforehand, from their team and their supporters, as we walked into buildings which were generally a lot older and more 'lived-in' than ours located in a new town. We mostly missed out on playing against the schools from the real inner-city area, because they had their own leagues and cups, but it didn't stop us knowing all about their reputation when someone mentioned places like Scotswood, Denton, Montagu or Cruddas Park. Their lads just looked harder and they acted and talked tougher than any of us. Somehow, we never felt like that against our rival county teams, wherever they came from.

Hard lives grafting in coalfields and shipyards bred a regional resilience and resistance to pain and the feeling on the football terraces was that it just wasn't the same if you were from places like, say, Ipswich or Norwich, Shrewsbury or Brighton. As the home crowd put it while promising to take any visitors outside for a 'howking' after a game: 'Come and have a go if you think you're hard enough.'

Football clubs were built on the backs of industry in working-class areas, which meant there were plenty of challengers to any Geordie claims of being 'hard' from the likes of Liverpool, Leeds, Manchester, Sheffield, Birmingham, Stoke and, yes, even London. They weren't all stockbrokers.

Around the ground, there would be rounds of 'come and have a go at the Geordie aggro', and even the kids, ever eager to fit in, joined in with a chorus of 'you're going home in a St John Ambulance', because it sounded daft, though mode of transport for offenders was more likely to be in a Black Mariah owned by the local constabulary, for there was no shortage of takers who did want to show they did, indeed, feel hard enough.

The summers may have been sunnier, Tudor Crisps packets fuller and Twix fingers longer but the late 70s did have plenty of negatives, too. There was a global energy crisis, terrorist bombings and hijackings, military coups, the Cold War and threat of nuclear extermination which would at least save us from more strikes, inflation, inner-city strife and the rise of Margaret Thatcher (mentioned here only because her one involvement in football was in response to escalating issues with stadium violence, which were accompanied by headlines and news coverage backed by cries of 'National

Service' or 'bring back the birch' from people who had never stood on a terrace).

Personally, I never 'got' the excitement provided by the promise of a good scrap. I was never going to be a fighter (I didn't have a big brother as back-up, for a start), though I loved to see footballers knocking lumps out of each other in a game. Scrapping is like wanting to play in the front row of a scrum or enjoying spine-chilling rides at theme parks; you're either for it and do or you're against it and let the ones who are in favour get on without you.

My enthusiasm for fighting was restricted to watching the gloved variety on television during the closing years of the Muhammad Ali era and the reign of champions like Sugar Ray Leonard, Roberto Duran, Thomas Hearns and Barry McGuigan which followed. If I wanted to see bloodshed on a Saturday evening, I switched on to ITV's coverage of a bout featuring Alan Minter or Charlie Magri.

Violent incidents at football started to make regular headlines in the 60s, the first full decade when youth of the Western world supposedly identified as something more than just a younger (or Mini, to suit the era) version of their own parents. The journalist John Moynihan, writing a best-selling book in 1966, was particularly scathing of the behaviour of Liverpool fans while hoping his beloved Chelsea would never follow in that direction (cough cough). Newcastle were not immune, either, with newspaper coverage of clashes in and around city pubs on matchdays. The rioting of Rangers fans at St James' Park during their Fairs Cup defeat in 1969 raised further awareness and fear in the public so close to our doorstep.

As early as 1971, club captain Bobby Moncur had declared in his autobiography this was 'the time of the bovver boys', using the expression of the day. 'He's giving the fan a bad name,' Moncur continued. 'Pick up a paper virtually any day of the week and you'll read of violence on the terraces or in the city after a match. It seems to be spreading like a disease.'

To be fair, the long-serving United skipper also urged a sense of proportion, identifying the perpetrators as a minority of supporters. That was how most of the public saw football hooliganism at the time, despite the headlines, and that was exactly what we thought as young lads when we started to join the crowds on matchdays. Don't bother them and they won't bother you.

The pitch invasion which halted Newcastle's FA Cup tie with Nottingham Forest in 1974 made national news and hit the front pages locally after the referee took both teams to the safety of the tunnel as home supporters ran on from the Leazes End with their team trailing 3-1 and tempers fraying. Commentary noted that these incursions were made not just by over-exuberant kids, feeling the wind in the fake fur of their green Parkas, but also by grown men whose intentions were possibly less innocent.

When the pitch was eventually cleared, the sixth-round fixture resumed and the Magpies, down to ten men after the dismissal of defender Pat Howard for disputing a Forest penalty, staged a remarkable comeback to level the scores and then dramatically secure a 4-3 win, with Moncur among the scorers, finishing from a lay-off by Macdonald.

With the invasion hogging headlines, the Football Association ordered a replay, deeming the first game null and void, and sent the teams to play again on neutral territory at Everton's Goodison Park. There, they produced a goalless draw and had to try again three days later on the same soil – to the bemusement of all and the fury of Forest, who felt a replay should go to their City Ground. Whatever, Newcastle finally sealed progress over their Second Division opponents with a goal from Supermac.

Chastened by the experience, the club were among the pioneers in investigating segregation for supporters, who up to that point had mixed in parts of the ground. On TV, you would often spot pockets of opposition colours next to the black-and-whites in the Gallowgate, with one group celebrating a goal while others stood still. But the days of standing cheek by jowl were numbered, other than for the few who liked it that way and yearned for it to kick off in the crowd as well as on the field.

Just about every regional newspaper around the country carried stories of pitch invasions or football violence on their patch during the middle years of the 70s and there was extensive coverage of another cup incident at Newcastle, when fans got on the field in a game against Manchester City in 1977. In the same year, a news crew arranged to follow the Millwall mob for BBC's *Panorama* programme, during which they called football hooliganism 'the trench warfare of the terraces'.

While the description showed outrageous disrespect for a generation who had lived through the unimaginable horrors of the trenches of northern Europe, its sentiment did show where national opinion lay when it came to football and its issues. The failure of the national team to qualify for two World Cups in the decade did nothing but add to the general negativity around the game from around its periphery.

'A good game of football, a good punch-up and a good piss-up,' was how one of the fans from the south London dockyards described his perfect matchday on camera for *Panorama*. If anyone knew, it was Millwall, even then.

Some clubs did not bring much of a travelling support in those Second Division years, put off by the expense, the mysteries of the far north – Newcastle was not a party destination then – or by the standard of facilities in the corner enclosure which awaited them. Being so severely outnumbered by home fans and facing a notoriously sketchy trip back to the railway station didn't help swell their numbers, either. There were taunts of, 'you must have come in a taxi' or 'on a skateboard' from home fans who asked, 'Shall we sing a song for you?' and, if the visitors suddenly woke up to mark a shot or a goal, they were met with 'it's nice to know you're here', followed by the united instruction to go away.

Whatever the strength of away support, there were frequent flare-ups, though from our perspective they seemed like flashpoints involving like-minded lads and did not go much further than that.

There was always a heavy police presence around town; you heard their dogs and saw the black vans parked along Barrack Road and nearby streets. You heard and saw and smelled the horses. You could usually pick out the likely lads in a crowd who would want to get involved but we posed no threat and, being small enough and agile enough to get out of the way, we were among the thousands who felt a bit more grown-up just by going to watch our team and who remained largely unaffected by anything that happened on the fringes of the occasion.

It was almost impossible to avoid contact with bother here and there, though. Flying fists and boots would break out in pockets outside the stadium and on the terraces, where a loud cheer during a lifeless part of the game would signal something happening somewhere other than on the grass, followed by files of police sent in to investigate. Our route around the outside on the way back to town put us on the periphery of some close combat or stone and bottle-throwing, too, including in the streets behind the New

Stand, though the tidal flow of fans invariably kept us out of harm's reach.

On non-matchday trips into town, we always called into W.H. Smith to scan through the magazines and the records and there was one time we got locked in on the ground floor of Eldon Square shopping centre (which would have only been a few years old after developers effectively put a roof over the city in a foretaste of what would follow elsewhere) when the security shutters came down in response to football fighting nearby. There were sporadic outbreaks outside, too, especially on the routes for visiting fans to and from the stadium. But it was usually in small groups and never appeared to last long – or at least we didn't hang around long enough to find out.

This, then, was the era of 'Boot Boys' well before the advent of the 'casual', a term used to describe fashion sense rather than attitude towards violence, which included custom-made calling cards and prearranged meets between rival 'firms', who compiled their own league tables of results not connected with the actual football.

We had started going to games unaccompanied but never feared the consequences. Who wanted to fight a 13-year-old anyway, other than another 13-year-old? Also, our experience was still confined to home games. It would be another few years before I had a taste of the issues as an away fan around the country.

I had moved away from home just as the more organised violence of the 80s kicked in, where flashpoints spread further away from football grounds and became more difficult to judge as an innocent bystander. Wearing your colours was dangerous if you were on your own or in a small group and the expert advice was to never open your mouth if your accent was likely to betray you as 'not from around here, are ya mate?' You were told never to respond if someone pointed at their wrist and asked for the time. Either that or practise your language skills in different accents before leaving the house.

Challenges were laid down even before away fans entered the stadium and, once they got inside the turnstiles, corralled into their spartan segregated pen, they would be serenaded with an early chorus of 'Geordie boot boys, Geordie boot boys' or 'you're laughing now, I don't know why, cos after the match …' A bit of a scrap, or even just talk of it, was part of that ritual, a sport within a sport. For some of the lads, it was part of the fun. For us, it wouldn't have been.

Our understanding from the edges was that trouble was simply groups of lads coming together, fuelled perhaps by a few pints but mostly by partisan support for their team to the exclusion of all others and of being young and daft and seeking excitement. Some of the workforce still picked up a weekly pay packet and many aimed to get through it by Sunday evening before the drudgery started all over again. For some of them, scrapping side by side with mates was part of the agenda. Others were just caught up in it and gave it their best shot. It was simply 'aggro' or 'bother' in our everyday vocabulary, 'scrapping' in the days before 'radge' became all the rage.

All around the ground, heads would spin as flailing arms and clouds of dust like real-life versions of *The Beano* cartoons betrayed the location of rival groups coming together – the adult version of 'scrap, scrap, scrap' heard in the playground. This would mean either home fans had infiltrated the other end just for the sheer hell of it – a moral medal to wear with the bruises – or visiting fans had broken cover by cheering their team from somewhere other than their enclosure. When home fans started trouble in the away section, they were cheered all round for their commitment, especially if they refused to go quietly or tried to escape into another paddock as they were being escorted round the cinder track by police. Offenders from the away support were dragged out and taken round the edge of the pitch, where they suffered more verbal abuse on the way to their own areas of the ground or to be slung out into the streets, where they would have to watch out for the natives. Serious troublemakers went to the charge room and to the waiting vans, destined for the police station downtown.

The environment was as abusive of others as it was supportive of our own. Fans mockingly whistled the theme to *Laurel and Hardy* when the police moved into position and cheered mercilessly if one got involved with a scrapper in the crowd. There were police sentries on steps and terrace tops, with the mounted brigade outside or assembled in one corner as a show of strength.

Resistance was regular, too, with fans closing ranks to protect their kin whenever officers moved into the terraces from the edge of the pitch or via the fenced corridor which ran front to back on the Gallowgate. The acts of obstruction could grow more violent, too, if the police managed to grab their target.

Travelling contingents like Chelsea and Millwall, who had earned and enjoyed a dubious reputation, were escorted in a police cordon as they marched through the city. Their walk to the stadium looked like a protest rally as they were dutifully delivered to their end of the ground, the one with even more limited facilities and views than ours.

It was at this time that rumours would repeatedly surface about Chelsea travelling north with bigger numbers, swelled by the presence of notorious fighters from other London clubs, and this would mean a real war. Their visits appeared to take up the entire Northumbria Police workforce, trying to maintain the herd along the route from the station to St

James' and back. There would be posturing and verbals from both sets of fans, a few flare-ups along the way and the police giving an unfussy push to anyone who tried to get too close or broke ranks from within. Sparks would ignite, fights would start and end, then the parade would be directed around half a lap of the stadium to their designated corner of the Leazes while the baying continued from the other sides.

While witnessing a fight was seen as just part of matchday for some, its extremes still stopped everyone in their tracks on the day during the 1979/80 season when a petrol bomb incident during a visit from West Ham became the most notorious episode in the club's terrace history. Things had suddenly turned a whole lot more sinister.

Long-serving full-back David Craig, who had been a Youth Cup winner soon after his arrival from Northern Ireland in the early 60s before racking up more than 300 first-team appearances in something like 18 years at the club, once said demolition of the Leazes End had 'pulled the heart out of the club' and it was terrible to see an incident like that taking place on those steps. It also signalled an evolution from toe-to-toe blows to something far more unpredictable and frightening.

The shock and the headlines outweighed any previous trouble and there were photos of the incident splashed across the front pages. The image became an unwanted icon of Newcastle's terrace culture – at least until that bloke punched a police horse on derby day. The West Ham incident was Tyneside's landmark in lunacy, joining a shocking gallery which included that image of a dart sticking in the nose of a Manchester United fan (which dates from February 1978 but has been used so often that it feels a lot older) or of Millwall ripping out seats at Kenilworth Road during a televised cup tie against Luton ten years later.

* * *

Football's problem with violence, and the focus placed upon it from media and authorities, increased throughout the 70s and 80s, with incidents all over the country. But the spotlight was inescapable after the attention given to the huge numbers who followed Manchester United in their Second Division season, where they outnumbered home fans wherever they went and made the most of the opportunity.

As their fortunes on the pitch dipped with the end of the Matt Busby era, United's fans provided their own entertainment off it. Their reputation had been growing for several years before the team's stunning fall from grace, with the Red Army tracing its roots back to clashes with West Ham in the mid-60s. As a world-famous club with a media profile to match, they attracted more interest, which attracted more trouble, which brought more media reports, more interest and so on.

Objects including a knife were thrown in the crowd during their game against Newcastle in 1971 and, as punishment for crowd misbehaviour, they were ordered to play the opening two home games of the following season on neutral grounds, at Stoke and Liverpool, respectively. It is unsurprising to learn that the decision signalled more crowd trouble, with pitch invasions at Anfield and smashed windows in local houses. At the start of the 1977/78, they were kicked out of Europe, then reinstated, but only if the next 'home' game was taken to Plymouth, as far as you can get from Old Trafford on the mainland. What the good people of these neutral venues thought about it no doubt made decent coverage in their local press but didn't seem to matter to the football authorities. In my own experience of games on neutral territory, it usually meant inviting three sets of fans to the party, including one who could choose which side they were on.

But misbehaviour was by no means exclusive to the Red Army. Chelsea and Millwall were among other early adopters; West Ham, Arsenal and Tottenham had other violent groups from the capital; Birmingham, Cardiff and Bristol City had reputations in other major cities. Middlesbrough is still named in polls of dodgiest destinations during that era and Leeds became as unpopular for their crowd as they had been for their team, with various incidents forcing them to play the first four games of 1971/72 outside their own city. That run included a clash with Newcastle who, while we're casting stones, had some troublemakers as well. But just about every club, along with every town or city they played in, experienced some disorder on a Saturday.

A North-East newspaper described pre-match fighting with Liverpool supporters as 'a running battle' after trouble apparently started when a policeman's helmet got knocked off as he was the target of numerous boots. It may sound like sticking your tongue out with your fingers in your ears but the action was no doubt based on the widely held view that you couldn't get arrested if the copper didn't have his hat on.

A few years after I'd left home, I went to a heated derby between Preston and Blackpool when both teams were in the Fourth Division and watched as a policeman in full motorbike leathers waded into a load of trouble which had been initiated by fans banging holes in the corrugated wall at the back of the away end. I was in the paddock to one side (like 'E' Wing, just for old times' sake) and watched the copper push his way from front to back. I could also clearly see the punches which rained down on his full-face helmet as he collared whoever had been identified as the main antagonist. His head must have been ringing by the time assistance arrived but it was an interesting tactic, certainly better than the protection offered by a peaked cap, and there's no way anyone was flicking a motorbike helmet to the floor.

'Animals' was the term used in association with trouble which spread from stadiums and surrounding areas into town centres and beyond. The 'Football Special' trains, which began journeys as glorified cattle trucks, often ended them in considerably worse state, with stripped and dismembered carcases for carriages. Windows were routinely smashed, seats slashed and bathrooms reduced to dust.

The authorities thought they could fix football with segregation, limited ticket sales to away fans and all-ticket fixtures. Later, the Tory government proposed the introduction of identity cards, which was all well and good if you also believed that deception and forgery had already been eradicated from society.

Earnest debates ensued on the possible causes of what became known as football hooliganism – also the 'Football Disease' or, even more naively, the 'English Disease' – while panel participants failed to understand that their grandstanding chatter on the subject also helped to advertise and glorify it.

Some of these experts described football fighting as out-and-out mindless thuggery which should be stamped out with a show of even greater force. Or another 'Enemy Within'. The other viewpoint believed that, while not condoning violence, football and the actions of the people who followed it merely reflected the dissatisfaction, loss of hope and decreasing standards in society as a whole and should not be viewed in isolation.

The 'Winter of Discontent' coincided with Newcastle's first season back in the Second Division in 1978/79 when a mid-table finish – after dropping as far as 16th place before Easter – did little to help the mood and average crowds remained just above the 20,000 mark. By then, a bit of aggro had become a fact of life. 'Aggro' covered any kind of aggravation or inconvenience as well as aggression and violence of any scale, though I'm not sure it was ever used by the BBC who referenced 'hooliganism' as if it was a religious belief system. Maybe it was for some.

Later, stiff wire fences were added as a desperate response to pitch incursions and, tragically, we all know how that ended.

At St James' Park, with standing on three sides by the mid-80s – benches replaced standing at the front of the New Stand – there would be no shortage of fencing, looming high over the top of anyone standing near the front and adding another layer to the hatch-marked view from low down, especially if you stood directly behind the goal and also looked through the net at anything in the penalty area.

Fences also produced a tell-tale pinging sound which betrayed missiles being thrown towards the opposition. It was strange at first, with little high-pitched tinging but then you worked out that these were objects flicking off the fences. Coins mostly. I know because I took one 50p piece behind the ear at a game against Chelsea as we edged towards the escape routes in the closing minutes.

Visiting winger Mickey Thomas was the intended target as he went to take a corner in front of the Gallowgate and I just happened to be in the way, having left my usual post in the middle to edge nearer to the exits. The strike stunned me momentarily but then I noticed the collection of loose change bouncing back off the fence. Wrong place, wrong time. A pity we hadn't gone contactless by then.

These were the Wild West days of terrace culture and Thomas was known as the kind of player who would give and take in equal measure against rival players and fans. But it was still no excuse.

The incident gave me something to talk about, though my story has nothing compared with that of Thomas himself, who also served Manchester United, Everton, Leeds and a prison sentence after passing counterfeit bank notes among apprentice professionals during his time at Wrexham, for whom he also scored a famous goal in a giantkilling victory against Arsenal. One of the characters of the game and always a good talker in the media, Thomas once quipped about one of his Old Trafford successors: 'So, Roy Keane's on 50 grand a week. I was on 50 grand a week until the police found my printing machine!' He also carried on playing into his 40s, was stabbed 15 times during an assault while in a parked car with his ex-wife's sister-in-law and, in 2021, announced that he was cancer-free after a two-year battle with a huge stomach tumour. A life well and truly lived.

* * *

'Basic' would be about the kindest description for the limited facilities on offer inside a football stadium in these years, a million miles away from the glamour of the modern Premier League and orderly redevelopment below that level. Even before the barbarism of anti-hooligan fences around the pitch, a football ground (a term more fitting than 'stadium' in most places) had little to recommend it other than the atmosphere and, if you were lucky, the match itself.

Travelling through town to see our team, through streets which still carried the remnants of their industrial heritage, where concrete chaos had been uneasily coupled with Victorian planning, football grounds of the 70s and 80s had their own intimidating aura. There were no plazas or fanzones but, instead, threatening tall brick walls, barbed wire, aggressive graffiti, narrow entry points and a few no-go areas.

All around the chanting, singing, swearing and, sadly, the racism were at full volume. But, as lads who were there, we will still talk warmly of the experience and of standing in all weathers to be part of it on the terraces. Of gambling on whether to go in front of a crash barrier so you couldn't get pushed forward from there or to stay behind and take advantage of the chance to lever yourself up on your elbows when your view was impaired by someone bigger (and tougher) in front, despite knowing you would also get squashed whenever everyone else moved.

Modern stadia can still claim volume – especially under total cover, which allows the noise to reverberate – but the all-seater cannot compete with the excitement of the movement of a terrace in full flow.

Scarves stretched between two hands, or swung around from one wrist, everyone bouncing together in celebration has a colour and a vibrancy that is impossible to replicate. And there is nothing in an all-seater stadium to compare with the spontaneous surges of energy experienced within a standing crowd. A shot on goal, especially one that looks like it is going to hit the net but instead produces a save or desperate defensive block, would see the whole stand on the move. The surge started from the back, where fans moved forward in expectation of seeing the net ripple, and would instigate a human wave down the steps. Seconds later, everyone casually moved back to where they started.

Goal celebrations meant moving forward, back or sideways, cheering and jumping with strangers before shuffling back to somewhere near your starting position, reclaiming the hat or scarf or programme dropped inside the noisy mob, then getting ready in the hope of doing it all again. If anyone hit the deck, they were helped up, dusted off and did their best to find their starting position as if nothing had happened.

Unless, of course, you were unlucky enough to get close to a terrace pisser. Unable or unwilling to vacate a position among the masses, the beered-up fan would simply go where he stood and, if you didn't get out of the way, at least you were assured of a double seat to yourself on the bus home, though, unlikely to have many close friends for the duration of the journey. It happened to a member of our group once and it had to be on the day he was wearing light-grey trousers and matching shoes!

Whatever the overtime bonuses, you didn't envy the police officers on duty. When they did wade into the crowd to extract a fan, they would emerge with phlegm-streaked uniforms to go with an earful of more figurative bile. The lads in the crowd were no revolutionaries but this was a way of giving it back to what the Americans call 'The Man' without inner-city rioting or going on strike again.

Away from the misbehaviour, though, there was always humour or at least light-hearted banter, beginning with a welcome to the opposition. Goalkeepers were an easy and obvious target, shown the famous northern warmth with a generous round of applause as they ran towards the Gallowgate goal before kick-off, only to be greeted with a variety of gestures and a gravel-throated 'aaaaaaaaaaaaa' when they acknowledged it. Not for us the Kop's generous appreciation of the visitors. As regular champions, it was easy for them to be magnanimous in triumph. We didn't have that luxury. Some keepers simply smiled knowingly, others kept their head down. They couldn't win, whatever they did.

Players spent a lot less time on the floor than in the 21st century non-contact version of football and, in the days of clear divide between the sexes and attitudes towards them, we always laughed at chants of 'she fell over' when a visiting player was fouled, acknowledging how important it was in our young lives to be seen as real men, though it would not be alone in being described as inappropriate now. If the opposition physio ran on from the dugout, they were accompanied by cries of 'let him die, let him die' booming out from the terraces. 'Dig a hole, dig a hole' was an alternative. In the end, a cold water sponge and a cold spray usually negated the need for undertakers.

At a point in the game where there appeared to be little to get excited about, we were regularly treated to a Native American war cry from the New Stand. Described as cultural appropriation in the 21st century, it was always met with a great cheer from the rest of the ground then as we craned our necks trying to spot the owner of the best vocal cords in the north.

His warbling cry was as much a part of matchday as cricket's Barmy Army band, the bell ringer at Portsmouth or the guy who used to crank up an air raid siren at Lincoln City – I went to Sincil Bank once just to see/hear it and was not disappointed.

Although it had no historic grounding or relevance, the owner of the war cry enjoyed his few seconds of fame each Saturday. Social media has since identified season ticket holder 'Davey T' as the man responsible and he remained at the front of the East Stand seats close to the Gallowgate corner for many years. We looked forward to it each week, which shows exactly how much we anticipated the team's performance on the pitch, but we only ever saw a fleeting glimpse of Davey with his arms in the air, acknowledging his public before retreating to his seat.

A couple of years ago I saw a post on Facebook concerning terrace culture which said: 'I'm glad I got to experience it but there's no way I would want to go back.' I agree only with the first half of the statement. For all its faults, and there were many, there is nothing to match the excitement of being right in among your football family on those steps.

The passion and the partisanship are unmatched in any other environment. It's what our matchday was all about. But something also had to be done about safety, about kicking out racism and about making matchdays more inclusive. Some of it has been accomplished, some of it seems to be forever a work in progress.

* * *

The hard edge to the game in the gap between the glory days of post-war and the later commercial obsession was reflected in the game's vocabulary, where romance was almost dead.

Looking at biographies from the dusty days of the 50s and 60s, no one was anyone in football until they had a monicker. More than a nickname (which is what team-mates shout when they want a pass), a monicker adds a description of appearance or talent, producing a game watched by our forefathers inhabited by 'Lion of Vienna' Nat Lofthouse, 'Wizard of the Dribble' Stanley Matthews, 'Gentleman' Jimmy Dickinson and 'Gentle Giant' John Charles. They also had 'the Galloping Major' Ferenc Puskás of the 'Mighty Magyars' alongside the affectionate 'Wor Jackie' Milburn and 'Bobby Dazzler' Mitchell. The 60s featured 'Golden Vision' Alex Young, Peter 'The Cat' Bonetti and 'Crazy Horse' Emlyn Hughes. And were any names more fitting than 'Iron' Tommy Smith or Ron 'Chopper' Harris? As terms of endearment, respect and affection, they told you so much more than 'Gazza' or 'Keano'.

Whole teams were adopted as 'Busby Babes' and 'Lisbon Lions'. Significant matches, too, were given their own handle, as in the 'Miracle of Bern' and 'Battle of Santiago' but what they all had in common was creating a mental image in an era before wall-to-wall television and they were used freely by journalists who often had equally colourful pen names.

By the time we got stuck into football, they were nearly gone. At Newcastle we'd had 'Jinky' Smith and, of course, 'Supermac' but we then had to be content with 'Bomber' Blackhall and the predictable 'Rocky' Hudson, despite neither being long-term first-teamers. In the wilderness years, Mick Martin became 'Zico', affectionate if inaccurate. I was confused when I thought I'd heard Brighton fans sing the same during their cup run year, only to learn they were calling out their club's nickname, 'Seagulls, Seagulls', instead. We also had 'Fingers' Saunders and, later, 'Sarge' Goddard, which at least hinted at a story to tell. In our school team, we had a 'Skinner', which had nothing to do with his surname, but where were the 'Lions' and the 'Choppers?'

* * *

Finishing eighth in 1978/79 after the ructions of relegation and an emergency team rebuild could be seen as a decent platform from which to start a proper promotion push, with some stability in the management and squad, and well into the new year of 1980, hopes remained high that we could reach that goal in just our second season of Second Division competition.

Four wins in a row during September took the Magpies to the top of the table for the first time and we went top again in the best possible style with a 3-1 derby win on the opening day of the year, inspiring thoughts of a thrilling and successful concluding half to the season.

Even after the shock of an FA Cup exit in a home defeat by minnows Chester in the third round – with teenager Ian

Rush scoring for the visitors – this Newcastle team managed to maintain league form and were still in a promotion place by mid-February. Then, though, the goals suddenly dried up and, with them, any real hope of an escape. With just one goal scored in a run of seven games, a dip in form hit at the worst possible time and, for a second successive season, early promise had faded, replaced by puzzlement and frustration.

A single win in the final 16 games of the campaign was a remarkable record, even by the falling standards set by this team. They finished ninth, a place below Cambridge United, who had only been in the Football League for a decade and were rookies at this level. Worse still … no prizes for guessing who went up in second place despite spending the first half of the season stuck in mid-table and also enjoyed a League Cup derby win on penalties at St James' after a pair of 2-2 draws in the first knockout meeting for more than 20 years.

Alan Shoulder had come in from non-league football the previous season and, rather than just settling quietly into professional football after getting his chance in his mid-20s, the former pitman was soon among the best players in the team. He missed just one game all season and finished with 20 league goals. It was a fairytale introduction to the pro ranks, which could have been bettered only if the team had been at least a half-dozen places higher.

This was also the season in which United had a look at a Wallsend teenager on a trial basis but decided not to take up the option of offering a contract and, instead, it was former captain Bob Moncur who took the young Peter Beardsley to join his Carlisle United line-up, predicting the lad was going to be a star.

The Magpies went in the opposite direction in terms of experience by bringing in central defender Stuart Boam during the first weeks of the season – rather than getting business completed in the summer – after more than 300 league appearances for Middlesbrough. The big man made an immediate impact, too.

Boam was not only in the team but also on the front cover of the match programme when I made a season's debut for the win over Wrexham – the *Match of the Day* cameras joining us one year on from their cup battles with both the Magpies and Spartans – and the game was sealed with a Shoulder penalty. It was one of the nine spot kicks he would convert during that league season and it earned at least a small portion of payback for his bitter memories of Blyth's defeat a year earlier.

The club then played its 3,000th game in the Football League and celebrated by sitting on top of the Second Division table with the point gained from a goalless draw at Birmingham.

From a position of relative strength, McGarry continued to add to his options as experienced striker Billy Rafferty came in from Wolves – we'd been aware of him from BBC regional reports of his earlier spell at Carlisle – and Peter Cartwright signed from North Shields for the kind of money that would change hands in the small ads of *Exchange and Mart*. The midfielder settled in almost as quickly as Shoulder and made more than 35 appearances in his debut season.

Defeat at lowly Watford eventually loosened the grip on top spot but the team continued to leading places three or four places in the table before climbing to the top again for another month in December as spirits rose again on the terraces. It remained a tight contest with the table in a constant state of flux thereafter and in February, when I set out for the rearranged game against Birmingham, Newcastle were just a point behind the top three of Luton, Chelsea and Leicester. A win, therefore, would be enough to jump from fourth to first yet again.

Birmingham had been widely tipped for promotion under 'Bald Eagle' Jim Smith and, with the quality, even in their twilight years, of internationals Colin Todd, Frank Worthington, Archie Gemmill and Willie Johnston, they seemed a good bet. Points were shared in a goalless draw but more costly damage was done in defeat at Shrewsbury a few days later. While the writing was not exactly on the wall, nerves were jangling, with so many teams tied so closely together and, as it turned out, this was the last we saw of our name in the *Final Score* graphic of the top four.

The frequency of my appearances in the crowd increased just as the players were reducing theirs in front of goal and they drew another blank when we returned for Watford's first-ever league visit to Gallowgate. Under superstar chairman Elton John and up-and-coming manager Graham Taylor, they were on a journey which would ultimately take them to second place in the Football League in 1982/83, just a few seasons after leaping out of the Fourth Division.

My main memory of the Watford game is the programme – one I still seem to stumble upon whenever a box or a cupboard is opened at home, distinguishable by its front cover, which showed three blurred images of the Newcastle squad in training. It's not the faces that are memorable – with all respect to the likes of John Connolly, John Bird, Colin Suggett, David Barton and John Brownlie, who are prominent – but the paucity of facilities at Benwell where they went to work each day.

One image shows a muddy, uneven pitch rimmed by a row of bare trees, reminiscent of the countless welfares and public park pitches across the region. A second picture has the players at what appears to be the end of a training session picking up a bag of balls while wearing two different kits under their bib tops. The third is inside what looks like a derelict council leisure centre, all bare breeze blocks and inhospitable concrete floors, with a couple of simple pieces of weights equipment and the players – still caked in mud – going through their paces on filthy floormats. The best piece of kit in the picture is a rogue dining chair.

Television crews did not go to training grounds for soundbites to throw into rolling new channels back then and it was just as well. This was home to the club's prized assets but, even after a century of league football, training facilities were still very basic. Kevin Keegan insisted on having the place fumigated in one of his first changes when he returned as manager.

Benwell looked limited but was probably not too dissimilar to many other training grounds up and down the country. Liverpool's base, where the cameras did occasionally visit, was nothing to write home about, with the quality of the playing staff far outstripping the level of facilities at their disposal. They had a famous rebound wall which they used for working on reactions, with quick passing movements, but, in reality, it was 'just like any other wall' to use Terry Collier's description of Hadrian's finest. The Reds' wall was the same as the garage blocks we used for games of SPOT, a football version of Hangman in which every missed kick cost you a letter until you spelled the full word and where the strategy was generally to get close in and play laterally along the wall so you could boot play as hard as possible along its length and across the road, making the next shot dangerous, as well as near-impossible.

To complete the picture of the Newcastle United environment on this programme cover, the 'star face' on my copy (a sticker in the corner of the page) was Stuart Robinson, a young forward who did not make a first-team appearance in the whole season and then left on a free that summer. It felt like you always got someone out of the reserves that you'd never seen in action when you scratched off that little silver panel, a forerunner of lottery scratchcards and just as messy but even less rewarding.

That front page to me, even now when it turns up randomly in my eyeline, showed just how quickly Newcastle had taken on the look and feel of a dispirited, rudderless Second Division club.

In the days long before parachute payments were introduced to safeguard relegated clubs faced with large wage bills and reduced incomes, Newcastle had lost what remained of their big names. In their place, McGarry recruited a trio of non-leaguers to join the youngsters Barton, Mitchell, Carr and Wharton (to name a few) and journeymen like Connolly, Suggett, Rafferty and Shinton, who at least brought in some experience. Keith Armstrong, a former Sunderland man with not much of a profile, also joined after a short spell in Finland but he never got a look-in at first-team level and soon left professional football.

Unfortunately for McGarry, he also lost the know-how of Suggett and Jim Pearson to career-ending injuries in a decade littered with similar misfortune. After the keenly felt loss of Tony Green, a midfield magician with less than a season's worth of games for the club but always mentioned in conversation around its greatest-ever players, injury also forced the retirement of fellow favourites John Tudor, Jimmy Smith and Terry Hibbitt, the classy David Craig and promising youngsters Peter Kelly and Derek Bell, as well as Suggett, Pearson and centre-forward Ray Clarke in rapid order. It would be interesting to know how many would have been able to continue with modern medical knowledge and rehabilitation and whether they could have helped to rewrite a few painful chapters in the Newcastle United story.

Of the players available to the manager, only targetman Peter Withe appeared likely to move upwards again, with or without a black-and-white shirt on his back. He had already won a league title with Nottingham Forest but could never have dreamt that, after a couple of seasons in the Second Division, he would celebrate a second championship medal, a winning goal in the European Cup Final (with his right foot/shin) and an England call-up for a World Cup.

Shoulder, a professional for just two seasons, must take some measure of credit for Withe's resurgence, as the duo worked so well in tandem after taking divergent and circuitous routes to get there. He'd arrived in the professional game approaching his 26th birthday but still managed to amass nearly 300 league games, spread across three clubs, before returning to the part-time ranks. Strike partner Withe would have identified with the late-starter story, as he had experienced a faltering start to his own career with Southport and Barrow before both clubs dropped out of the Football League altogether but he fully deserved his second chance and the honours which followed.

At centre-forward for United, like the legends before him, Withe was the focal point of the team and he contested everything pumped up towards him. I'd watched No.9s scoring goals and doing their damage in the opposition penalty area but he was the first to make a big impression on me for his work with his back to goal, dropping deep to provide a target and unselfishly holding up play before laying off possession to others and then making his way to the vicinity of the far post to wait for the cross. When play reached him in forward positions, Withe had a physical presence, a deep determination and the heading skills to either go for goal himself or set up an accomplice.

In those dark days, Withe provided a rare shaft of light, with his Clint Eastwood stubble and Supremac sweatbands. He also intrigued us in the paddock because he was the only footballer we knew who ever seemed to get a haircut. Once every six weeks or so, he'd run out with a fresh, sharp look. No one else in football ever looked like they'd been for a cut, except for the victims of the excruciating perm craze in the late-'70s. Knowing how much stick we took at school after a trim ('clips, nee avengies' and a slap on the head), perhaps the rest of them had a trim every Sunday bath night rather than a drastic cut at the barbers every couple of months.

The goal famine which ended the promotion hopes during February and March – it spread into the reserves, where top scorers Gary Walton and Brian Ferguson had just four each approaching the last quarter of the season – was finally broken with a 3-1 win over Bristol Rovers in a game I watched with my dad from 'E' Wing.

The veteran Stewart Barrowclough was an old-fashioned winger who dad always referred to as 'Floorcloth' while also showing an appreciation of his playing ability, and that afternoon, we were just yards away from him, playing in long sleeves as always, as he repeatedly tantalised full-back John Brownlie.

An international in a strong Hibernian team a few years earlier and a target for Tommy Docherty's Scottish revolution at Manchester United before his career was stalled by a broken leg, Brownlie finally got his move south of the border when he joined Newcastle and he soon became owner of one of St James' worst-ever perms (though David Mills fans may contest this). But he was also a bit of a crowd favourite. As successor to the popular Craig and Nattrass at right-back, he was keen to get forward and also provided some valuable know-how in a new team, for a while lining up alongside former Hibs colleague John Blackley, who had played at the 1974 World Cup finals, though he was clearly not quite the player he had been earlier in his career.

The visit of Rovers had attracted a crowd of under 10,000 the previous year, when fans were still getting used to relegation, but that figure more than doubled as Withe scored twice past future Magpies goalkeeper Martin Thomas to secure the win.

The paddock gave us a close-up view of the squad even before kick-off when they set up for a commemorative photo. We didn't know why at the time but it duly appeared in the pages of the programme for derby day at Roker Park a week later and was notable for the contrast between the home side's polished squad photo, taken indoors in front of a wood-panelled wall with their 21 men grinning for the camera, and the Newcastle version featuring a bitterly cold matchday 12, arms crossed over their chests in short sleeves, wind blowing through their hair, all willing the photographer to just get on with it and take the picture.

In the photo, captain Hibbitt is holding a white or, more accurately, nearly white and well-beaten panelled football. It looks not much better than any you'd see on a park pitch, at least at the start of the season before being booted repeatedly into trees, streams, car parks and assorted animal waste. The ball presumably came from the warm-up, which also resembled the pre-match potshots of non-league teams, with players drifting out from the dressing rooms whenever they felt like it to pass gently in small groups, occasionally performing a juggle, while defenders either played long along the touchline or headed out balls thrown to them from a couple of yards away. You half expected the shortest player to be lifted on to Stuart Boam's shoulders to fix the nets ahead of kick-off.

Part of this routine saw the goalkeeper get a feel for the back of the net by retrieving miscellaneous shots which nestled there and become acquainted with the crowd by acknowledging their return of others which did not. He then claimed a few crosses, often struck by the worst crosser of the ball in the squad or staff. Warm-up balls, perhaps making up for a lack of original paintwork, always seemed over-inflated, bouncing with a ping on hard-packed ground or off the hoardings behind the goal.

A white Minerva-branded ball was the St James' weapon of choice, though very occasionally we got to see a swish new Adidas Tango after its groundbreaking appearance at the 1978 World Cup and then the Sondico red-striped 'Berwick Cockle' for a couple of seasons, a ball whose thick single red stripe around its circumference created an illusion of appearing too big to kick. It was obviously a regulation size five but when Alan Shoulder was in possession, it looked like it came up to his knees.

Many years later, I read a history of football's origins by the poetic Uruguayan author Eduardo Galeano in which he described how the ancient Aztecs sacrificed winners in their games by cutting off their heads and painting red stripes on their bodies: 'The chosen of the gods would offer their blood so the earth would be fertile and the heavens generous.' Whoever convinced the authorities to adopt a ball with the red stripe must have had a background in literature rather than commerce because I never saw a single one outside of a Football League ground. It was an iconic eyecatcher, though, particularly with the gold maker's mark stamped on the red panel like a medieval king's seal or heavyweight reference book. The boring plain white editions then returned before the red-darted Mitre creation which heralded a start for ball designs being unveiled as frequently as new team kits.

(For the uninitiated, the Berwick Cockle is a cream-coloured boiled sweet with red/pink stripes. They were made in the Northumberland border town for more than 200 years, most famously by the Cowes family. 'Entirely different from imitations', said the tin, which was the same size as the one containing Black Bullets we got for my grandad at Christmas. Modern incarnations, apparently, are more like crumbly mints. No thanks. Jesmona Black Bullets, meanwhile, originate from the North-East, although the tin now carries a Sheffield address. They were good for helping to keep warm on cold days and were, apparently, popular with miners.)

The win over Bristol Rovers came at the end of March and, with still more than a month of the season to run, it provided fresh hope of a push for the top three just as other contenders started to drop points. League leaders were Chelsea, where World Cup legend Geoff Hurst had replaced Danny Blanchflower as manager in mid-season, but Leicester, Birmingham, QPR, Luton, West Ham and Sunderland were all still in with a shout alongside us, now in fifth place.

But as we dared to dream, suddenly form failed and we couldn't even stay that close to the top three, eventually limping in to finish ninth thanks to a catch of just three points in the last seven games. One of the defeats was at Roker, where Stan Cummins grabbed the only goal in front of a 41,000 crowd – four times the attendance of their previous game at Notts County and double the Newcastle gate against the same Midlanders in midweek.

The Newcastle fans were, though, saved from ringside seats at someone else's promotion party for a second season running as Luton sat three points short of the top three when they headed our way on the final day and their hopes had gone, too.

Big man Withe deserved and received a big send-off ahead of his club record £500,000 summer switch to Aston Villa and he was smothered by fans on a lap of honour after the Luton draw. In my regular position in 'E' Wing, I was joined by a school friend who had neither played football nor, as far as I know, been to a game before or since. He did, though, have the distinction of being sent off for stamping during our first season of playing rugby as 12-year-olds, proving it is the quiet ones you have to watch. The two of us debated whether we should get on the pitch with Withe until we finally compromised by moving up to the front next to the cinder track as he trotted past and waved. Completing his lap of honour and his fond farewells, he was draped in black-and-white scarves, Mardi Gras-style, and I was determined, much as I valued him as a player, that he wasn't going to add mine to his collection, so I held on tightly.

* * *

Raw with the emotion of seeing my two previous favourite players leave at what I saw as the peak of their careers and faced with a struggling team robbed of headline grabbers or potential world beaters, I didn't have an absolute favourite player for a while after Malcolm Macdonald and Alan Kennedy.

Young full-back Peter Kelly, though, caught my eye as he started to claim a place in the first team as Newcastle made it into Europe again and, for a while, he looked like he could be the new Irving Nattrass in terms of ability and the new Kennedy as a poster on my wall.

We'd caught fleeting glimpses of a stream of players from the youth teams and few established themselves as big hopes for the future but Kelly was quick, could tackle and there was always positivity in the commentary on Radio Newcastle, even if I wasn't watching him in the flesh. He even started to earn a mention as a potential future Scotland international, providing another link with the club's glorious past and the teams that featured a rollcall from north of the border. Most romantically of all, he was involved in the squad that faced Bastia in the UEFA Cup, a name which forged a lasting impression on me and a soft spot for the Corsicans even when the island club suffered the indignity of relegation. An all-to-familiar tale.

Sadly, a knee injury cut short Kelly's professional career before its prime and another good man was gone. In a strange twist, he went into business with right-back predecessor Craig, a man who could have become a valuable mentor in his football career rather than as a newsagent if the dice had landed differently. That selling cigarettes and sweets, while hoping paper delivery lads would turn up at 6.30 every morning, is where he saw his future outside the game is as much a sign of the times as was having to retire with a knee problem.

With Kelly now gone, I had to look elsewhere and it was another defender who fitted the bill as my personal favourite. As part of Blyth Spartans' famous FA Cup squad, playing alongside his older brother, Steve Carney turned professional during October 1979. The records show he cost Newcastle £1,000, which would not have made him a major signing even 75 years earlier.

After first taking striker Alan Shoulder into the pro ranks, United soon added Carney and also midfielder Peter Cartwright, who had been at North Shields. It shows all you need to know about both the Second Division and the Northern League that they all made a fair fist of it, too; in Carney's case, sometimes literally.

Carney became my personal favourite – to be joined by battling midfielder David McCreery – in those Second

Division years. Where McCreery was all workrate, scuttling stride, astute reading of the game and ball-winning tenacity in all areas of the pitch, Carney was a Northern League defender playing professional football. And that is not meant in any way as an insult.

He'd learned the game the hard way. Working as an electrician after rejection at Football League level as a youngster, there was no flash car, no cigar-smoking agent and no airs and graces. But Carney had a strong will born from that initial disappointment and a very decent turn of pace, which allowed him to survive in some good company. And he didn't stand on ceremony if anyone tried to get in his way.

He hadn't made the grade as a youngster at West Bromwich Albion, so Steve started again as a part-timer before earning a second chance and he was 22 years old when he was first named in a Newcastle team. At under 6ft, he was hardly tall enough to play in the centre of defence, but Carney still amassed nearly 150 games for the Magpies as the club found its way again and he proved a useful foil for Jeff Clarke and Glenn Roeder or slotting in at right-back when required and occasionally being pushed into a combative role in midfield.

Carney had an upright, scuttling running style, aggressive tackling and a very keen competitive edge. He played like he didn't want to let anyone down and never appeared to be overawed by anyone or anything. There were a few red mist moments, too, for which he was loved just as much by the masses. It seemed to me that he saved many of them for games against Sheffield Wednesday, who played a direct and confrontational style which suited him down to the ground but also ignited the sparks from time to time. Perhaps it was growing up as the younger member of a footballing family that did it, brother Rob being a long-standing figure in the

Northern League with the likes of Spartans and Blue Star, or just that he had to grow up and prove himself in part-time football, where respect was hard-earned, but Steve always stood his ground.

Part of the personal appeal was that he was in complete contrast to how I saw myself as a schoolboy footballer, being little and quick with a cheeky side but not that keen on a 50-50 with players like him. Steve was the sleeves-rolled-up, committed-to-the-cause type who challenged opposition to 'come and have a go if you think you're hard enough' so that he could prove he could be their match. It was an attitude which kept him among my all-time favourites and it was awful to hear of his early death during 2013.

* * *

In middle age, I've often shared the story that I went into journalism as a career because we didn't have a video recorder when I was a kid. When a big game was on telly, I wrote a match report so my dad, who worked shifts, didn't have to miss out.

But in the spring of 1980, on a red letter day for our South Northumberland household, we became proud possessors – not owners, because it came from Radio Rentals – of a VHS recorder. We'd taken delivery of our first-ever colour television on the morning of the 1973 FA Cup Final and it was another big game in red and white which became the first recorded programme on our top-loader, complete with its plug-in remote control (still more hi-tech than a neighbour in later years who changed channels from their armchair using an antique snooker cue).

England had just beaten Argentina at Wembley and were 18 months from qualification for a first World Cup finals since 1970 when they went to the Racecourse Ground in

Wrexham for a clash with Wales in the traditional season-ending Home Internationals tournament. Larry Lloyd, who had left Liverpool just as they were turning into an all-conquering force to join Coventry, who would never be one, had made such a success of his resurrection after moving on to join Nottingham Forest that he had earned a recall to the national team and he had a hand, or a head, or a leg in a scrambled goal by Paul Mariner as Ron Greenwood's team took an early lead.

But Wales, who had identified the big defender as a potential weak spot, carved open their rivals to score four times in reply, completed with a hapless own goal by skipper Phil Thompson in front of a crowd who could barely believe their eyes. It was their first home win over old foes since 1955 and I watched it multiple times – that and an episode of *Record Breakers* – on a free 90-minute tape we'd received with our new arrival.

I watched not because I enjoyed the match or the result but because we'd recorded it and this was how you tried out such revolutionary technology, shuffling forward and back, pausing play occasionally, though the picture was not exactly super slo-mo and there was little chance of ruling on any potential offside or finding out which part of Lloyd's ample frame had led to the England goal.

Coincidentally, we went to Llandudno on our family holiday in the same year and dad bought me the replica Wales kit (I know, but our school stipulated red shirts for games lessons), which stood out so much with its silky shorts, complete with wide side panels, that my one run with the ball in a trial match at the start of the new term got me a place on the team for the start of the season. I must have been less conspicuous in the official school-issue red, though, and was left out in the next two years. And I still blame the Welsh.

The best strike force we never had, the author (home) and mate Alan (away) in the revolutionary Bukta kit, 1977

Our escape route into a different world: the turnstiles and Gallowgate shrubbery, 1982.

Peter Withe (left, with Billy Rafferty) carried the number nine shirt well but he wasn't leaving with my scarf, 1979.

The Old Stand and its scary press box provide the backdrop as David Barton and John Connolly challenge against Charlton, 1979.

McGarry's men – the trio who shared promotion (Carney, far left, back; Carr, fourth from left, middle, and Wharton, third from left, front) would be outnumbered by team-mates forced into retirement by injury, 1980.

Ray Clarke, with Alan Shoulder in support, misses a chance to put Newcastle into the quarter-finals of the FA Cup at home to Exeter City, 1981.

The gaps in the paddock behind record signing John Trewick provide a picture of going nowhere in Division Two, 1981.

The Constabulary spoil the view from the Gallowgate steps of a win over Orient on the last day of the season, 1981.

A beacon of light by way of Tow Law Town, Chris Waddle and the truncated Leazes End with an empty section operating as crowd segregation, 1982.

The exciting and unpredictable Imre Varadi outscored his more famous strike partner in their season together, 1982.

Beginning of a love affair: a European Footballer of the Year announces his arrival in the Second Division with a debut winner, 1982.

Penned in by new fences, we could at least anticipate a First Division future after a 4-0 win over Derby, 1984.

The chipped concrete look of the original New Stand, built in 1972.

A different world: the size and shape of the redeveloped Gallowgate End for a new era, 2024.

Chapter Five

Don't Want Tomorrow to be Like Today

UNDER NEW manager Arthur Cox and with the city enjoying its 'Newcastle 900' celebrations, the Magpies improved in the 1980/81 campaign but only in respect of finishing above Cambridge. In a Second Division season dominated by West Ham, who finished 13 points clear of the rest (still in the days of two for a win), Newcastle were marooned in 11th with 42 points from 42 games and similarly symmetrical form of 11 wins at home and 11 defeats away. It added up to a finish eight points short of the promotion places, with Notts County and Swansea City in position to step up with the Hammers.

Notts County were the season's first visitors to St James', where I and my 13-year-old mates formed part of a 17,000 midweek crowd cheering an Alan Shoulder goal which officially launched a new strike partnership with journeyman Ray Clarke following Peter Withe's departure. Support, though, fell to just 13,000 at the end of the month for the first Saturday matchday, when Luton were beaten 2-1.

At the same time, football launched something called *Fight for Survival*. Billed as a blueprint for the future of the game and compiled in consultation with leading managers and administrators, this document included the proposal of three points for a win in response to the perceived negative tactics of teams playing away from home and falling crowds. The plan also proposed and agreed an end to the poaching of managers from other clubs during the season, thinking it would halt the hire-and-fire approach of certain chairmen. This move met with considerably less success than increasing the number of points awarded for a win.

Bill McGarry hadn't even had a chance to get his trusty sheepskin out for the autumn, leaving St James' with the season just a month old after defeats by Sheffield Wednesday (2-0) and Bolton (4-0) away alongside the draw with County. Former captain and manager Joe Harvey was dusted off to take on a temporary role in charge while the board waited to appoint Cox, previously at Chesterfield and an unknown quantity to the fans.

The directors obviously had a 'type' they liked, as they replaced noted hardnut McGarry with the quietly menacing Cox, who looked and talked like an army PT instructor. His playing career had been cut short by injury as a teenager at Coventry but he stayed in the game with a move into coaching, first with the Sky Blues and then at Walsall and Aston Villa, also breaking out of his Midlands patch to try his luck at Preston and Halifax before working with Bob Stokoe at Sunderland; he was sat next to him on the bench when they beat Leeds at Wembley in 1973. Chesterfield had been his first job as a manager, though with his immediate predecessor at Newcastle landing via Saudi Arabia and, before that, Richard Dinnis taking the job after starting out as a teacher, there had been stranger routes to the white wooden dugout.

Cox started just as Gordon Lee had done, talking about Newcastle's place among the top six clubs in the country, and described himself as 'desperate' (giving him something in common with the rest of the club) to get the job, while also being appreciative of Harvey's place nearby as a sounding board and adviser.

'My job is to take a long, hard look at the club and take it from there,' he said, hoping to be given time to do the job thoroughly and properly. Just four seasons on from his managerial debut, the board had placed a lot of trust in the new man and his statement hinted at being given a blank sheet of paper to sort it out, which was not the club's usual style. Despite the wary reaction towards a relative unknown from the lower divisions and ongoing doubts over the ability and ambition of the directors, Cox would prove more popular than his trio of predecessors, though the wisdom of his work would still take a couple of seasons to gain full approval.

The team now ran out in Umbro shirts, boasting an open collar and tell-tale diamond design down the sleeves. The shirt also carried a sponsorship logo for the first time (Scottish & Newcastle Breweries), though teams still had to wear plain shirts for any televised games, with sponsorship not yet permitted.

Even more pronounced than the previous rash of Bukta kits, the Umbro diamonds broke out like a rash, with the likes of Everton, Manchester City, Chelsea, Bolton and Burnley adopting a similar style. It seemed only Liverpool held the handbrake, surviving for years with only a small Umbro diamond on the chest and the club was met with pitchfork protests when they dared to replace the traditional round neck with a 'V' before eventually grasping the nettle full-on and adding pinstripes.

The new diamond sleeve design looked good on our away strips as well as the stripes, though not quite as classy as the Scotland second-strip white shirt I got from Dixons

Sports that year (textured material, long sleeves, embroidered badge, lovely).

We had started to think our new look was cursed until Terry Hibbitt, almost at the end of his career, and Dutch Under-21 international midfielder Frans Koenen, whose never really got started, scored against Luton to secure a first win of the season at the fourth attempt.

The line-up included a couple of former non-league players, homegrown hopefuls and not a single international. Peter Kelly, who started the season in the No.2 shirt, made just a handful of appearances before his career-ending injury, while Hibbitt and Koenen got only as far as halfway in the season, to be replaced by Mick Martin and a £250,000 record signing, John Trewick, in the centre of the pitch.

West Ham had been talked up as promotion favourites from the outset and duly won eight in a row, including a League Cup run, before the goalless draw on Tyneside in October. They were expected to rip it up with a team including Phil Parkes, whose half-million-pound transfer from QPR made him the world's most expensive goalkeeper, alongside full-backs Ray Stewart and Frank Lampard and the loyalists Billy Bonds, Alvin Martin, Alan Devonshire and Trevor Brooking. So, the draw was another step forward for Cox and his team. An extra point from a win would have been handy, though, even this early in the campaign, as the top four began to open a gap on the rest, with Howard Kendall's Blackburn Rovers still unbeaten and in even better form than the Hammers on top of the pile.

* * *

I had been truly bitten by the bug and had enough pocket money to get into 'E' Wing of the Old Stand for almost every game. Unlike the Gallowgate, where you parted with your cash at the turnstile, we used to get tickets to produce to the gatemen in the paddock. The ticket office was just a few yards across the car park and the queue for kids was always shorter than at the adult window, especially as we got there while the pubs were still open.

Every kid wants to look and act older than they are, except, of course, when it is cheaper to be younger! As the oldest but shortest in our usual group, I could be trusted not to get bumped into the adult prices and getting to the front of the queue to stand at that intimidating window was a big moment, the request for 'a junior in "E" Wing' like Oliver Twist holding out his empty bowl. Through the thick glass, you could see a pair of specs looking back at you and a club calendar on the wall but that was about it. In my experience, there is always a club calendar on the wall of a ticket office and, back in 1980, it would have featured one team photo with tear-off monthly pages. Artistic photography, graphics and artwork didn't exist in the First Division in 1980, let alone the backwaters of a level lower.

Technology, though, did arrive on Tyneside in the form of an electronic scoreboard at the Gallowgate End, which at least gave the impression of some planning for the future. Perched above the advertising hoardings at the back of the terrace, it brought us into the modern age, albeit a limited-pixel one. At first, the board showed the score for 'Magpies' and changed the name of opponents underneath each week, until letters started going missing and the second line simply became a permanent painted 'Visitors'. The little icons which jumped up and down for a goal proved a hit, though we also soon noticed blinking and broken bulbs with regularity. It was a problem which never happened with its predecessor, a wooden half-time scoreboard – A 1-0, B 0-0, C 0-2 – which you could decode using the fixture list printed on the back page of the programme at Newcastle as at matchdays everywhere for decades.

Disappointingly, my prolific season of match attendance coincided with one in which my team scored just 22 times in their 21 home league games. Top scorer Bobby Shinton finished the season with just seven goals. All seven had been scored by the end of November. Kai Havertz finished the 2022/23 Premier League campaign as Chelsea's top marksman with the same number but only one of the pair earned a £65m summer move to Arsenal. Mind you, the Blues had spent £71m on the German just four years earlier.

No top scorer would stoop lower than Shinton's tally until John Barnes claimed a mere six during 1997/98 when Alan Shearer was ruled out by injury. To be fair, Shinton's season did end in early February due to injury and he later also had to cope with a health scare involving his new-born daughter while he was still sidelined.

Behind Shinton, Mick Harford was signed from Lincoln City in the Fourth Division for goalscoring potential and collected a three-match ban alongside his four goals, the same number as Shoulder, who was used deeper or wider than in his more prolific seasons. Clarke had a pedigree, with spells at top-flight European duo Ajax and Club Brugge, but barely registered a namecheck in his home country before his arrival, though apparently he had been linked with the club when Dinnis was in charge. He scored just three times in 18 games as a No.9 before injury ended his career. The young and raw Harford was soon on his way out, too.

It was, therefore, no surprise that Newcastle were never more than bit-part players in the league drama and the finishing place of 11th was the lowest since tumbling out of the top division. It meant facing a fourth season at this level, which is how long the 60s team had taken to escape upwards.

There was, though, the start of some optimistic talk about prospects in the longer term, that perhaps this was Newcastle bottoming out and that Cox had at least started to shape a team.

Kevin Carr had started to establish his place as goalkeeper, Kenny Wharton was now a permanent fixture on the left, Martin and Trewick were a reliable duo in midfield and there was also the surprise emergence of a young, gangling forward recruited like Shoulder and Carney from local non-league.

I was there when Chris Waddle made his debut in the centre-forward shirt for a midweek win over Shrewsbury and the newspapers lapped up his story, which featured a job in a sausage seasoning factory to supplement any income from part-time football with Tow Law.

Acknowledged as the coldest place to watch football in the North-East (and that's coming from a regular at Blyth's Croft Park), Tow Law Town had been proud members of the region's non-league scene for decades and their Ironworks Road home carried the scars to prove it. It was like a time capsule tribute to the days of long shorts and hobnail boots. Eventually, having noted the link with Waddle, curiosity got the better of me and I made the pilgrimage on the day they clinched the Northern League title in 1995, a full 70 years since their previous championship win. (We, of course, know all about waiting 70 years and more!) I wore my attendance that day as a medal, braving monsoon rain for the whole afternoon to see a team in black-and-white finally lift a trophy, led on the field by Steve Howard and Jason Ainsley, who both went on to have careers as professionals.

Chris Withe, younger brother of former centre-forward Peter, made his Newcastle debut on the same night as Waddle, picked at left-back in the absence of Ian Davies, a moustachioed Welshman memorable mainly because he had Claude as his middle name.

The two newcomers kept their places for a weekend trip to Chelsea, only to be left out again after the 6-0 defeat at Stamford Bridge. It took a while for Waddle to properly become a first choice but he did eventually find his feet (or at least the left one) and, when he did return to the first team and discover a level of consistency to go with his undoubted raw talent, he was on his way to becoming a star, first on Tyneside and then on even bigger stages in London and beyond.

The younger Withe, though, never wore the club colours again. Instead, he played regularly at Bradford City and Notts County among others before a final stint at Shrewsbury, ending his career with the team against whom it had all begun.

The left-back spot, instead, went to the fair-haired Peter Johnson, signed from Middlesbrough as Cox's first purchase for a fee of £60,000. He made an immediate impact, especially with his willingness to get forward, but then mysteriously faded from the scene just as quickly as he had arrived on it. A dozen or so games later and Davies, twice demoted, bounced back again to reclaim the No.3 shirt. Johnson, like Withe junior, had come and gone.

I had already noticed Waddle in the pages of *The Pink* on Saturday nights while he was going well in the reserves playing in the Central League. Sometimes, their matches mirrored the seniors, so they would be at home to Everton when the big boys were at Goodison. A friend from school, despite being a full-on Manchester United fan even when they were glamorous but not very good, went a few times to these second-team games – mainly, I assumed, because entry was free – and the club printed a teamsheet instead of a programme for the few hundred who turned up. Liverpool seemed to win the Central League title year after year, while just about everyone else could win well one week and lose heavily the next, depending on how many senior players each team called upon and how motivated they were if they were included.

On his way to becoming a first-team regular, Waddle was a handy goalscorer in the reserves. Also hitting the net with regularity was Gary Walton, who was doing it with the youth team in the Intermediate League too. Although he did get a few mentions as potentially one to watch, he never did get his chance in senior football.

Paul Brayson in the 90s, Michael Chopra a few years later and then Adam Armstrong were similarly high-scoring strikers with the second string, though at least the latter two did get to play some first-team football for their hometown team. In a long professional career, Chopra did particularly well in two spells with Cardiff, where he remains popular, and played Premier League football as a £5m signing at Sunderland, while Armstrong had many admirers at Southampton and a couple of bites at the top flight. Brayson made his Football League debut on loan with Swansea and, after being let go by the Magpies, he went to Reading and Cardiff, followed by a succession of non-league clubs closer to home. At the age of 45, he was still banging them in for Newcastle Benfield.

Once Walton disappeared from the sports pages, I didn't see his name in *The Chronicle* again until, sadly, reports of his violent death near home in County Durham in his mid-30s. Alan Shoulder, an old friend and a link in his signing for United as an apprentice, was central to pulling together the senior North-East clubs for a fundraising game in support of the family.

* * *

Sharing a league with smaller clubs like Shrewsbury, Orient and Cambridge or with struggling set-ups like the Bristol duo didn't really matter to me. I didn't go to watch the opposition. Of course, I wanted to see us put Liverpool and Manchester United in their places and have a sniff of some glory – we all did. But I never understood it when someone asked, 'Who we playing?' before confirming whether or not they would be joining us in the crowd.

A neighbour spotting us on the way out to a game would invariably base comments on the day's opponents rather than on our team. 'It's just Millwall,' or 'It's just Grimsby,' he'd say, implying that the Magpies would roll over them even without our support from the sidelines.

I didn't care who they were, where they came from, what colour kit they wore and if they were likely to win or not; I was there to watch my team. It didn't matter to me if it was a league game or a cup tie – no manager changed selection much between competitions then anyway – because every game was a chance to see my team and show them my support. Who knows, it might also just be the day when everything turns around and you could be there for the start of something special.

The anticipation of going to the game fuelled the whole week and post-match conversation kept you going until there was something to say about the next one. When every weekend fixture was a three o'clock kick-off on a Saturday, with only brief highlights occasionally of a midweek cup replay on BBC's *Sportsnight* and no television previews until the next Saturday lunchtime, it left a lot of the week to talk about what you'd seen.

Where football had been my everything almost from starting school – 'eat, sleep and drink football' as my parents and grandparents would say – going to the match was, by my teenage years, everything and more. Even if the team were not pulling up any trees, it was still an occasion and the excitement was in being part of it.

We were too young to understand cynicism or appreciate the use of gallows humour as a defensive shield. We took it all personally and, as we saw it, Newcastle United still provided the heartbeat of the city and neighbouring county, even if the club was in need of intensive care.

I read Arthur Hopcraft's 1968 book *The Football Man* again recently and know exactly where he is coming from when he says: 'There is more eccentricity in deliberately disregarding it [football] than in devoting a life to it. The way we play the game, organise it and reward it reflects the kind of community we are.' I would barely speak to classmates who were not interested in football or didn't kick a ball about at break time in the course of my school day or on the local fields after it. We had no common ground to share. I couldn't get my head around why anyone would not be interested in the game or obsessed by our team or, for that matter, any team.

My grandad was a relation of Ray Pointer, the league title-winning forward with Burnley and an England international in the early 60s, but his only real interest in football came through the Littlewoods Pools or recalling the names of his many contemporaries from the villages of the South Northumberland coalfield who had made their way in the game as professionals or starred in the local amateur leagues. He knew where each of them had gone but had no idea how their careers had turned out once they'd got there or how good or bad their clubs were, either.

Without knowledge of the game, grandad's pools picks were based on fancy, not form book. But he never missed a week. Listening to *Sports Report* on a Saturday tea-time remained a 'quiet please' event, though he knew the teams only by virtue of whether they had matched his selections for score draws worth three points on the coupon or let him down with any other result rather than through any implications their results had in a league table or cup run.

* * *

As established matchgoers in our early teens, our Saturday build-up now began in front of *Football Focus* and *On the Ball* (later *Saint & Greavsie*, of course) before we went to catch the bus to town. These days, it is all replica tops and colour-matched leisurewear but back then the only accessory you needed was a black-and-white scarf, fastened tie style around your neck. There were a few fans with black-and-white tartan or printed silk scarves fastened around a wrist as an option to spin in the air or stretch out for 'You'll Never Walk Alone' on the occasion of overwhelming victories, and there were a few striped shirts but nothing like the proliferation you see now.

Like many others, I started with a homemade scarf, which was knitted, like my school jumpers, by my grandma. It had black-and-white stripes only at the ends, with the middle section in plain black – she must have had more black wool spare than white or perhaps she had spotted, like grandmothers do, that I had a dirty neck.

Nevertheless, it was a big thing to get your first scarf and then even bigger to actually wear it at a game. Within a short space of time, I progressed to a shop-bought item, a really smart one, too, the stripes running along the scarf's length rather than across-ways. It was big enough to go round an adult neck, too, and, when I grew out of my first black tracksuit, Mam unpicked the stitch-on club crest and transferred it to the scarf in the style of the day. It looked a lot more grown-up that way, too, like I'd been among the terrace foot soldiers for many years.

I was devastated when I once misplaced the treasured scarf. A few weeks later, I spotted someone I knew wearing it at the bus stop as we headed home from a game. I ran down from the top deck to claim it back, which was pretty good going for a kid of about seven stone and usually averse to confrontation. Thankfully, it was returned without incident. I still keep it safe and I'd still wear it if I was bound for St James' Park.

I had a knitted bobble hat to go with the original scarf – my grandma bashed out a hasty lime green and white one, too, in time for me to watch Blyth in their FA Cup run – but it didn't go to many games and was consigned to the cupboard under the stairs unless it was snowing.

Among the woolly hats, with or without pom-pom, flat caps were a thing, too; not the whippet-fancier type but the printed black-and-white type, carrying a club badge or a name or a face, with the obvious drawback that any player good enough to be featured on club merchandise was liable to be sold before it could be worn out. There were tartan versions on the terraces, too, alongside random woolly hats, a few plastic bowlers and a handful of flags on special occasions.

Alongside the denim jackets and butchers' coats, which started out all white but had stripes painted on or names and slogans added in marker pen, these were the days of the donkey jacket. Worn at the pit, shipyard and building site, some versions carried black or orange shiny waterproofed shoulders and some had National Coal Board branding. The donkey jacket kept St James' Park wrapped up long before South Shields-based Barbour became a metaphor for the region, preserving the warmth on the inside against challenges thrown at it from the outside.

Other than that, matchday was plain shirts, jumpers, jeans and trainers unless, of course, you preferred a Dr Marten or monkey boot.

We always started our trip with a look in the supporters' shop at the Haymarket, just a few yards from where we got off the bus. It was a little flat-roofed unit with a smell of musky programmes. Its innocence would look rank amateur now but it was our Aladdin's cave, with anything you wanted in any colour you wanted, so long as it was black-and-white, to paraphrase Henry Ford.

Dozens of the better items were piled up in the window display, each with its own brightly coloured price tag, alongside notices about booking away coach travel in coming weeks. Many of the programmes passed along to me by family and friends over the years have the corner of one page missing where the travel token has been cut out, part of a loyalty scheme for booking places. I've still got a couple of coupon sheets, too, which were inserted into the first few editions of the programme each season.

The shop window always carried the standard replica team shirts (first and second strip), a variety of T-shirts, hats, 'silk' (more accurately nylon or other man-made fibre) rosettes dedicated to individual players as well as to the team, and scarves of various qualities, not on mannequins but pinned to the wall and stored in clear plastic bags behind the counter. Almost all of the shop, in fact, was behind the counter, where a couple of white-haired assistants tried to keep up with the changing minds of young fans counting their pocket money pennies.

There were plenty of pens, stickers, badges, darts flights, beer tankards and ties but modern supporters would be shocked by the absence of hoodies and baseball caps, which had not yet arrived from the States. Foam hands, golf club covers, replica training kit and technical warm-up shirts were still far off in the future, too.

On non-matchdays, when we were just killing time by going to town for a mooch around, we sometimes also went to Stan Seymour's sports shop, where none of us ever bought a single item, and we would always, without fail, race through Eldon Square to check out the football boots and shirts at Dixon Sports.

We paid particular attention to any that we were unlikely to ever actually own, like Puma King boots in kangaroo leather or the intriguingly rare foreign team shirts. Someone I knew had a Strasbourg top and it gave him an almost superstar following locally.

Also, we'd never miss Virgin Records (before it became Virgin Megastore or some such), sometimes followed by a detour to the darts shop in the Green Market. Time was too limited after *Football Focus* and *On the Ball* for a full run-through on matchdays, though, and you would never want to take a bag of shopping to the game and be unable to clap your hands or sing with your arms above your head. No, the only things you took into a match were in your pockets, plus the programme, which I stored up a sleeve, and whatever sweets you had left, though by that stage of the afternoon they'd usually be firmly stuck to the paper bag.

The direct route to the ground from our bus stop passed a few pubs on Percy Street and they were almost as scary as passing the away end at the ground.

There was the Hotspur Hotel, all dark paintwork and equally dark windows, where the only sign of life was the door banging open and closed, though you could barely see anything inside anyway through the crowd and the fog in the days when smokers stayed indoors to light up rather than gather on the front doorstep, ankle-deep in ash.

I think the Haymarket pub, near the cinema at the university end, looked the same, though it became famous for the quality of its jukebox, which was much more up to date than the decor. When it was demolished in 1987 as part of university expansion, I read that its bar was relocated to a room at the Cumberland Arms in Byker.

There was the Percy, too, and the Farmers Arms on the corner, which had more glass and light but somehow looked even more intimidating, as the occupants could see you from within. Both were covered in a layer of grime distributed by city traffic and the idling engines in the bus station right outside the front door.

We headed upwards to St Thomas Crescent, with its immaculate period brickwork and paintwork, and there was another pub on the top corner, the Trent House, before we turned left and then right towards St James' Park and past the front door (though usually on the opposite side of the road) of the famous Strawberry.

Here, the crowd was swollen by supporters converging from all directions and the pub looked nowhere near as welcoming as it is now, with frequent outbreaks of aggro followed by temporarily closed doors, the arrival of the police and the exit of any troublemakers. Like road traffic accidents, there were many among us who slowed their pace to crane a neck at what was going on while still trying to make steady progress towards the turnstiles ahead of the post-pub crush.

Just for variety as we got older, we sometimes used an alternative route through Handyside Arcade, though only on the outward journey, as it was often closed on the return to avoid any trouble – there was too much glass and not enough elbow room for the owners to allow it to become a battleground. Sometimes, on non-matchdays, we'd call at the joke shop there for some Snap-its or, in later years, when we were a tiny bit cooler, look in the patchouli-scented Kard Bar to check out the posters, pin badges and hippies. This was their natural habitat, along with the grass area of Old Eldon Square just around the corner, though having such habitual hang-outs did make them easy targets for bored bovver boys, like bewildered wildebeest at a watering hole. It was horrible to watch but at least it was over quickly.

* * *

With no great goal threat and just 13 points gained away from home in the entire 1980/81 season, it was no surprise that Newcastle remained, at best, on the fringes of the real action.

Sitting around eighth or ninth in the second-tier table now may be enough to give hope of a late-season surge into the play-offs but when promotion went only to the top three, you knew you could not afford to be so far off the pace and there would be no room for manoeuvre in making up for a bad patch.

We could only look up jealously as Notts County and John Toshack's Swansea joined champions West Ham in securing a return to the top flight, three more teams living the dream while we were stuck, half asleep, in the Second Division. There was at least an FA Cup run, my first 'live' experience of cup fever, though it took us only as far as the fifth round, which shows just how short of thrills we'd been since relegation.

Every fan knows that the FA Cup provided Newcastle's second golden era during the 50s, winning the trophy three times in five years with a team led by local hero Jackie Milburn. Although the competition is dominated by a handful of clubs these days, it was a remarkable achievement during a decade which otherwise featured 13 different finalists and eight winners.

It was all the more noteworthy in that it immediately followed the club's longest spell out of the top division. Ashington-born Milburn and the other locals, including fellow three-time winner Bobby Cowell alongside Bob Stokoe, Charlie Crowe and Tommy Walker, had all grown up with United stuck in the Second Division before making their mark as players. Maybe there was hope for us yet.

The club's greatest heyday had been early in the century, with three league championships in five years from 1905, when they also could have achieved a double but lost to Aston Villa in the FA Cup Final at Crystal Palace. Similar falls at the final hurdle became an unfortunate habit, even in that successful era, with just one win in their five finals between 1905 and 1911, but the club was well and truly on the football map after seeing rivals Sunderland collect three league titles of their own during the latter years of Queen Victoria.

Relegated for the first time in 1934, it was not until 1948, with Joe Harvey as captain and Milburn in his first full season in attack, that St James' Park again welcomed top-flight football, though there was obviously a break due to the war. Home crowds averaged more than 56,000 in the promotion season as the public came out of the shadows cast by a world conflict and the Magpies immediately made their presence felt by finishing fourth, fifth and fourth again in the league during their first three seasons back on the way to that Wembley hat-trick.

Newspaper coverage shows flat-capped men in overcoats enveloped in cigarette smoke crammed into St James' and being entertained by a team including Bobby Mitchell, a left-winger to match any of the day – 'I didn't know he had ankles, you could only see him from the knees up,' my dad said, describing the view of players on the opposite wing from the front of the Boys' Enclosure – and an attacking verve supplied by the likes of Len White, Vic Keeble, George Hannah, Ernie Taylor and the Chilean-born George Robledo, as well as local hero Milburn. The defensive colossus of Frank Brennan, the craggy Jimmy Scoular as captain in succession to Harvey, and full-back Cowell were just as influential in front of the reliable Jack Fairbrother and his goalkeeping successor Ronnie Simpson, a man who would collect a European Cup winner's medal in 1967 as a veteran with Celtic's lauded 'Lisbon Lions'.

Club historian Paul Joannou says national newspapers made the 1951 final sound like a one-man show, with Milburn claiming both goals against a Blackpool team which included Stan Mortensen, Harry Johnston, Bill Slater, Jackie Mudie and George Farm alongside national treasure Stanley Matthews. 'It was anything but that,' said Milburn in reaction to the reports, published in Joannou's *First 100 Years* in 1991, though his goals have been acknowledged among Wembley's finest, hit in a five-minute spell just after half-time. The opener illustrated Milburn's greatest asset – a flat-out pace befitting his J.E.T. initials – and a low right-foot shot beyond Scotland international Farm, while he thumped in the second with his left foot from a backheel by the 5ft 4in Taylor, who was described by the hero of the hour as his favourite inside-forward.

A year later, the holders beat Arsenal with a late header from Robledo, who had been joined in the team by his brother, Ted. Their family had settled in Yorkshire during the 30s following revolution in Chile and, after leaving his job as a miner, George started to make a name for himself with Barnsley before the pair joined Newcastle for a combined fee of £26,500. Ted was more of a squad player, selected for that one cup final, while George bagged 91 goals in 164 appearances before the pair departed in 1953, heading home with the Colo Colo club in the capital city of Santiago.

The Magpies' winning run ended with a shock fourth-round defeat at home to Rotherham in 1953 and they reached the fifth round a year later before bouncing back to complete a Wembley hat-trick in 1955 with a marathon run featuring ten games across six rounds.

With Harvey by now on the sidelines and tough guy Scoular the driving force on the pitch, it took three games to get past Nottingham Forest (sounds familiar) in the fifth round, another two against Huddersfield and a pair which ended the fairytale for York City of the Third Division North in the semi-finals after a replay hosted on enemy soil at Roker and an incredible aggregate crowd of 120,000 over the two ties.

It was Milburn again who stood up at Wembley, despite controversially not being included in the team initially submitted to the board of directors by the manager. Wearing the No.8 shirt, with Keeble at centre-forward, Milburn scored after just 45 seconds, which remained the fastest goal in cup final history until Chelsea's Roberto di Matteo floored Middlesbrough 42 years later. Mitchell and Hannah were also on the mark in a 3-1 win over Manchester City and their deep-lying centre-forward Don Revie.

Finishing eighth in the league in the same season, that was as good as it got before relegation at the start of the 60s and four years in the Second Division, during which Harvey returned as manager and brought through a group of players who would become the backbone of his team for the next decade, including goalkeeper Iam McFaul, full-backs David Craig and Frank Clark and skipper Bob Moncur. Harvey also persuaded the directors to spend well, breaking the club record three times in ten years to bring in Wyn Davies for

£80,000 and Jimmy Smith at £100,000 before splashing out £180,000 for Malcolm Macdonald. He also polished some rough diamonds who cost considerably less but offered almost as much in an entertaining if inconsistent team which won a European trophy and reached another Wembley cup final before he finally left the job in the mid-70s.

In his 1971 memoir, Moncur refers to 10,000 Geordies turning up to watch if a set of black-and-white shirts were hung on a clothes line across the pitch, while during the confrontations between fans and management, my dad would often say one of the biggest issues was having 20,000 fans who would turn up to watch the grass grow at St James' Park. The point being that there would always be support, even in times of hardship, so there was never any real pressure on the people who ran the club to change.

An updated expression of the same sentiment was expressed on a giant banner displayed during the protests against a later owner, which said: 'We don't demand a team that wins, we demand a club that tries.' The distinction between 'team' and 'club' was both deliberate and obvious. Aimed at leaders off the field, the fans were begging for investment in a struggling squad again located towards the foot of the Premier League and the club discounted as unambitious makeweights in the richest competition in world football. Newcastle United – the club which had given its people the thrills of Gallacher, Milburn, Supermac, Keegan and Shearer – were seen as irrelevant. That is what hurt most.

Only the laziest elements in the national media maintain that expectation weighs down the club. Expectation has always been tempered on Tyneside. With no league title since 1927 and no domestic trophy in 70 years, fans have got used to not winning. The vast majority have never seen their team lift anything major but there have still been some great times within the seasons of famine. It is desire – not expectation – to break the drought which increases every year.

During the Amazon documentary series *We Are Newcastle*, shown in 2023, new chairman Yasir Al-Rumayyan said: 'I remember the first time I walked into St James' Park [in October 2021]. It was like, you cannot ask for more, right? But the team were ranked number 19 [out of 20].' A Magpies fan during the same episode put it simply, saying: 'All we ever wanted was hope.'

By the time I became a matchday regular, the European adventures and the spectacular Macdonald had gone. After a relegation of humiliating proportions, the glory days seemed like they belonged to not only a different time but a totally different club. The team I first followed from the stands featured some of the least likely signings and least impressive recruits in black-and-white history at a rundown stadium in one of the most depressed areas of a struggling country. Was it any real surprise so few of them made an impact in such a challenging environment?

If ever there was a bad time to be born under on Tyneside, this was it, in the trough between the peaks of the 50s and the Messianic mania of Kevin Keegan and what became his 'Entertainers'.

At the start of 1980/81, we'd had fleeting glimpses of promotion form which raised heartbeats during each of the first two seasons back in the Second Division but we were not even halfway through the term of the club's stay there.

That is the context into which my expectations were born, not of Wembley heroes or nights of European conquest, and don't let the national media tell you any different. It didn't make us any less passionate in our support and, while there was always the hope that somewhere down the line the good times would come around again, we also had to make the most of any victory when we could, which is why the cup run of 1981 remains a high point in an otherwise historic low.

* * *

In the seasons immediately before I became a terrace regular, the team did go close to glory, though in the end it proved a passing acquaintance when we were looking to settle into a lasting relationship. First, there was the run to Wembley in the FA Cup in 1974 (after a 19-year gap) and, just two years later, there was a return south for the League Cup Final. Newspaper cuttings, previews and posters from each campaign were pinned on my bedroom wall before being transferred to a scrapbook in the hope of making wall space for the next one.

In 1974, with Labour leader Harold Wilson back in Downing Street and *Whatever Happened to the Likely Lads* a ratings winner with the BBC, the club set an FA Cup record by reaching an 11th final, though the run had been anything but plain sailing, with replays required to remove Hendon of the Isthmian League – whatever an Isth is – and Scunthorpe from the Fourth Division, despite being given home advantage in both rounds. Newcastle United have always been oblivious to the obvious.

Before the infamous win over Nottingham Forest in the quarter-final, Joe Harvey's men did hit their straps with a 3-0 win over a potentially dangerous West Brom side who were in the Second Division but could call on the likes of Tony Brown, Asa Hartford, Len Cantello, John Wile and Scotland winger Willie Johnston.

The BBC cameras were there, too, no doubt seeking another spectacular exit against a team of lower status, but instead captured Newcastle's best performance of the season. The third goal, headed in by workhorse striker John Tudor, was a joy to behold and well worth checking out on YouTube even 50 years later. It is a classic team goal, subtly finished by a player who ran his socks off for the team while also still finding his way to supply a steady stream of goals alongside Macdonald.

When Forest were finally felled, it was Supermac – with assistance from Terry Hibbitt and a huge travelling support – who did for Burnley in the semi-final at Hillsborough. Liverpool, who had won the league title a year earlier and were on their way towards becoming the era's all-conquering force, slugged it out in a replay with Leicester City before booking the remaining place under the Twin Towers.

Cup fever quickly infected another generation of Magpies supporters, forging a new link in a chain which stretched back to the early part of the century and, of course, the magical days of the 50s. 'The North-East saluted these wins with raucous enthusiasm,' wrote John Moynihan in *Soccer Syndrome*. 'Somehow, football had always seemed half to belong there, so suited to the mass enthusiasm of Tyneside, the salty shipyards where Newcastle [and] Sunderland, although far less forces now, have always been hailed as kings in the working men's clubs.' Not bad for a Chelsea fan.

In the run-up to Wembley, there were shop window displays all over Tyneside, printed souvenirs in the newspapers and stripes everywhere you looked. It was all set for the big day out. Sadly, Wembley Way is where the excitement ended.

As legendary boss Bill Shankly led out his Reds, the famous Black-and-whites strode behind Harvey in purple-and-gold tracksuit tops, black shorts and white socks (replacing the hooped version worn during the rest of the season). On the eve of the game, the club had apparently received and rejected a set of white towelling tops from outfitters Burton and had to arrange urgent replacements from Gola, despite having playing kit supplied by Bukta. Beggars cannot be choosers and, with no black-and-white availability at short notice, purple would have to do. Those tops remained the most out-of-place Wembley wear until Liverpool's 'Spice Boys' showed up in white suits and shades in 1996.

Supermac had scored in every round – in the Hendon replay at Watford's Vicarage Road, twice in the Scunthorpe replay, the opener at West Brom and the only goals in wins over Forest and Burnley – and he vowed that he would do it again at Wembley. His words were reportedly pinned up around the Liverpool dressing room and Shankly's pre-match motivational talk was pretty much done, though it's hard to believe the loquacious Scot had nothing to add.

On the day itself, Macdonald had just two shots and both flew well wide of Ray Clemence's goal, while the image of Shankly conducting with his hands while sat next to the chain-smoking Harvey has become iconic.

We'd received our first colour television on cup final day a year earlier and it was the afternoon of the year when everything else stopped. Unfortunately, that meant there were no distractions as Newcastle were dismantled by a team still on the lower slopes of their ascent to domestic and European dominance. 'Undressed,' said the BBC's legendary commentator David Coleman as he described the team's performance. In my view, then and on repeat viewing since, only Terry McDermott in that team fully justified his place on the stage, a fact not lost on Liverpool, who soon took him back to Merseyside and helped him to develop into one of the game's finest attacking midfielders with an eye for a pass, an incredible workrate and exquisite timing when it came to attacking the penalty area.

The final in every one of the previous ten years had been decided by a single-goal margin but, after reaching half-time with nothing between the teams, Liverpool cut loose to win 3-0. Kevin Keegan contributed a double and Steve Heighway added the other. It could have been even worse as the best 'goal' of the day, one that would have gone down among the best in final history, was wrongly disallowed when full-back Alec Lindsay crashed in a great second-half volley.

The players knew they had let down the fans and admitted afterwards that they half expected a tough time on their return home. Instead, they were blown away by the reception. This was only five years after lifting the Fairs Cup, so you can only imagine the scenes when they can deliver some silverware again.

Two years later, the Magpies dared to dream of a cup double. The long slog of the 1975/76 campaign featured 16 fixtures on top of a league programme in which they finished only 15th, despite scoring ten more goals at home than champions Liverpool.

The League Cup run began with Alan Gowling – replacing Tudor as Macdonald's striker partner – scoring four times in a 6-0 win over Southport of the Fourth Division. After beating Bristol Rovers in a replay, there was also a very impressive 3-1 win away to QPR, a team that would miss out on the league title by a single point despite winning 13 of their last 15 games. The TV cameras were there to capture it in all its glory, with goals from Macdonald, Burns and Nulty ensuring progress on another 'up late on a school night' *Sportsnight* occasion.

Notts County were knocked over in the next round and then attention switched to the FA Cup at the start of the new year. There, the fates paired United and QPR again, the outcome settled in a replay with a Gowling goal, one of the 30 he netted that season. North-East writer Harry Pearson was unkind to the curly-haired striker in *The Far Corner*, offering the opinion that he never looked like a footballer. He said Gowling 'couldn't kick a ball properly but he looked good in sweatbands!', though his Newcastle record stands up to comparison with many better-known names.

Just three days after beating QPR again, Gowling added a hat-trick in a 5-0 league win over Everton to lift confidence ahead of a trip to Tottenham in the first leg of the League Cup semi-final. A goal from John Pratt gave the Londoners an advantage but tables were turned with a 3-1 home win back at a raucous St James' Park to book a place in February's final.

In the fortnight before that trip, the team edged through a three-game saga with Bolton to earn a place in the FA Cup sixth round, where they would meet a Derby outfit who were the reigning league champions.

As league form suffered amid the emotion of knockout football and the fatigue of a heavy fixture list, a flu bug felled a number of players in the build-up to the League Cup Final. It was so serious that the squad did not even travel together to London, with the bed-ridden staying at home for an extra day or two.

The 1976 final is almost lost in anonymity, with a full league programme still dominating the headlines on Saturday evening and the only television coverage consisting of recorded highlights on Sunday afternoon, 24 hours after the event. Our only live television coverage at the time was of the FA Cup Final (on both BBC1 and ITV), the European Cup Final, England versus Scotland in the Home Internationals and the annual schoolboys match against Scotland at Wembley, a game I attended in 1977, catching a 'Soccer Special' train (though not a smashed-up one) on a long day trip with school.

What the Wembley footage does feature, though, is the huge noise from the stands when Gowling scored to cancel out the Manchester City opener. The contrast in volume between this and the celebration of a Peter Barnes opener at the other end is obvious and overwhelming. Sadly, though, the last word went to Dennis Tueart, a Newcastle-born former Sunderland winger whose overhead kick took the three-handled trophy to the North-West. I still say his effort was dangerous, though, as Glen Keeley's head was the closest defensive object to his boot.

Not helped by having to watch highlights when we already knew we'd lost, there was further hurt as we tried to copy the Tueart volley in the weeks afterwards. Still, there was always the FA Cup.

Despite two more goals from Gowling, a team shorn of Mahoney, Nattrass and Tommy Craig went to Derby a week after the Wembley defeat and lost 4-2 just two steps short of another big day out. I'd had a bad feeling about the game, with the combination of yellow shirts, blue shorts and *Match of the Day* cameras. While the Brazilian resemblance suited a Derby pitch holding as much sand as Copacabana, it was the hosts in white and dark blue who went through.

Young full-back Ray Blackhall deputised for Nattrass, the inexperienced Ray Hudson took Craig's spot in midfield and goalkeeper Eddie Edgar made his first and last senior appearance for the club. None could be apportioned any blame but the toll of the season made its presence felt at the worst possible time. Bruce Rioch scored twice in a Derby performance which bordered on bullying. There was simply nothing Newcastle could do to turn the tide and the Rams, under Dave Mackay, were never going to let us off lightly. Their run ended in the last four as Gordon Hill scored twice for Manchester United, taking Tommy Docherty's Red

Devils to the final for the first time since the pre-George Best days of the early 60s.

The occasion of the FA Cup third round draw was the day of days to go skip school dinners and run home. Without internet, mobile phones, rolling news channels or even Teletext, the only way to catch the draw live was on the radio. It was like wartime revisited but it just wasn't the same if you learned the outcome second-hand at four o'clock in the afternoon. Like the pop charts on a Tuesday lunchtime, the cup draw had to be absorbed as it happened.

Every stage of the competition held its own attraction but nothing compared with the third round, the day when regular giantkillers like Yeovil, Altrincham and Enfield, plus any other surviving non-league minnows and a bunch of lower division clubs punching above their weight, hoped for their day in the sun alongside the giants of the top two divisions. There was the chance of a David versus Goliath as the plumbers, electricians and civil servants went into the hat alongside the big-name professionals. With a bit of luck, a few of the heavyweights would be thrown together and improve the odds of a decent shout if your team made it through safely.

Newcastle, we were told in the build-up, had been victims of giantkillings in the past. Hereford, we were reminded every single season, had been non-leaguers when they put out Newcastle on their Edgar Street ploughed field. 'Who could be the Hereford – or the Newcastle United – of this year?' Yeah, yeah, yeah, thanks for the reminder.

The draw was broadcast live on BBC Radio at 12.30 on a Monday lunchtime in early winter, beginning with the famous line: 'The first voice you will hear is …' before handing over to Ted Croker, secretary of the Football Association. No celebrities, no music, no on-the-spot interviews, no multi-coloured moving captions, just a few old men from the establishment in a (no doubt wood-panelled) committee room at London's Lancaster Gate and the legendary velvet bag of numbered balls. I scribbled down the draw as each ball was pulled out and couldn't wait to pass round the little piece of paper on the return to afternoon lessons in a school which had a few outliers looking for Manchester United, Liverpool or Leeds alongside the masses of Newcastle supporters.

Following the quarter-final trip to Derby in 1976, we were knocked out in successive seasons at the fourth-round stage by Manchester City, Wrexham and Wolves, and then were dumped by Fourth Division visitors Chester in the third, so we could be forgiven for feeling nervous, though spirits lifted slightly when Newcastle's name came out as a home team in the third round draw for the 1980/81 competition. The ball which followed belonged to Sheffield Wednesday and they would come to St James' on the first Saturday in January. At least we'd avoided Hereford.

The teams had already met twice in the league, with the Owls winning in what was their first game after promotion from the Third Division and one of Bobby Shinton's seven seasonal goals securing the points for the Magpies in the return. The cup tie was settled with a double from Waddle in front of a 22,000 crowd (the Christmas defeat by Derby a week earlier had been just the second 20,000-plus gate of the league season at Gallowgate) and, after repeating the lunchtime routine the following Monday, we learned the next round would also be at home and also against a Second Division rival, this time from Luton.

The Hatters were on a good run of form and well in the promotion race (before missing out by just two points at season's end) but they were beaten by goals from Ray Clarke and Mick Martin. A crowd of more than 29,000 went home happy, the attendance almost double the average figure for the league programme, which said everything about the magic of the cup on Tyneside.

Another Monday lunchtime, another draw, this time for the last 32 survivors in the competition. Newcastle's ball came up first again and then we waited … 'will play' … Exeter City from the Third Division. The game was made all-ticket at a 38,000-capacity stadium, with a kid's ticket in 'E' Wing costing £1, the club perhaps surprisingly sticking to the prices for league games despite the increasing momentum.

Although we had to wait for a full week to get into town and head to the ticket office window to book our places, we made sure we were there extra early on matchday and I made my mark as the first fan on to the terraces.

Coinciding with the final series of *When the Boat Comes In*, which gave the North-East a national profile again and peak-time audiences, we had a fourth home game in succession in all competitions and fans were already talking about going further in the competition. I don't think any of us really believed 'this is our year' but Fulham, Southampton and West Ham, not to mention a team from not too far away, had all got to Wembley as Second Division teams in the past few seasons, so why not us?

Daring to dream, a lad from our school turned up for the Exeter clash wearing a black-and-white tail coat, despite a noted absence of engagement in any sport previously. He was best known outside our immediate group of mates for referring to 'spectators' when we watched a video recording of a rugby match during a games lesson after being forced indoors by deep snow. But, suddenly, it was like 1974 all over again.

Alas, the dream went south in the replay down in Devon a few days later in my first experience on the wrong end of a giantkilling. So, with Newcastle out of the way, Tottenham and Manchester City went to Wembley and Ricardo Villa enjoyed his greatest day, scoring twice in the replay and running almost all the way home in celebration, with the rest of the Spurs team desperately trying to grab his billowing shirt-tail.

* * *

English football had fallen in love with overseas signings from the moment Tottenham landed Ossie Ardiles and Ricky Villa after the 1978 World Cup, signed by manager Keith Burkinshaw, who had been a coach at Newcastle and been tipped as a possible successor to Joe Harvey but never got the call and, instead, headed south.

Sheffield United broke their transfer record in spending £160,000 on uncapped Argentine midfielder Alex Sabella and he became a folk hero there before a single-season spell with Yorkshire rivals Leeds in another southern hemisphere swoop.

World Cup winner Alberto Tarantini, though, lasted just one season with Birmingham, where his name became synonymous with wasteful spending on foreign talent, while in 1979, an eye-catching fee of £320,000 took Claudio Marangoni to Wearside, where he played in a promotion team alongside 'Pop' Robson, Jeff Clarke and Stan Cummins before bidding 'adios' after just a handful of opportunities in the top flight.

Yugoslavs were in even bigger demand, with Sarajevo-born Božo Janković moving to Middlesbrough, over-enthusiastic goalkeeper Petar Borota joining Chelsea and full-back Ivan Golac starting a long stint at Southampton among many who traded Balkans for Britain. Raddy Antić, whose moment of glory would come later, had already been abroad with Zaragoza in Spain before David Pleat took him to Luton.

From other parts of Europe, the Dutch duo Arnold Mühren and Frans Thijssen became key to Ipswich Town success and Kazimierz Deyna, with nearly 100 caps for Poland and often viewed as his country's greatest-ever player, joined Malcolm Allison's Manchester City. He showed some of his midfield class there but enjoyed fresh fortune with a switch to the North American Soccer League two years later.

Away from the headliners, there were also unheralded Europeans all over the Football League, many making little impression but some earning cult hero status with the fans who celebrated their point of difference.

The all-conquering Liverpool resisted – they either already had everything they needed or else value for money in the market was not as important a commodity as class – while Arsenal and Everton were among others who paused. Manchester United merely dabbled, playing Yugoslav international hulk Nikola Jovanović alongside Kevin Moran in an uncompromising central defence. Newcastle United, as they did in the approach to signing black players, waited.

Earlier generations had welcomed with open arms the Robledo brothers from Chile and celebrated a Fairs Cup Final goal from Danish midfielder Ben Arentoft while St James' Park would later become home to a galaxy of overseas stars including Philippe Albert, Tino Asprilla and David Ginola, Alain Saint-Maximin, Alexander Isak and Bruno Guimarães (though there were a large number of misses, too, often from South America). But in our Second Division days of the late 70s and early 80s, we saw only the Dutchman Frans Koenen – and, even then, only for a little while.

It looked like there would be more cosmopolitan recruits, including Finland international Leo Houtsonen, who joined the squad on tour in the summer of 1980. The defender impressed observers, though obviously not the manager of the team or perhaps the bank, as he was not taken on permanently. Ray Xuereb from Malta had been given a trial by Richard Dinnis but never got beyond the reserves and we saw South African-born striker Andy Parkinson in second-string reports in *The Pink* but rarely in the flesh. These were the only other foreigners who came close to a Magpies career in this period.

From my earliest memories of watching football, I had been a disciple of the Dutch so, naturally, I took to Koenen, even before I'd seen him.

Inspired by Johan Cruyff in 1974, enthralled by Robbie Rensenbrink in the Cup Winners' Cup Final against West Ham two years later and on to Johnny Rep with Bastia in 78, I loved what the Dutch did with a football. After seeing Arie Haan's long-range missiles at the World Cup in Argentina, it was wonderful to watch Mühren and Thijssen weaving their magic for Bobby Robson. In later years, I became a fan of Clarence Seedorf and enjoyed watching Edgar Davids and Marco van Basten, though, like most Englishmen (even ones like me who find it hard to blindly support the national team), I hated Ronald Koeman no matter how good he was at 35-yard free kicks. Then there was that long-haired bloke with the moustache, the one who married Cruyff's daughter and dropped 'King Al of Tyneside' for a local derby.

After learning that Koenen had been the Netherlands' Under-21 captain while playing with NEC Nijmegen, we noted that he was stocky and all left foot and he wore white ankle pads outside his socks in the way only continentals could. I was among those willing him to make a success of the move.

But after a run of just a dozen games, Koenen was gone, setting a trend for a number of Netherlanders in subsequent years, with fleeting glimpses of Siem and Luuk de Jong and even less of Patrick van Aanholt, Brian Pinas and John Karelse. Even midfielder Gini Wijnaldum, a standout in a struggling team, and the relatively regular Patrick Kluivert and Jetro Willems lasted a single season each. Their countryman, Tim Krul, made more appearances than all the rest added together in his 12 seasons on Tyneside.

* * *

A highlight of every summer was the appearance of the pocket-sized fixtures card in the *Evening Chronicle*, complete with its Newcastle Brown Ale back page advert, which heralded the end of the boring close season. Unlike the television age, once the fixtures were on that card, they stayed on the date given and, of course, there was no need to wait for kick-off times, with the only deviation from three o'clock on a Saturday being Bank Holiday weekends and a couple of early season midweek dates. Only postponements for bad weather or a long cup run meant any alteration. The list always included the reserve date for the FA Cup Final, too, and its mere presence in print brought a tinge of anticipation.

After checking for the opening game of the season, a derby was the next one you looked for. There is nothing like a derby game but, in 1980/81, there was nothing like a derby for Newcastle United. The neighbours had won promotion at their third attempt and, with Middlesbrough well established around mid-table in the First Division, we were left alone one step lower, looking lonely on those printed fixture pages. I had never been to a Tyne-Wear derby but that did not mean I wouldn't miss them. We could have done with the payday, too, with the club well into a bank overdraft of £500,000 when changes in the boardroom led to the departure of former chairman Lord Westwood.

During the six-year wilderness period from 1978 to the moment Newcastle returned to top company, there were just four Tyne-Wear league meetings. Under Bill McGarry in the opening season after relegation, United finished four points behind neighbours who just missed out on promotion. A year later, when we could only manage ninth place, they won promotion as runners-up. They joined Boro in the top division and, suddenly and all too obviously, Newcastle were the poor relations as the lowest-ranked of the trio. The black sheep of the North-East football family.

The Wearsiders stayed up thanks to wins on the last day of two consecutive seasons, while Boro went through the trapdoor in 1982. Both have, of course, experienced life at the third level of English league football, a point worthy of a gratuitous mention here and on occasion of any other comparison.

At points in Newcastle's six-year spell in the second tier, meetings with Carlisle United became our derby events, though the cities are 60 miles apart and have little in common other than an ancient wall, a cross-country railway line, regional television 'for the North-East and Cumbria' and Peter Beardsley.

Carlisle famously topped the First Division after three weeks of the 1974/75 season but they still went down at the end of it. That 22nd place, nevertheless, remains their highest finish in a century of club history. But they were a really competitive outfit in the early 80s under Bob Stokoe, the former Newcastle player who led Sunderland to their 1973 FA Cup win. Alan Shoulder and one-time Geordies skipper Tommy Craig were among their key men as the minnows chased the big names of Newcastle, Chelsea, Manchester City and Sheffield Wednesday in the promotion frame. Bobby Moncur, 'Pop' Robson, Aiden McCaffrey and David

McCreery also all played for Newcastle before joining the managerial merry-go-round at Carlisle, with varying degrees of satisfaction and frustration.

Sheffield Wednesday provided the next-closest thing to being derby rivals in this period, thanks to shared frustrations and volume of support as much as geography. Under Ashington hero Jack Charlton, they got out of the Third Division in 1980 with an up-and-at-them style and went on to finish tenth, fourth and sixth in the Second Division before finally gaining promotion, alongside Newcastle, under Howard Wilkinson in 1984, ironically the same year that 'Big Jack' went home for his shortlived spell as Magpies manager.

It is a curiosity of North-East football that two of the region's biggest heroes never played in a Tyne-Wear derby. Malcolm Macdonald's six years on Tyneside coincided with one of Sunderland's Second Division spells and then, when Kevin Keegan took the mantle, our neighbours were enjoying a five-year stint in the division above (the Wearsiders, of course, made up for it in the next few years, plummeting to the Third Division before the decade was out).

Neither man got to experience playing in the derby. Mac had to make do with scoring all of Arsenal's goals in a win and a draw against north London neighbours Spurs while Keegan, who knew all about Merseyside rivalry earlier in his career, would only see the North-East's biggest head-to-head battles from the sidelines long after his playing days were over.

We were reminded of just how far Newcastle United had slipped when the pages of *The Pink* printed its league tables every Saturday evening with the names of the local clubs highlighted in bold text. Though neither of our closest geographic rivals pulled up any trees, even sitting in the bottom half of the First Division put them higher up the page than us and I am not ashamed to admit that, after watching the regional highlights programme on Sunday afternoons, it was obvious our nearest rivals had better teams than us.

Boro had a quality keeper in Jim Platt, who had been there since the age of the steam-powered wireless, they had the brash youngsters Craig Johnston and David Hodgson before both moved on to Liverpool, midfielder David Armstrong, who literally never missed a game, and the balding import, Janković, who finished the season as their top scorer. Remember midfielder Billy Askew? They had him, too.

Down among the pyjama-kitted men at Roker, manager Alan Durban had Shaun Elliott in defence and the dynamic duo of Alan Brown and Gary Rowell up front. They also had Stan Cummins. At 5ft 6in (that's what it said in the yearbooks, though he looked shorter on a pitch where even the big men were just a shade over 6ft tall) and less than nine and a half stones, he was all close control and 'impish' skills, as the newspapers would call it. He could also take the knocks and bounced back like a rubber ball in the days when grievous bodily harm was an occupational hazard for any striker.

Sunderland were no longer the 'Bank of England Club' of old but they did part with some serious money to sign Cummins from Boro, though still a long way short of Jack Charlton's valuation when he predicted 'Little Stan' would be the first million-pound Englishman. Cummins, though, did have the distinction of scoring against Newcastle in both Tyne-Wear and Tyne-Tees derbies and I was not alone at the most northerly of the three clubs to secretly admire his skills, though obviously a lot less after his transfer.

Chapter Six

Worked Off My Dues

I HAD always been a note-taker, list-maker and scrapbook-sticker but by the summer of 1981, I'd started writing a daily diary. It was nothing special; there were no passages of teenage revelation or angst (other than what was contained in *Final Score* on a Saturday teatime), as I considered it more a record of what I'd been up to, what we'd done at school, where I'd played football, who I'd gone with to St James' Park, that sort of thing; just the important stuff of being in my early teens. I'd done holiday diaries before but this was more serious, inspired by a couple of books I'd read around that time and an unspectacular BBC drama based on the journal of an old woman.

I remember clearly the first day of the diary because it coincided with a North-East double in the transfer market. Quoting directly: 'Sunderland signed Ally McCoist from St Johnstone for a club record £400,000. Newcastle bought Imre Varadi (who?) from Everton (who?) for £150,000.'

Clearly, sarcasm had started to surface as a personal quality, nurtured in the cynicism of another season watching a team splashing around in mid-table in the Second Division, as far away from the top as at any point in my (short) lifetime.

I watched *Match of the Day* without fail, I never missed *Football Focus* and *On the Ball* on a Saturday, I regularly read *Shoot* and the new *Match Weekly*, so I must have seen something of Varadi. But I still expected Newcastle to do better.

He sounded exotic (we were told he had Hungarian heritage) but Varadi was born in Paddington, London, and I read that he had played non-league football with Letchworth. He had tattooed forearms when they were the exclusive preserve of the manual labour force and squaddies and he'd so far scored ten goals in his Football League career. So far, so what?

With Alan Shoulder no longer an automatic choice (though he was around the 20-goal mark with the reserves in the Central League, which was about five times more than any other striker), Bobby Shinton making his way back from a six-month injury absence and Chris Waddle only a dozen games into his first professional contract, boss Arthur Cox must have seen something in Varadi that us experts on the terraces had not. It would not be the last time he would demonstrate his superior knowledge and shrewdness in the transfer market.

Varadi had already been over to Portugal to discuss a potential move to Benfica, the two-time European champions and dominant force in their own country, after deciding the time had come to leave Everton. He'd started his pro career with Sheffield United and it was Gordon Lee who took him to Goodison Park after just a handful of senior games in the Second Division. He netted the winning goal against Liverpool in his first Merseyside derby – in the FA Cup, too – though the story goes that he also copped ('Kopped' if it hadn't been played on Everton turf) a pie in the face from the crowd for his troubles. The high-profile goal could have been the platform to go on to greater glories – and there are Evertonians who still talk warmly about his contribution – but when Howard Kendall replaced Lee in charge and the club brought in Newcastle-born Mick Ferguson and the Rod Stewart lookalike Alan Biley as options up front, his time was up. Thankfully for us, Cox was ready to step in.

* * *

Over the previous couple of seasons, we had followed the action mainly from the paddock in the Old Stand, while also being brave enough – with falling attendances – to occasionally sample life behind the goal. But for the start of 1981/82, we became full-time Gallowgate graduates and waved goodbye to the paddock apprenticeship, never to return.

I took to standing halfway back on the main home terrace, in line with one goalpost, next to an imposing concrete crowd barrier, built like the tank traps still visible on our Northumbrian beaches.

Years earlier at the other end of the ground, the capacity of the Leazes had been savaged when the Safety of Sports Grounds Act insisted upon the use of better crowd barriers. Simon Inglis, in his first guide to the *Football Grounds of England and Wales* in 1983, described how the original Leazes barriers had been concreted-in during stadium updates over the years but the metal rails were still attached underneath to a wooden strip installed 70 years earlier. Replacement work had been priced at £150,000 in the 70s and, with the entire new East Stand erected at a reported cost of £420,000, the decision was taken that a rebuild would be more cost effective and more appropriate than repair. Half a million pounds was spent on removing the roof, the floodlights and the terrace. Sadly, though, that was as far as it got.

So, the Gallowgate became the busiest part of the ground, home of the home fans. Standing on the terrace did have its downsides at times, especially as the shortest member of our group and, therefore, only ever a step away from seeing nothing at all, but there was no turning back. This was now our spot, in the middle of it all and, for comfort's sake, also close to the access corridor which ran front to back, just to one side of the centre of goal.

From here, now considering ourselves seriously experienced operators, we would take a guess at the attendance figure before it was revealed on the electronic scoreboard during the second half. About as scientific as a competition to 'guess the number of sweets it would take to fill this Ford Fiesta', we would cast an eye around, assess the strength of travelling support, look for empty seats in the corners and come up with a number. Mine always ended in the digits 812 for no good reason at all and, as far as my O-level maths could make out, I had as much chance of being right as anyone who changed the last three digits up or down week to week.

A more serious challenge, though, was working out why our team had never scored from a corner. From our vantage point in the Gallowgate, we'd see two tall centre-halves make their way forward in anticipation of the set piece but, for the life of me, I can hardly recall a goal scored from a corner in this period. We had some decent headers of the ball at times, too, and some players with a good delivery, just not simultaneously.

Years later, I read that Newcastle topped the list in the Premier League stats for goals scored from corners, I think in the 2010/11 season. They totalled four. So, perhaps it isn't the dulling of memory through time; perhaps we were always crap from corners. And by the sounds of it, the rest of the country were even worse.

Outside, the presence of police horses around the Barrack Road entry points often seemed more processional than practical but they got through more work in the street directly behind the Gallowgate most weeks. Back in the Ladybird books of my childhood, I remembered a picture of a mounted bobby equipped with an extra long baton, used to reach villains from an elevated position when the pocket-sized truncheon would have been inadequate. So, whenever we (carefully) crossed paths with the horses, I looked out for it, ticking it off like an item in the I-Spy books. Matchday mounties, tick; oversized baton, tick; watch where you're walking, tick.

The horses and their riders ushered fans around often enough, blocking off one way or directing to another, usually in the half an hour before kick-off when we would already be in our places inside, sometimes standing right at the back before it filled up just to observe events unfold outside and monitor the build-up of aggravation before stepping forward towards our more regular positions.

We selected our turnstile entrance depending on the look of whoever was in front of us in the queue rather than blind faith to a lucky number or a particular entry. The operator often pushed little me and a slightly bigger mate through on a single click, allowing him to pocket one of the admission prices.

Reaching the turnstiles was the point where nervous tension gave way to sheer excitement, regardless of the team's form or the likelihood of a win.

That excitement remained every single time I got to those gates, league or cup, sunshine or showers, Withe or without. Some will say all forms of entertainment stimulate this kind of buzz – a 'frisson of excitement' as the heavier newspaper critics used to say, on entering a cinema, theatre or concert hall – but there is nothing to compare with the click of the turnstile of a match, where the plot and finale are yet to be written.

On the slopes at the back of the Gallowgate, filling areas between our terrace steps and the outdoor urinals, we made a surprise splash of mysterious inner-city greenery. At a stretch, you could call it a shrubbery, though not a nice one. It looked more like an unloved motorway embankment, more of dust and rubbish than of foliage. Nowadays, it would probably have a sponsor and a gang of community service gardeners trying to keep on top of the litter. These unattractive bushes were presumably there not just to catch litter blowing around the stadium or fag ends flicked from the steps but as landscaping to hold the soil in place and break up the run of concrete and brick. Through the deepest winter months, this little slice of urban landscaping, its bushes and soil, assumed the same grey colour as the steps but the plants somehow survived, testament to a resilience shared with supporters.

Part of our growing-up process was a requirement for body searches in the Gallowgate once you got through the turnstiles and before you tackled the zig-zag staircases upwards. Performed by the police, they were pretty thorough and I did worry about providing a convincing explanation if the little piece of souvenir concrete from the terrace in my pocket was ever discovered. The conformist within me eventually decided it would be best left at home.

Full gentrification of football would have to wait until the advent of the Premier League in the early 90s and the commercialisation which came with it, so the stadium bowl of our time remained the preserve of the working man and keen young lads. There was more hostility than hospitality as the 'prawn sandwich brigade' was restricted to a handful of directors and their guests who, we assumed, did not have to make do with a Bovril. There were no corporate suites, no lounges, no executive boxes – not until the builders' huts were added at the back of the benches in the New Stand – and only one 'experience'; the one of being at matchday alongside several thousand similar supporters.

Fans in search of sustenance could find burgers or pies if they were lucky. There were crisps in a limited range of flavours – what I would have given for Tudor's pickled onion or the curry ones in the Indian-styled bag – and 'chocolate-flavoured' Wagon Wheels when they were still wagon wheel size. I was never a fan, feeling they didn't look like chocolate, didn't feel like chocolate and didn't taste much like chocolate either, though as they were kept next to the tea urn they did at least melt like chocolate. Or there were packets of Clix (Klix?) chewing gum. I never saw them in a newsagent but whatever they were, they seemed to corner the market in matchday confectionery, sold in a pop-out plastic wrapper like Rennie indigestion relief tablets.

Tea and Bovril were served in little plastic brown yoghurt pots which melted in your hands – 'If we win promotion, they've promised a new tea bag' was a regular review – there was a selection of 'fruit' juices in various neon colours contained in flimsy transparent containers with a short straw you popped directly through the lid, thereby taking any dirt or germs from the warehouse directly into your drink and your mouth. It was a very rare day indeed when any of our group parted with any money at the kiosks.

We were a bit late for 'peanuts, tanner a bag' of the 50s and 60s but the sellers were occasionally still visible around the ground, walking the perimeter of the pitch with an usherette's tray hanging from their shoulders. Curiosity got the better of me on one occasion when I moved towards the front to buy some nuts. Wrapped in a paper cone, it was the day that I discovered peanuts did not always come in a golden brown colour, covered in salt like in a tin at Christmas. These were straight from the kernel, like you hang out for blue tits in the winter in the garden. I think we ended up surreptitiously lobbing most of them around the crowd and never fell for that one again.

It was pretty desperate when that was about all you could get from your standing position, though at least whenever I went with my dad he would be prepared, taking a packet of Smith's Salt & Shake crisps (the ones with the little blue bag inside) and an Oxo cube. Hey presto, beef-flavour crisps!

As the hawkers made their circuits, they picked their way around the toilet rolls thrown from the terraces and around the photographers who took their positions just to one side of the goalposts, sitting a yard or two from the white line and mostly in their normal workwear of shirt and jacket or anorak, casual dark trousers and shoes, desperate to get their shots and the film back to base – down in the Bigg Market for the local rags – in time to develop and print for the papers. Around them, the edge of the pitch was dotted with little wooden stools, there for the police, stewards, St John Ambulance and the ballboys who had unbeatable views of the action as reward for having to wear blue nylon tracksuits which were either slightly too big or much too small for any of them.

Very occasionally, if the queues outside the centre section of the Gallowgate had ground to a halt, we would chance our arm by entering a different part of the stand and weaving through the dividing fences to assume our usual positions. Usually, this held no drama but on the odd occasions that stewards or police decided this was not going to be allowed, we had to find somewhere to stand on the flagpole side, where the concrete terrace rose to a point in the corner.

There, the swaying seemed even more exaggerated than in the middle section, with the crowd leaders standing on top of the concrete barriers. Their plunge forward and downward was all part of the excitement, though you only really saw the aftermath, prompted by ironic cheering, rather than the fall.

In the centre section, you stood still only during the pre-match warm-ups, thereafter moving to and fro, left and right in sync with what was happening on the pitch. A pass flicked out wide required craned necks and tiptoes or a choreographed little shuffle to one side and a sea of eyes following the flight of the ball towards the penalty area, then a chorus of oohs and aahs, frustration or celebration, followed by a reset, ready to go again. Even when your team attacked at the other end of the field, a sea of heads and shoulders moved this way and that, with massed heads involuntarily snapping forward to connect with any dangerous cross, neck muscles tensed and teeth clenched. We'd all scored a good few 'virtual goals' at that end but never got our names printed in *The Pink*.

There were flare-ups round and about but the most frequently threatening part of that crammed centre section was the industrial-strength sulphuric farting which gave away whoever had spent their pre-match in a session at the pub. Experts could probably identify the brewery, especially with a major one literally across the road from our end of the ground.

But no matter what was happening all around, I never felt anything other than safe. It was only later, with the more organised face of violence, that matchday got a bit hairy.

The Gallowgate End was frenetic and passionate, but it was not a gigantic terrace by the standards of the day. It hadn't been built as the 'home' end but inherited the title by default when the Leazes was lost in the relegation year. In appearance, the Gallowgate looked stark but that was just because it was grey and open. It was not of a size to rival the Kop at Anfield, Aston Villa's Holte End, the South Bank at Wolves or giant Spion Kop at Hillsborough. The steps had a shallow rake, too, which meant there was no 'wall' of faces but rather a gradual embankment. But it was still a sight to behold in its prime.

There would be a few likely lads you didn't fancy standing next to and a few boring ones who didn't join in the singing but, by and large, we were all similar, there to give what we could for the team. If you stumbled on a step as your foot failed to make contact with the ground, there was usually someone bigger and heavier to stop your fall before it had even started and, if there was any disturbance, it was mainly down at the very front or at the very back where the entrances and exits were easier to locate for away fans looking to claim new territory.

There were plenty of smokers before the public bans, so you had to do your best to keep polyester jumpers and nylon kagoules out of harm's way. With fag ends clenched ever more tightly between teeth as the action intensified, plumes of smoke drifted upwards from everywhere, eventually absorbed into the output from the brewery chimneys. You could see steam rising from the masses on damp days and the vapour of breath on cold afternoons of deep midwinter, especially in evening matches.

It wasn't just anticipating the next move of the masses that required you to keep your wits about you. The state of the toilets – and levels of inebriation – meant there were some fans who didn't see any reason to move from where they stood if they needed to pee. Given the scene that awaited them if they did make it to the uncovered black wall at the back of the stand, it was perhaps not a tough decision to make.

Stories of people peeing in your pocket were untrue, like getting your head flushed down the toilet on your birthday at big school, but we were on the receiving end once, when a friend went home with one warm, wet ankle and shoe. There were plenty of other occasions, too, when groups of fans were required to move a few steps to one side as someone decided the designated painted wall was too far away.

There was more noise and more movement all-round in the Gallowgate compared with the paddocks but you could still hear the chatter, too. Some of the better-natured comments would keep us amused for the rest of the week. I always enjoyed when someone pushed their way through the crowd or stumbled into an innocent bystander on the steps, which triggered a Geordie chorus of 'how man, hey man; how man, hey man' from the vicinity, together with friendly barging of anyone adjacent. It felt great at the time but I appreciate that it sounds odd when describing the behaviour of grown men out of context now.

During the game, the response to a 50-50 challenge which resulted in the ball flying over the touchline would be led by someone screaming 'wor baal' and a group response of 'whose baal?' (my grandad's Northumbrian dialect would have asked 'wee's baal?') and a mightier roar of 'wor baal' from unified United voices. I'm not sure it would work in any other accent but it always brought smiles around the crowd and often from the pitch, too, where a player in stripes would hold his hands out for the ball and the referee felt under pressure to give him the benefit of the doubt in deciding the direction of play to get the game restarted.

There was, of course, also plenty of abuse directed at the opposition, the referee and linesmen, visiting fans and the police. At least there is some reasoning behind disliking the forces of law and order or for venting against the opposition and officials but it was confusing to hear 'friendly fire' thrown down among different sections of the home crowd. 'Why's the corner full of shits?' enquired the centre section of the Gallowgate on a regular basis, while the corner responded similarly. It usually raised a bit of a laugh but it was an odd approach to someone in the same scarf who just happened to be standing further along the same concrete steps. Likewise, the challenge to and from home fans in the Leazes End if there was nothing else to sing about.

In the section closest to the Old Stand, there always seemed to be a disproportionate number of Scottish Newcastle fans (as well as Scottish & Newcastle fans, who downed their products on matchdays). The successful teams from the club's very earliest days had always included Scots and the first golden era had been dominated by them. In my time, you could also buy woolly hats which featured half-and-half colours, black and green for Newcastle and Celtic or black and blue if you were a Rangers man. Chants of 'Celtic, Rangers; Celtic, Rangers' rang out in the Gallowgate for a time and I've never encountered fans elsewhere who call out the names of alternative clubs without adding comment or expletive.

I can only ever remember standing in that corner on a very small number of occasions, including once when we only got into the ground with seconds to spare ahead of kick-off for a New Year's Day game against Carlisle because we'd been caught in traffic on the Great North Road through Gosforth as it was down to one lane due to the Morpeth-Newcastle road race, which was usually won by Mike McLeod from Elswick Harriers. During the game, getting carried away by the occasion and the beer fumes, fitting in with the general mood one of our group – I know who but will save his embarrassment – called either an opposition player or the referee a 'basket' and, about two seconds later, one of the Scots around us leaned forward and barked: 'If you're going to swear, then ****ing swear properly,' with a fag end still clenched in his teeth. I've never forgotten his words. Or his breath. It was New Year, after all.

* * *

We never, ever left a game before the final whistle but as the 90-minute mark approached we would sometimes shuffle nearer to a gate so we could be in the right place to beat the bulk of the crowd for our dash back down to the Haymarket. There were no laps of honour or throwing shirts to the crowd at the final whistle, the players simply clapped towards the crowd, none of whom had handmade signs begging for a shirt or a photo, and they disappeared down the tunnel towards the old communal baths. Within minutes, the place would be empty, though on good days the singing continued into the streets, at least until we started to thin out as the procession reached the first pubs.

Outside, there were discarded newspapers pulped against the stadium walls and kerbsides, random loose horseracing pages blowing down the street alongside unwanted Golden Goal tickets and empty beer and pop cans, chip wrappers and other food packaging, together with an overwhelming smell of tomato ketchup and boiled onions. There was also always the chance of standing in something soft and slippery. If you were lucky, it was the remains of a ketchup-soaked piece of bread from a hot dog or burger.

The back of the Gallowgate was closed off to traffic at full time as we all walked straight down the middle of the road, with fans stretched out from kerb to kerb. Occasionally, a startled driver would somehow find their way in from the end near the Strawberry, only to realise their error as they reached a point of no return. There was nothing to be gained in a car anyway because we were walking faster than they could pick a way through and male rogue drivers could expect a few glares and what my parents would describe as 'choice words', while unlucky or unwitting red-faced women were greeted with a few slaps on the bonnet as they yearned for a hole in the ground to swallow them up and provide an escape from the embarrassment. All of them, though, just had to wait it out.

Blue-and-white vans (the only mention of 'Keegan' on Newcastle matchdays up to this point) lined the streets outside, selling their boiled hotdogs, boiled hamburgers and boiled onions. Lazily, I was going to say 'greasy burgers' but that would be inaccurate when describing something which came in tins and had the pallor of school's spam fritters. The rival Westler's burgers were among those available in some streets, though for obvious reasons it is the Keegan ones which have stuck in my mind over the years since.

Vendors stood freezing in white butchers' coats, warmed by endless clouds of steam, all the while handling coins and notes as well as the food, enveloped in a smell of the onions and runny red sauce. It is the image that still comes to mind when I see the words 'street food', though a million miles away from the modern trend.

No matter how long it had been since breakfast, a burger stop was never my priority, though there was occasionally one in the group who would be tempted. In all honesty, it was probably the size of the queue or having enough money left which informed the decision on whether to buy or not, rather than any thoughts based on the food, though I did wonder what his mam's cooking was like if this was the preferred option on Saturday teatime. It also meant a race against time to eat and start to digest before we jumped aboard the bus home at the bottom the hill.

Given the choice between allocating pocket money for a match programme or an overpriced burger from an undersized van, I'd rather have eaten the programme.

On occasion, time permitting, someone would manage a sausage roll at Carricks bakers or Greggs, when it was still 'Greggs of Gosforth' (our alternative bus route actually went past the front door of Greggs *in* Gosforth on the way home). Vegan sausage rolls, like all-seater stadia and mobile score notifications, were still decades in the future.

The food vendors reminded me of the ice cream man we used to see pushing a hand barrow around the streets of Fawdon near my grandparents' home on Sunday afternoons. He sold only the yellow ice cream you bought in bricks to add to your tinned fruit, rather than cornets and lollies. He had the first fingerless gloves I'd ever seen outside of television period dramas and his appearance, complete with constant running (one step up from dripping) nose, raised a number of questions in my head: Where did he push the cart from? Did he take his company vehicle home in the evening? What did he do with the leftovers at the end of each day? And has he heard of tissues?

We continued our downhill run after the final whistle to grab prime seats on the X25 Blyth-bound bus, sitting peacefully as other representatives of Cramlington and Annitsford attempted to settle tribal scores outside. I'm not sure any of them went to the game or were even football fans but they became part of the matchday ritual, regardless.

With half an hour between bus departures and tea almost certain to be on the table by the time you got home, you didn't want to miss this one, so we were rarely among the crowds who gathered at the windows of Granada, Radio Rentals, Dixon's inside Eldon Square or any other electrical stores to check the rest of the results as they appeared on

Final Score, unless someone had to go back into town to do some shopping. Nevertheless, it was rare that we got all the way home without finding out all the relevant scores from elsewhere, starting, of course, with our derby rivals.

If you were near someone in the crowd with a radio – using a cream-coloured plastic earplug or a pocket-sized wireless held up against their head – you could sometimes overhear commentary of goals going in and, by the time we got to the bus, everyone was able to swap what snippets they'd heard, so we ended up with something close to a full set. Even better, if there was a transistor radio somewhere on the bus, there would be a deathly hush when the results check was read out, with shared reactions up and down the seats.

Anyway, not long after we got home, we had *The Pink* edition of the *Evening Chronicle* delivered. With all the fanfare of the digital age, among the greatest disappointments is the loss of seeing all the results, all the tables, the match reports, photos and round-ups from your most relevant games all printed in one place so quickly after the final whistle. I've seen the operation up close from behind the scenes but even the people who worked on them as journalists or printers are still in awe of how it all happened so quickly and so efficiently, ready to hit the streets while many supporters were still on their way home.

The new world of seven-days-a-week sport and coverage from all over the world has a great number of plus-points but I'm not alone in missing the impact of that front and back page of *The Pink*, with the consequences of football's full programme on a Saturday afternoon all mapped out in front of you. It could make or break your weekend.

* * *

The 1981/82 season saw Football League's landmark introduction of three points for a win, so it was typical of Newcastle United that they opened without a goal in a defeat by Watford at home and followed up with the same outcome on a revolutionary new 'plastic' pitch at Queens Park Rangers.

Bottom of the table after two games, a goal from John Trewick – the last North-East native to hold the position of club record purchase until Sir John Hall authorised a rather more significant cheque to bring Alan Shearer home from Blackburn – provided the first points of the season at the expense of Cambridge United. The visitors were only a decade into their professional history but in another ten years would narrowly miss out on becoming founder members of the Premier League after a fifth-placed finish at this level. They were not, though, a big draw for the Magpies, who had already announced season ticket sales in excess of the announced crowd figure of 15,000 and must have feared the stay-aways had started already.

Chris Waddle had the distinction of netting the 5,000th goal in Newcastle's Football League history during a defeat at Norwich before the team registered back-to-back home wins against Shrewsbury and Orient – who would finish bottom of the table – and then brought the first month to a close with another loss at Bolton.

I was there for Kevin Todd's debut as a substitute in a 3-0 win over Derby but by the time I returned to the Gallowgate a few weeks later, we had slipped to 12th in the table with six wins from the opening 14 games. We had also been knocked out of the League Cup at the hands of Fulham, beaten in home and away legs by a team that manager Malcolm Macdonald was taking to promotion from the Third Division.

Big Stuart Boam had been a crucial part of the team the previous season with experience, know-how and bulk to tether the defence following a surprise move from Middlesbrough but in the summer he opted to join his hometown club, Mansfield, as player-manager. In a typical Newcastle way, rather than sign a replacement of equal or better quality, the club instead kicked off the season with the youthful partnership of David Barton and Bruce Halliday in defence. Both were from south of the river but with Kevin Carr, Steve Carney, Alan Shoulder, Kenny Wharton, Nigel Walker, Peter Cartwright, Peter Haddock, Wes Saunders and Waddle also making a significant number of appearances during the season, it would be hard to find a squad in the club's history with a stronger North-East flavour.

After retaining a settled side for the first months of the season, Arthur Cox started to shuffle his pack. Shinton made just one appearance in the seven months after October, Walker was out, Carney and the young Peter Haddock formed a new defensive pair, Wes Saunders ousted Ian Davies at left-back and we had the added excitement of seeing successive loan players given a chance to stake their claim to the No.7 shirt as the manager evaluated his options without a wallet to go to market.

Loan moves possessed a sense of intrigue and drama and, therefore, some glamour, especially at Newcastle, where they hadn't happened very often up to that point. It was obvious, too, that we, as supporters, could help make or break a player's temporary stay. Win over the fans early on and you got at least as far as a second interview; lose the public via attitude or ability and you might as well shake hands over the desk and say goodbye.

The system has changed over time and now loans are arranged in terms of finance and politics, as well as novelty and convenience, but the concept was used more out of necessity by Cox. This wasn't the 21st century Chelsea sending out 20 players a season on loan because there was no space for their blacked-out Range Rovers or all the zeroes on the Financial Fair Play statements. Neither was this manufactured to manage game time for young players on the fringes of first-team selection, offer development opportunities in a testing new environment or to find match fitness after long-term injury. This was all about taking players on approval before committing to spending hard cash.

Like mail order fashion, the club could take a look, try on for size, even carefully wear for a night out and then make up their minds about longer term, pleading 'there's nothing wrong with the product but it's not quite the right size, please refund my money', or 'the quality did not meet my expectations from the pictures in the brochure'. In the event of a good fit, however, it came down to finding a place in the wardrobe at the expense of a previously loved but now worn-out item.

Newcastle had never been prolific players in the loan market after first dipping their toes in the water to bring Viv Busby up north in 1971. Busby had been a strike partner of Malcolm Macdonald in their days at Luton and, when they both scored in the first game of the reunion, the transfer seemed like a deal waiting to be done. Busby also provided the only goal of a win at West Ham before being named in the team beaten at non-league Hereford, a blow which proved terminal to his Tyneside trial. It was Busby who supplied the cross for Macdonald's far-post header to put Newcastle in front, though the camera angle from the Edgar Street gantry is so tight that he hardly gets into the frame on the right touchline. Not that it mattered; even with perfect camera work, his contribution would have been lost for all eternity under replays of Ronnie Radford, Ricky George and kids in green parkas.

Busby did gain personal compensation by going all the way to the FA Cup Final in 1975 with Second Division Fulham and led the line in a team featuring international veterans Bobby Moore and Alan Mullery. The underdogs fell short of a fairytale finish, however, with Alan Taylor netting twice for West Ham in his first season since leaving Rochdale in the Fourth Division.

Alex Cropley, a typically lightweight and light-of-touch Scottish midfielder who earned rave reviews early in his career at Hibernian, moved south as a hot prospect with Arsenal and then Aston Villa but had been hit by injury, including a broken leg, by the time Newcastle took a punt on a loan deal during the Second Division years. It was an opportunity for him to gain some confidence and consistency away from the top flight and a chance to become a key cog in a new team while the manager checked out an obviously decent performer who just needed a chance to show he was fully up and running again.

There were some glimpses of the quality there, undoubtedly, when he pulled on a striped shirt but Newcastle were not convinced any further commitment would be worthwhile and he was gone after just three games. Still, that was three more than Irving Gernon, a defender from Ipswich who was once announced as a loan signing in the local press but never made an appearance and didn't even register as a Magpies player with the editors of *Rothman's Football Yearbook*.

First in the queue for Cox's audition slots in 1981/82 was Alan Brown, a blond striker at Sunderland who nevertheless had made an impressive start to his career before being stalled by injury. Although still just 22 years old, he had already played more than 100 senior games after making his breakthrough as a teenager. We had seen plenty of him in the regional highlights, so we knew he was quick and positive around the penalty area, with a good touch and an eye for goal. He had been hotly tipped to go far in the game and, if that meant turning his back on Wearside, even better.

Brown was the first player in my time to dare to go direct from Roker to St James' and he looked good despite obvious concerns about the long-term status of his troublesome back. He received a warm welcome, seemed to have an infectious attitude and big smile when things were going well and he scored three times in five games in an interesting partnership with the livewire Imre Varadi. Few defenders would have fancied matching either of them for pace and, for a moment, there was a hint that the good times were coming again and that this duo could really work.

After making his debut in defeat at Chelsea in November 1981, Brown claimed his first goal in a 4-1 win over Charlton Athletic which also featured a top-class strike among a pair from Varadi. The fans obviously approved, too, with an extra 6,000 added to the gate in time for a 3-2 win over league leaders Luton a week later when Brown scored twice, to go with another from partner-in-crime Varadi, in front of a 21,000 crowd.

The positivity in attack started to inspire confidence, not only on the field but in the crowd, but then, in a shock almost as great as his arrival, the back page of *The Chronicle* revealed that Brown was on his way back Wearside way. Club historian Paul Joannou has reported conflicting tales behind the outcome, with claims of injury issues on one side and a lack of funds available on the other. Whatever, Brown went back down the road and played a handful of times in another successful fight against relegation from the First

Division but then left for good in the summer. Rather than Tyneside, he went to Shrewsbury where, naturally, he netted a winner against Newcastle and then played out his career at Doncaster.

It would be a lie to say there was never a dull moment in testing times but we were already into an amazing five-year run without watching a goalless draw in league football at St James' Park. After a stalemate against Leicester at the end of the previous season, it would be November 1986 before we had another one, which must be something of a record. Flicking through the yearbooks, we didn't draw too many blanks in front of goal in those years either, which was quite a shock after the drought of 1980/81. The watching public, though, were still picking their games in the Second Division and attendances would only pick up again for the late-season dates with Chelsea, Crystal Palace and Leicester.

With Brown gone and a striker-shaped hole still to fill, Cox tried again and this time he managed to bring in a former British record transfer signing.

Born in Whitby on the North Yorkshire coast, David Mills was a Teesside hero in a classy Middlesbrough team assembled by Jack Charlton and he needed very little introduction to the Geordie public. Despite the chemical cloud and the ancient ground, Boro boasted a decent squad, including a midfield which was the envy of many up and down the country, with Graeme Souness, David Armstrong and European Cup veteran Bobby Murdoch, plus the quality of Willie Maddren at the back and Mills operating up front.

Like Keith Houchen and Bob Newton at Hartlepool, Alan Walsh at Darlington and Gary Rowell in red and white, Mills seemed to get a mention every week in our Saturday evening sports round-up on local television and was on his way to claiming 100 goals in a 300-game spell with the

Ayresome club. After a record move to West Brom, where he was used more as an attacking midfielder than an out-and-out striker, the goals dried up and, unfortunately for him, Mills became a regular inclusion in lists of players whose transfer values had not been matched by their results on the pitch. But he had long been on Newcastle's radar, including as a target for Gordon Lee during the push for Europe just a few years earlier, and had huge experience which could come in useful. Mills had also started the season in the Albion team in the First Division, a campaign under Ron Wylie in which they would finish 17th but also reach the semi-finals of both cups before losing to London duo Tottenham and Queens Park Rangers.

This time, rather than checking the paintwork and taking a quick test drive around the block, Cox got his new motor with an extended warranty. Unusually for the time, Mills spent five months on loan, playing in every one of the last 23 league games of Newcastle's campaign. But, after months of sizing each other up, he surprisingly returned to the Midlands in the summer before a cut-price move to Sheffield Wednesday, where former boss Charlton was now in the driving seat.

It was not the last we'd seen of him, though, as he returned – in part of a deal which took one of our favourites in the opposite direction – in a season which finally brought the outcome we all so craved.

***

Lingering snow and ice – which we obviously experienced a lot more than now, this being the 'good old days' – meant only three league games were played through December and January of the 1981/82 season, alongside a dour home draw with Fourth Division visitors Colchester in the FA Cup. But, with the Magpies making a strong start to the new year, the clash with Sheffield Wednesday was eagerly anticipated.

In only their second season back from an even lower level, Wednesday were on the up and the meeting represented the start of a rivalry which served as a pseudo derby for both clubs in the absence of their nearest and dearest. The 130 miles separating the two industrial cities meant little to the ranks of supporters who travelled to their respective away games. Wednesday came out of the Third Division in 1980 with Jack Charlton's direct style and they finished tenth, fourth and sixth before gaining another promotion under the World Cup winner's successor, Howard Wilkinson, in 1984.

Games with the Owls were always dramatic, played in front of the massive Kop End at Hillsborough or a full Gallowgate, and they sometimes tipped over the edge. Steve Carney's was among the red cards I remember in one of these clashes and any trip to Hillsborough provided a jolting reminder of a thrilling cup semi-final triumph there with a very different team just a few years earlier. There was also a steady stream of players who alternated between the stripes in black or blue with David Mills, Imre Varadi, Ray Blackhall, Tony Cunningham, Gary Megson, John Ryan and Pat Heard among the men to serve both clubs.

It was Varadi who got the only goal of the game in the midweek win over Wednesday at St James' and, with a strong run through February and March, our hopes remained high of a proper promotion push.

By now, Kevin Carr was undisputed No.1 and, over the next few years, he was several times named among the best of the rest behind England's international keepers. A habit of adjusting the back of his shiny short shorts with a huge white-and-blue glove could be off-putting for those of us standing behind him on the terrace but he was an unfussy last line of defence with good reactions and plenty of reach to command his penalty area. In front of him, Barton and Halliday were edged out by Carney and new boy Haddock, who had come from our school and whose sister was just a year or two above us. He did not look the most physical defender, with a peculiarly stiff running style where his feet seemed to slide along the grass rather than lift off it, but he nevertheless established himself in the squad and enjoyed a lengthy pro career.

Waddle and Wharton were now firmly first-teamers but Varadi remained the eye-catcher. He was a far more popular wearer of the No.9 shirt than his immediate predecessors and actually got his picture up in the famous Number Nine bar of the social club opposite the ground as personal reward for hitting 20 goals in a season. As a centre-forward, he brought excitement whenever he faced goal. He was as quick as anything we'd seen in years, probably since Macdonald, and was sharp around the penalty area, relentlessly sniping around the ankles of defenders. He was brave in the thick of the action and, for a man with a slight frame, he also worked for the team in holding up play and chasing into the channels. With shoulders slightly rounded and head held low as he accelerated, he could have come from the indoor athletics at RAF Cosford that we saw on *Grandstand* each winter. He'd played non-league as a youth and had hardly started his pro career when he was whisked away to join the bigger time with Everton.

When he got his chance under Cox, Varadi was determined to make the most of it. He could be demonstrative, throwing his arms around at a lost opportunity or a misplaced pass, but he looked like he cared.

There are many parts of the game that can be coached but flat-out speed is natural-born and Varadi had it. A quick burst from deep raised anticipation for fans who'd been brought up on Macdonald going for goal in one-on-one shoot-outs with a keeper. Though half as wide as Supermac, Varadi was similar in operating style on the shoulder of the last defender and thrived on that kind of service, too.

He missed chances – sometimes doing the hard work of beating defenders or chasing what looked like a hopeful long ball forward to manufacture a shooting opportunity but not managing to beat the keeper or putting his finish wide – but that merely added to the excitement. Would he, wouldn't he? In his best form, the answer was 'yes he would', often enough for him to become a big favourite with fans and colleagues alike. Varadi brought hope where there had been despair, to quote the enemy in Downing Street.

It can be overlooked now as memory fades but Varadi was also only 22 years old when he took on the burden of wearing the No.9 shirt and leading the Newcastle United forward line in what we all hoped would be an overdue promotion chase. He'd played a very limited amount of league football when Cox brought him in and, although he would spend most of his career outside the top flight, the very least he deserved was to be forever linked with the resurgence of hope on Tyneside.

There is a social media account which regularly features long threads of conversation in response to a simple image and the simple question: 'Who is the first player you think of when you see this kit?' The shirt selected is usually from the Bergkamp, Yorke, Dublin, Merson era of the early Premier League years when kits were bold and bright, with voluminous sleeves. A particular look is attributed to a certain team, an era or a player and, as I worked at *MATCH* football magazine for a spell in the 90s, I can still visualise dozens of these images which we used for poster pages or front covers.

I cannot see Paul Merson in a figure-hugging technical kit, I only visualise him running with long sleeves billowing up over his shoulders like windsocks in the colours of Arsenal or Aston Villa. I see Jamie Pollock running with his tongue out in the laser blue of Kappa-era Manchester City, Dion Dublin in the broad stripes of Villa or Coventry, or Jamie Redknapp and Steve McManaman with three enormous stripes on one red shoulder, like a claw getting to grips with the pride of Merseyside. A few years earlier, it would have been Paul Bracewell and Kevin Sheedy in Everton blue with the filled-in V-neck (looking like a kid who'd put on a T-shirt under a school jumper), Allan Evans in the Villa version, Kenny Dalglish and Ray Kennedy in Liverpool's white change shirt with thick red V-neck or Tony Woodcock in Arsenal's hooped socks.

In the same way, some players are identified with each Newcastle shirt, no matter how many years they spent at the club or how many changes they went through. For me, the Umbro diamond-sleeved shirt will always be the Varadi kit. Other instant recalls include Paul Stephenson in a long-sleeved V-neck, Micky Quinn in yellow and green stripes, Gavin Peacock wearing the bar code edition and, oddly, Paul Gascoigne in silver/grey rather than black-and-white.

* * *

Just as things were going so well up to the third quarter of the 1981/82 season, the script hit the fan again with a disastrous run of five successive defeats in April, starting with the rematch at Hillsborough.

The losing run could not have come at a worse time, with just a month of the season left to play, leaving so little scope to make up for the defeats. As it ended any hopes of a return to the First Division for another year, we welcomed teenager Derek Bell into the team, celebrating his debut on the same day that Northern Ireland age-group international winger Paul Ferris made his mark as the club's youngest-ever first-team player.

The club's circumstances and the manager's apparent liking for picking potential could have provided a launchpad for them both but, sadly, their stories on the pitch would not last a great deal longer.

Bell, a midfield dynamo identified as definitely one for the future, ended his professional career due to injury before he'd even reached his 20th birthday and he would sadly but bravely later expose even bigger struggles involving someone in a position of trust.

Ferris wore Kevin Keegan's No.7 shirt in his single starting appearance before also suffering a serious knee injury. Recovery was long and ultimately unsuccessful but he then found a new calling. He retrained and returned as a physio, spending more than a decade treating the players who had followed him into stripes. The bright and resourceful Ferris also wrote a novel, gained a master's degree and gathered rave reviews and awards when he committed his own story to print. He also went into the sports industry alongside one of the region's most successful businessmen and the club's record goalscorer; he also had a heart attack, fought cancer and sat down to write it all down again.

Back in their debut season, consecutive wins over Wrexham and Crystal Palace in the last week of the campaign took Newcastle to ninth place, sitting above Chelsea for a second successive year, though still locked in a meaty chasing pack behind the promotion places. Luton, Watford and Norwich celebrated promotion to the First Division.

Credit where it is due for making the top three and having the consistency to stay there after 42 games but the upwardly mobile trio were not exactly noted names in the game. Luton's Kenilworth Road hosted crowds of barely half its 22,000 capacity through the season; Watford had been the Fourth Division champions just four years earlier and were now entering the top flight for the first time in their history; and the only major honour in Norwich's history was the 1962 League Cup. The trio had just over a dozen years of First Division experience between them in the previous century. All three have become familiar with promotion and relegation ever since, though this was Luton's last top-flight ascent until their surprise elevation to the Premier League in 2023.

Rotherham and Barnsley were among the other clubs above Newcastle. The duo had played their Yorkshire derbies in the Fourth Division just a few years earlier yet still had a better record than the Magpies in 1981/82.

Despite missing out again, only Sheffield Wednesday enjoyed bigger support at home, though they still averaged under 20,000 over the course of the season. In crowd terms, Newcastle's highlights were playing in front of 25,000 of us against Leicester and almost 27,000 for a win over Chelsea, secured thanks to a first-half Waddle goal. We also had 21,000 cheering goals from loanee Brown and Varadi against Luton and the same for a draw with Palace. Just short of that figure had trooped down to St James' for the opening weekend but it immediately dipped to 14,700 and 13,800 for visits from Cambridge and Shrewsbury – an alarming figure for Tyneside but still three times the number either of them attracted regularly to their home games – on the way to a seasonal average in the league of 17,250.

With my matchday mates, we were swimming against the tide, bustling up from the Haymarket desperate to get in and taste matchday independence just as thousands of others were turning their backs and getting the hell out. We were among just 10,700 lonely souls in the ground for the visit of QPR after promotion dreams had been shattered so close to the finishing line. Gavin Haigh's book on the team's kits reminded me that this was the game where the visitors had to borrow United's yellow away shirts, paired with their own shorts and socks, due to a colour clash which had been deemed unacceptable on the day by the referee. The Londoners' away colours were red and white halved shirts (Feyenoord style) but the unfortunate outcome at St James' may have been behind their move to wear all red instead for their FA Cup Final appearance against Tottenham just a couple of weeks later.

I would still go home buzzing, no matter how many or few had shared matchday, and I'd talk over tea with a slightly hoarse voice about the 'massive crowds' if we breached the 20,000 mark. That figure was better than we'd been used to during the previous couple of seasons but my dad would have chosen a different description for a ground which regularly hosted twice as many when he had stood on what was known as the Popular Side. Our biggest gates of the year were also around a third of the club record dating back to 1930 when Hughie Gallacher returned in a Chelsea shirt just three years after leading Newcastle to what remains the club's most recent league title win.

The issue of falling attendances, though, was not confined to Newcastle by any stretch of the imagination. With fans sick of poor facilities, hooliganism, the recession and the football, many clubs saw dramatic drops from previous decades. Everton announced just 12,500 for a top-flight game against Notts County and there were many more attendances of similar scale at Tottenham, Chelsea, Leeds, Forest, Leicester and others. While not completely self-inflicted, football did not help itself with the treatment of its supporters, the vast majority of whom were well behaved and the only fight they wanted to see was the one put up by their team on the pitch every Saturday afternoon.

* * *

The unpredictable dynamism of Imre Varadi and the maturing of Chris Waddle provided the highlights of our campaign but it was now four years since the drop, the point at which our last relegated team in the 60s had managed to bounce back. So, there was no escaping the opinion that Newcastle United had now become an established Second Division club.

With respect, that label might have been an achievement for Barnsley and Rotherham, for league rivals Cambridge and Shrewsbury, or for little Orient and Wrexham, who were relegated with gates of less than 4,500. But Newcastle United? Being seen as an 'established Second Division club' felt like an acceptance of what had come to be seen as the level of our club's ambition. Many of the signings were second division players (the absence of capital letters is deliberate) and many of the youngsters were given an opportunity because this was a second division team (here, too). Winning just four times away from home over the season also smacked of a second division (and again) mentality.

Some fans were going through this kind of despair for a second time, being old enough to remember the last spell in the Second Division just as England assumed the mantle as world leaders for entertainment, innovation and style in the 60s. Stan Anderson, an old-fashioned wing-half who won a couple of caps for England before joining Newcastle, has an interesting view on the club in the era (he was also one of only three men to make first-team appearances for the trio of major North-East clubs in the 20th century, a fact I used as a quiz question aimed at another Magpies supporter I worked with years later. 'Name the other two,' I said. 'Sunderland and Middlesbrough,' came his instant reply. He wasn't trying to be funny, but he'd managed it. The names I was looking for were Alan Foggon and pre-war winger Tom Urwin. Anderson remains unique in captaining all three teams).

Reflecting in his autobiography on his move from Sunderland, Anderson's words could have acted as a warning to those who followed. Recalling the experience of a heavy home defeat after a surprise move from Wearside to Tyneside, he said: 'I was surprised at how resigned the crowd was. If we'd lost 4-0 at Sunderland, the Roker Park faithful would have been outraged. At St James' … it was as if they didn't really believe the team could do any better.' Painfully, we recognised how many of those words could also describe how we felt entering the 80s.

* * *

Over the years, Newcastle had turned inconsistency into a fine art. At times in the club's history, they would be described as a 'cup team' but it is not always a compliment – after all, a run to Wembley meant five good results, not a sustained level of performances over 42 league games. As star striker Malcolm Macdonald once said: 'The colours of Newcastle United, two extremes, typified the way we played.'

To illustrate the point, a week after Ronnie Radford and Ricky George rubbed noses in the Hereford mud, the Magpies beat Manchester United 2-0 at Old Trafford. Likewise, after needing replays to get past non-league Hendon and lower division Scunthorpe after draws at home in 1974, the same team produced a superb 3-0 win at West Bromwich Albion in the next round. That same team finished the league season just two points above the relegation zone before running out at Wembley. After being humbled in the final, the fans sang 'we want our cup back' during a 4-1 revenge win over Liverpool in the first meeting afterwards.

I have neither the will nor the paper to relive all the ups and downs but I will add a couple of other examples. Only Newcastle United could lose one manager on the way to a fifth-place finish in the league and then another – who had been championed by the players – just 12 months later with the team on the way to relegation after six wins in the league season. A few years on, we barely had time to celebrate a long-awaited promotion on the back of one of the most celebrated players in the club's history and its most venerated forward line when we lost the manager to a team that had just been relegated to the Third Division.

When there was a consistency as 70s turned into 80s, it came in the form of finishing 8th, 9th, 11th and 9th again in those first four seasons in the Second Division. This run of mid-table finishes meant we were becoming used to playing Second Division football in a stadium unsuited for anything higher as part of a crowd which was starting to believe this could be our lot for a good while to come.

During one episode of *Whatever Happened to the Likely Lads*, there is a scene where Bob and Terry are poring over the advice pages of a gossip magazine described as a 'frank exchange of personal and private fears' when the soon-to-be-married Bob asks Terry about his fears. 'Apart from relegation and baldness?' he says. Like the best of the lines crafted by Dick Clement and Ian La Frenais, it got a laugh because its roots were in genuine everyman discourse.

By 1981/82, almost a decade after those two great philosophers had flicked through the pages of their titillating magazine, the biggest fear was that, just like baldness, relegation was, in fact, irreversible. 'It's just the way it is; some people get relegated when they're still quite young and for others it happens much later. Either way, there's nothing you can do about it. Now drink your tea before it gets cold,' as Terry might have said. It wasn't the bogeyman who lived under the bed in the North-East, it was the Second Division that started to give us sleepless nights.

There's another *Likely Lads* exchange which comes to mind. Sharing a bed on the night before his wedding to Thelma – millions of us watched Morecambe and Wise in their pyjamas in a shared mid-century modern double, too – nerves had got the better of the groom. Terry's suggestion is to tempt sleep by closing his eyes and having a fantasy. No more than a minute later, Bob admits: 'I've had my fantasy.' Terry, in striped cotton pyjamas, asks about its content. 'We won,' replies Bob, who wears a Magpies shirt to bed in another episode. 'Cup and league double … 4-1 at Wembley against Arsenal.' Absolute fantasy, indeed.

With lines like that, you can just about excuse the accents of the supporting cast of a show which took viewers on a tour of the north in every episode. The theme tune played over footage of kids climbing on the walls of terraced Tyneside houses during demolition still brings me to the verge of tears. 'The only thing to look forward to, the past' is unfortunately an accurate description of several eras of Newcastle United support, including the start of my own.

For all their genius as writers and social commentators, however, a few years later one of the Clement and La Frenais creations committed an unforgiveable sin in sending the lads of *Auf Wiedersehen Pet* to watch Sunderland in a pre-season game in Belgium.

In the debut series, Oz had already driven them to Germany in a Ford Zephyr complete with a Sunderland sticker, admitting he didn't follow them but couldn't remove it for fear of losing the bumper, so perhaps the writers were conscious of spreading the net wide across the region for viewers. It showed just how good the series was that sending two of the lads to watch the enemy did not ostracise Tyneside. Anyway, by the time the Geordie brickies reached the middle of their first working week in that Düsseldorf hut, they'd already been in Europe longer than Sunderland.

By way of redemption, Oz wears a Newcastle scarf or hat in many episodes of multiple series thereafter and, in the final episode of that opening run, the boys did return home, jobless and potless but optimistic like the rest of us after seeing the back page of the newspaper.

Newcastle United had finally made the headlines again.

Chapter Seven

What Became of the People We Used to Be

EXILE IN the Second Division would last a total of six years but, if *The Wilderness Years* is a play in two acts, there is almost a full change of cast and direction between start and finish. There is also a major alteration in outlook from the first four seasons into the final two. Even if the physical backdrop remains the same, emotionally they could not be more different.

In those first four seasons following the summer of 1978, when I first became a regular at St James' Park, significant breaks in the dark clouds were few and far between. This was a sequence of grey days for the Black-and-whites. The apparent acceptance of second-tier status and the shortage of any real drive to change made it hard to handle for all of us and it was difficult to see a rosy future beyond. In a region hit hard by recession, unemployment and a lack of hope, there was nowhere to turn for escape.

As fans, we know that winning every game is not possible, no matter who you support, but trying to understand the troughs along with the peaks only gets you so far when you know that your team really, really belongs somewhere else.

From the thousands who would have been content to 'watch the grass grow', we had become accustomed to shrinking attendances. We'd already been there on days when crowds were as low as the 10,000 mark. Gates of around 15,000 to 18,000 were frequent and on big days we went home talking excitedly about being in the heart of a 20,000-strong Geordie gathering.

You would be hard-pushed to pinpoint a single area where Newcastle United had moved forward in the four seasons up to the end of 1981/82 or, in all honesty, find where some genuinely positive headlines had been made on or off the field. Outside our four walls, though, the world was moving on apace, leaping into a new age and embracing it.

When relegation was confirmed in the 1978, the record transfer fee between British clubs stood at the £440,000 paid by Liverpool to Celtic for Kenny Dalglish. The record between Football League clubs was still the £350,000 which had taken centre-forward Bob Latchford from Birmingham to Everton in 1974.

A page in my *Scorcher* annual (as in *Tiger and Scorcher* comic, though it does, admittedly, sound rather more like something from the 70s top shelf) had a photo of the mop-haired and bearded Latchford in a feature about transfers, under which there was a graphic of a money tree with the numbers 500,000 and 750,000 drawn on its branches, plus one for £1m. The image stayed with me because it seemed so outlandish that it could never happen. 'What of the future?' the page asked. 'Shall we see the record doubled or will the tree begin to die back? Who can tell?'

John Trewick, a Bedlington lad who had played for Northumberland Boys and England Youth, made his breakthrough at West Bromwich Albion, and when the midfielder was signed by Newcastle to join the battle in the

Second Division in December 1980, the fee was a club record £250,000. At that point, the national mark was already six times more. At a quarter of a million pounds, Trewick remained Newcastle's most expensive purchase until 1986.

In January 1979, West Brom paid £500,000 for David Mills, who we have already met in this story. Within weeks, that record was not only beaten but doubled as Nottingham Forest made Trevor Francis the country's first million-pound man. He had been in the Birmingham City team since the age of 16 and was still only 24 years old but already had 120 league goals to his credit when Brian Clough added him to his team of rising stars. Just seven months later, that mark was beaten when Manchester City purchased midfielder Steve Daley from Wolves, who went out and spent the cash on Andy Gray from local rivals Aston Villa before the cheque had even had time to clear at the bank. There is some dispute on the actual fees, with different sources reporting anything from £1.1m to £1.4m but what is known for certain is that, in one calendar year, the domestic record had more than doubled. The national rate of inflation was around 10 per cent at the beginning of 1979, during the closing months of Jim Callaghan's residency at Downing Street, and rose to 17 per cent with a new Tory government by the year's end, but football even outstripped those eye-watering numbers.

Francis was a dozen caps into his England career and Gray had a handful of appearances for Scotland but it was significant that Mills and Daley would remain uncapped, despite being valued so highly by club managers and their supportive bank managers.

There were numerous other inflated exchanges, including the £250,000 paid by Manchester City for midfielder Steve MacKenzie before he had even made a league appearance for Crystal Palace. Clough, who had already managed to get his Forest directors to fork out seven figures on one striker, did it again after their European Cup win to land Coventry's Ian Wallace and repeated the trick a year on for Norwich City's Justin Fashanu after banking £1.25m from Manchester United for Garry Birtles.

In June 1980, Arsenal made Clive Allen their record signing at £1.25m, having never previously spent more than £500,000 on a player. Goal poacher Allen was then swapped for Palace left-back Kenny Sansom without making a single league appearance for the Gunners. Then, in the autumn of 1981, Bryan Robson became Britain's new most expensive footballer at £1.5m. Just a year later, Barcelona paid more than £4m for Diego Maradona and, although European clubs paid big sums for the likes of Mark Hughes, Ian Rush, Chris Waddle and David Platt, that Robson figure remarkably remained a record between English clubs until the mid-90s when Newcastle sold Andy Cole to title rivals at Old Trafford.

Maradona had missed out on a home World Cup win in 1978 when he was still a teenager but he was there four years later when Argentina were eliminated in the second-round stage in Spain and had to watch from the sidelines as veteran goalkeeper Dino Zoff lifted the golden trophy for Italy in one of the great tournaments (still *the* greatest for this fan, who watched it during O-level mocks). Newcastle, still slumbering in the Second Division, had no playing representative at either tournament.

Following the fortunes of Tommy Cassidy, now of Burnley, and his Northern Ireland colleagues was as close as we got in 1982. They had been outright winners of the Home Internationals for the first time two years earlier and then beat hosts Spain on a memorably hot and humid evening in the group stage of a World Cup which saw teenager Norman Whiteside thrust into the spotlight.

After being ditched by Don Revie, England made it to the European Championship finals in 1980 under Ron Greenwood, the former West Ham boss, and finally returned to the World Cup stage two years later for the first time since 1970 amid a huge changing of the guard. Debutants in the white shirt during the first four years of Newcastle's residence outside the top flight included Terry Butcher, Kenny Sansom, Glenn Hoddle and Bryan Robson, who would all become mainstays in the years to follow.

Under the unconventional Clough and his assistant Peter Taylor, this period also saw Nottingham Forest come from nowhere to bloody the noses of top clubs domestically and in Europe. Tony Woodcock went from loan spells at Doncaster and Lincoln to leading the line with a title-winning club and his country. He then spread his wings by joining Köln in Germany while international colleague Laurie Cunningham got a dream move to Real Madrid.

Kevin Keegan, a name which forms a thread in spirit if not in print through almost every page of this book, became a double European player of the year with SV Hamburger of the Bundesliga before returning to England to inspire unfashionable Southampton to sixth place in the Football League, all in the same four seasons that Newcastle sat in mid-table in the Second Division. Over time, the south coast Saints gathered together Keegan, Peter Shilton, Mick Mills, Frank Worthington, Dave Watson, Chris Nicholl and David Armstrong to join their local hero, Mick Channon, while Newcastle scratched around in the lower divisions for signings.

Terry McDermott made the most of his move to Liverpool as the first man to be named player of the year by both his peers and the nation's sports writers in the same year, though he did admit to being more at home in a working men's club than at glitzy presentation dinners.

Queens Park Rangers were relegated just three years after finishing runners-up to champions Liverpool, while Swansea's rise from Third Division to First was counter-balanced by Bristol City simultaneously making the same journey in reverse. Southport dropped out of the Football League altogether after losing a re-election vote, with Wigan Athletic becoming the fourth newcomers in the decade in their place. Consistent FA Cup giantkillers Altrincham missed out on election by just one vote. Proposals for regionalised membership for the bottom two divisions of the Football League were defeated.

Approval was given by the Football League for QPR, despite widespread scepticism, to install the competition's first 'plastic' pitch and players suddenly had to think about AstroTurf footwear and carpet burns.

ITV caused a sensation by picking up the rights to Saturday evening football highlights in a move branded in newspaper headlines as 'Snatch of the Day'. Court action followed and, eventually, a compromise deal was struck which involved ITV and BBC alternating in the primetime slot and *Match of the Day* moving to Sunday afternoons for the first time in 1980/81. Shirt sponsorship was introduced in a new commercial age but could not be worn for televised matches. I remember Hibs shirts carrying an oversized 'Bukta' text across the chest, with the club presumably spotting a loophole in similar regulations. None of this bothered us much at Newcastle, though, because there were bigger fish to fry with the broadcasters' money.

During this four-year period of change, the flamboyant Malcolm Allison came and went at both Manchester City and Crystal Palace, likewise Jock Stein at Leeds. Howard Kendall took over from Gordon Lee at Everton, Doug Ellis was ousted from his first spell as chairman of Aston Villa and

Sepp Blatter moved in as the new general secretary of FIFA. The Anglo-Scottish Cup disappeared and Glasgow's grip on the league title over the border was broken by Aberdeen in Alex Ferguson's second season in charge at the all-seater Pittodrie. Steve Archibald, Gordon Strachan and the former (and future) Magpies striker Mark McGhee were among their key men. Back on the Borders, Berwick Rangers provided one small part of Northumberland with something to cheer about with promotion to the Scottish First Division, sharing a stage with the likes of Hearts, Motherwell, Dundee and Kilmarnock in two seasons there.

Significant Newcastle United newborns included Shola Ameobi, Kieron Dyer, Scott Parker, Aaron Hughes and Craig Bellamy, while a future England squad of Steven Gerrard, Michael Owen, John Terry, Peter Crouch, Michael Carrick, Joe Cole, Rio Ferdinand, Ashley Cole and Ledley King were all preparing for their first days at primary school.

The Magpies had not yet signed a player of colour when Forest full-back Viv Anderson became the first black player to win an England cap. A league champion and then European Cup winner, Anderson was among the generation of pioneers who, despite often ugly opposition inside football and out, represented a brave new world for the game and for the country as a whole.

Change was visible wherever you turned in the world of sport. Only Newcastle United appeared to be standing still.

Muhammad Ali, the most recognisable man on the planet, regained the world heavyweight title for a third time and retired twice, all while Newcastle slugged it out unconvincingly in the Second Division. Ali initially announced his retirement in July 1979 after an uninspiring victory in a rematch with champion Leon Spinks but 'The Greatest' returned to fight Larry Holmes. In October the following year, with the Magpies on a three-game run of goalless draws against Oldham, Bristol Rovers and West Ham, he was stopped for the only time in his long career. He decided, though, to have one more go and this time lost on points to Trevor Berbick, a man who would link two great eras in the sport as the last opponent of Ali and then, in 1986, the first to lose a world title bout involving Mike Tyson. Two days after Ali climbed out of the ring for a final time, Newcastle were handed a knockout blow of their own with a 4-0 defeat at Swansea at the halfway point of another nondescript season.

A golden era for boxing bred more big names beyond the heavyweight division as Sugar Ray Leonard won his first world title, lost it and won again against Roberto Duran and also beat Thomas Hearns, while Marvin Hagler topped British hopefuls Alan Minter and Tony Sibson. Barry McGuigan, the 'Clones Cyclone', with fans on both sides of the Irish border, won a Commonwealth title before turning professional, and Jim Watt became Scotland's lightweight champion of the world. The sport, sadly, also made the front pages when Welsh fighter Johnny Owen lost his life after being knocked out in a title fight in the United States.

In Ali's wake, there were few more charismatic sporting champions than Spanish golfer Seve Ballesteros, who won his first US Masters aged just 23, a year after celebrating a maiden victory at The Open despite finding the rough from nine of his tee shots in the final round at Royal Lytham. One famously landed in the car park en route to the 16th hole but Seve still managed to make his mark as the first Open champion from Continental Europe since 1907 and he charmed audiences way beyond the world of golf.

In the space of six weeks during the summer of 1979, the 22-year-old Sebastian Coe set athletics world records at 800m, 1500m and the mile, putting the Loughborough University student on the long road towards becoming a Tory MP, chair of the London Olympics organising committee, president of World Athletics, life peer and potential chief of the International Olympic Committee.

In early July, he set the new mark for 800m, clocking one minute 42.33 seconds over two laps of Oslo's track to beat the previous best set by Alberto Juantorena, the charismatic Cuban who had become a global favourite after a unique Olympic double over 400 and 800 in 1976. His legend had only been added to by Ron Pickering's commentary: 'There goes Juantorena down the back straight, opening his legs and showing his class.' Less than two weeks later, the blue riband mark of the mile fell, again in Oslo, as Coe clocked three minutes 48.95 seconds, and he completed a remarkable treble with a 1500m time of three minutes 32.03 seconds in Zürich.

Coe went into the race over a mile with the slowest personal best time in an elite field led by John Walker from New Zealand. Marking 25 years since Roger Bannister's historic run through the four-minute barrier, the new record breaker strode to the finish line 11 seconds quicker than that magic mark. 'My world would never be the same again,' said Coe, who was named BBC Sports Personality of the Year and World Athlete of the Year.

Coe was devastated to miss out on Olympic gold over 800m in Moscow a year later, great rival Steve Ovett taking the honours, but he bounced back to win their head-to-head over 1500m. Daley Thompson and sprinter Allan Wells were among Britain's other champions in track and field, while Duncan Goodhew, Teófilo Stevenson, Nadia Comăneci, Miruts Yifter and gymnast Alexander Dityatin (who won eight medals) were the other showstoppers. Moscow, though, hosted the smallest Olympic entry since 1956, as the United

States led a widespread boycott following the Soviet invasion of Afghanistan. The hosts and their neighbours, East Germany, won more than half of the 200 gold medals.

World records and medal places helped to inspire a running boom and 'jogging' not only entered the vocabulary but also became a daily routine for tens of thousands of Britons. Following the example of American cities, including New York and Chicago, London staged its first public marathon around streets closed to traffic in 1981 and there were 7,000 participants on the start line. In the same year, the Great North Run was born, inspired and created by Brendan Foster, the Tyneside teacher and athlete whose 10,000m bronze had been Team GB's only track medal at the Montreal Olympics five years earlier and who won a pre-match race around Wembley Stadium in a black-and-white striped vest at the 1974 cup final. The first North Run attracted a 12,000-strong field on a course which crossed the Tyne Bridge on its way to a finish on the sea front at South Shields. Fittingly, it was Mike McLeod, a local international, who became its first champion.

Wales enjoyed their final years of dominance in rugby union's Five Nations, Hull won rugby league's final BBC2 Floodlit Trophy, Bjorn Borg earned the last of his five Wimbledon tennis titles and Martina Navratilova was just getting started on more than a decade of dominance on Centre Court.

Kerry Packer's World Series caused chaos and West Indies won the second cricket World Cup during a pivotal period in the sporting life of Ian Botham, during which he launched a football career at Scunthorpe, scored his first Test century, gained and lost the England captaincy and also produced one of the all-time great performances at Headingley on the way to Ashes victory over Australia. His county team, Somerset, also claimed the first trophies in their history, inspired by West Indian maestro Viv Richards and the giant bowler Joel Garner.

'Puissance' became familiar on BBC *Sportsnight* for one week each year during the high jump competition at the Horse of the Year Show and the equestrian names of David Broome and Lucinda Prior-Palmer were known to the common man. Pat Eddery rode the winner in the 200th anniversary Epsom Derby, then Willie Carson rode to successive victories for trainer Dick Hern before 19-year-old Walter Swinburn claimed his first on board equine superstar Shergar. Lester Piggott, meanwhile, had still not completed his record total of nine wins in flat racing's biggest day out. Top-class steeplechaser Aldaniti placed in the Cheltenham Gold Cup and Scottish Grand National then spent a year out of racing with a leg injury before an unlikely win at the Grand National under cancer survivor Bob Champion in a sporting fairytale.

The 'Crafty Cockney' Eric Bristow won the first of his five darts world crowns and Alex Higgins sobbed on live television as he lifted snooker's world title, his 'Hurricane' playing style in stark contrast to immediate predecessors Terry Griffiths, Cliff Thorburn and Steve Davis. Snooker was at the very height of its popularity, dominating daytime and evening TV schedules during various championships and its best players became national celebrities. I got to see Griffiths and Thorburn play in an exhibition match at Newcastle's Eldon Square Recreation Centre one night when the Canadian was world champion in 1980. Neither was known for an up-tempo style and the match went on for so long I wasn't sure if I'd be back home in time to collect my kit for school in the morning. For our own amusement, my mate Mike and I tried to be the last to clap a good shot, then got brave enough to 'danger clap' and be first, always with the potential embarrassment of no one joining in. It wasn't the same as starting a terrace chant, though, which brought with it a lifetime of respect on those concrete steps.

Canadian F1 driver Gilles Villeneuve lost his life in a crash during qualifying at the Belgian Grand Prix, while other sporting deaths included Adi Dassler, founder of Adidas, Merseyside football legends Dixie Dean and Bill Shankly and former England batsman Ken Barrington at the age of just 50.

The charismatic weightlifter Precious Mackenzie won his fourth Commonwealth Games gold medal at the age of 42, while the abrasive Bernard Hinault won both the Tour de France and Tour of Spain at his first attempt, succeeding Eddy Merckx as the most feared man in pro cycling. Kenny Roberts replaced Barry Sheene as the world's champion motorcyclist. Sheene, though, remained an icon, joining Henry Cooper and Kevin Keegan (who shared the racer's attachment to the number seven) in endorsing Brut for Men aftershave.

Cultural references, too, changed out of all recognition. Pop music is a perfect barometer not only of what everyone is listening to in idle hours but also what they are talking about, what they look like and which social groups they inhabit. Has there ever been as big a shift in such a short period of time as this one in the late 70s and early 80s?

When Newcastle's relegation was sealed in April 1978, the country's biggest-selling single was the soppy 'Matchstalk Men and Matchstalk Cats and Dogs' from one-hit wonders Peter and Simon, outselling global smash 'Night Fever' by The Bee Gees and 'I Wonder Why' by rock and roll revivalists Showaddywaddy. That season had kicked off to the middle-of-the-road sounds of Brotherhood of Man,

Abba and Elvis, yet 1977 was also the year of punk. The Sex Pistols gatecrashed the Queen's Silver Jubilee, accompanied by the sounds of The Clash's 'White Riot' and 'Oh Bondage! Up Yours!' by X-Ray Spex. It was the time of The Damned and The Buzzcocks and the release of *Rattus Norvegicus* by The Stranglers, while The Ramones blazed a trail over the Atlantic.

But by the end of a first season in the Second Division, punk had already passed a peak and, instead, ska started selling, with the two-tone revival led by The Specials, Madness, Bad Manners, The Selecter and The Beat. In turn, this led into the revival of the mods to a backing track of The Jam and Secret Affair, as well as the return of tribal fighting in the UK's beach resorts. By the summer of 1979, as writer Chris Hunt described it, 'parkas, scooters and target T-shirts were once again a regular sight in the high streets of Britain', with a second generation of mods going back to the future with a sound inspired by the 60s and given extra impetus with the release of the film *Quadrophenia* starring Sting, the artist formerly known as Cramlington teacher Mr Sumner.

Bovver boots and Harringtons joined denim and donkey jackets on football's terraces and its matchday violence but when the New Romantics arrived in 1981, they made little impression behind the goal. There may have been some Spandau Ballet haircuts and a few jumpers tucked into trousers but hair lacquer and make-up were conspicuous by their absence in the Gallowgate End.

Four influential major musical movements had played themselves out during a period of just four years alongside the explosion of disco with the release of *Saturday Night Fever*. You could make it five if you include NWOBHM (the New Wave of British Heavy Metal), which I followed closely in the pages of *Kerrang* magazine, which first appeared during

June 1981. A year earlier, I'd been at Newcastle's City Hall in full double denim to see Iron Maiden live for the first time. They were supported by the French band Trust, who made just as big an impression on this teenager jumping around on the balcony. Maiden were still champions of the London circuit but they also toured relentlessly and had already released a couple of albums. Then, just as Newcastle United's hopes of a promotion push died in the last two months of the 1981/82 season, they kicked into overdrive on their way to superstardom thanks to the introduction of new frontman Bruce Dickinson and a No.1 album, *Number of the Beast.* Platinum sales status, enormo-dome world tours and their own aeroplane followed.

With taste in music established, we got to see a few more rock bands at the City Hall, including UFO and the Michael Schenker Group, with whom Cozy Powell played a *Dambusters* drum solo, though the regular rock nights at The Mayfair closer to St James' would have to wait until at least one of us could carry off the look of an 18-year-old.

'Video Killed the Radio Star' by Buggles, fronted by Trevor Horn, who would become one of the most influential men in music production and presentation, earned a place in history as the first video played on the new MTV channel. If you ever need to know it for a pub quiz, and as a thank you for reading this far, the second was 'You Better Run' by Pat Benatar. The new 'Prince of Pop', Michael Jackson, followed the release of his breakthrough album *Off the Wall* with the record-breaking *Thriller*, integrating theatre, cinema, drama and dancing to full effect through the new medium of video. Blissfully unaffected by cutting- edge taste or talent, Bucks Fizz scored another European title for the Brits, while Ireland's Johnny Logan and Germany's Nicole, the little girl with the big white guitar, also hit Eurovision winners.

In the weeks following the end of the 1981/82 season, St James' Park welcomed a rare sell-out crowd as 38,000 fans gathered to welcome the Rolling Stones to the first-ever rock concert at the venue. With the band coming to the end of their second decade together and Bill Wyman the only member already past his 30s, Sting and members of Genesis were among the backstage VIPs. The *Evening Chronicle* reported that a fleet of 26 trucks transported their equipment, including an 80-metre stage. Queues formed in the early hours of a warm and drizzly June day, ahead of doors opening in early afternoon. Support acts George Thoroughgood (and the Destroyers) and the J. Geils Band warmed up the crowd while the headliners travelled in from the Holiday Inn at Seaton Burn to arrive around seven o'clock.

It was not the first trip to Newcastle for the Stones. They had first visited a year after their formation in 1962 – coincidentally when United were also in the Second Division – when they performed at the Odeon and had also fulfilled matinee and evening slots at the City Hall in 1971. They returned in '73 and then completed a St James' double in 1982 and '90. The Stones may have sales topping 85 million albums worldwide (and still counting, as well as touring well into old age) but on their debut at the home of Newcastle United, they were out-sold by Blyth Spartans.

While Mick Jagger and Keith Richards would run and run with their band, during this period of Newcastle United's wilderness, the Volkswagen Beetle ceased production after 20 million sales. We also said goodbye to the sixpence, the Vauxhall Viva (we had a P-reg bright yellow one for a while), MG cars, Laker Airways and Radio Caroline, while also watching final flings for Basil Fawlty, *George & Mildred* and *Citizen Smith* on our televisions. John Lennon, and Sid

Vicious of the Sex Pistols died in New York, the latter aged just 21, and we also lost film director Alfred Hitchcock, actors Peter Sellers, Steve McQueen, Natalie Wood, the tragically young Richard Beckinsale and madcap John Belushi, one half of the *Blues Brothers*. Pope John Paul died after just 33 days in the Vatican, leading to the appointment of Polish cardinal and football fan Karol Wojtyla as Pope John Paul II, the first non-Italian to be elected head of the Catholic Church in 450 years. In May 1981, he survived a shooting, suffering wounds to his left hand and his stomach.

Violence and killings continued through the Troubles of Northern Ireland, with Lord Mountbatten of Burma, a cousin of Prince Phillip and relative of the Queen's father, becoming a high-profile bomb victim just over the border. MP Airey Neave, the first successful British wartime escapee from Colditz, was another, in the car park of Westminster, as the casualty list on all sides mounted. Republicans instigated blanket protests and ultimately hunger strikes in Maze Prison during campaigns against internment without trial and the removal of political status for paramilitary prisoners. More than 400 deaths were directly attributed to the Troubles in the four years from 1978 and the figure for 1982 alone would be the heaviest of the remaining years before the Good Friday Agreement.

An estimated 20 million trees died in the UK due to Dutch Elm disease, commercial whaling was brought to an end and the supertanker *Amoco Cadiz* broke apart in the Channel, spilling oil into the sea, polluting more than 100 miles of coastline.

New arrivals included the Social Democratic Party, Wetherspoon's pubs, Alton Towers theme park and 'test tube baby' Louise Brown, the first human conceived through in-vitro fertilisation. The first printed edition of *Viz* emerged on an unsuspecting public from its understated Newcastle base, while the entertainment world created *The Deer Hunter, Grease, Watership Down, E.T.* and Indiana Jones. Audiences at home sat back with small-screen newcomers *Blankety Blank, Dukes of Hazzard, Shoestring, Worzel Gummidge, Family Fortunes, Tenko, Postman Pat* and the *Mork & Mindy* catchphrase 'nanu nanu shazbot'.

Not the Nine O'Clock News provided a weekly dose of irreverent humour in an updated version of The Goons, Peter Cook and Dudley Moore or *Monty Python* for my generation. Mel Smith, Griff Rhys Jones, Pamela Stephenson and County Durham-born Rowan Atkinson introduced us to Gerald the Gorilla, Constable Savage (being reminded by a superior officer that it is not an offence to 'walk in a loud shirt in a built-up area' or 'with an offensive wife'), parodies on darts, truck-driving and living in Wales. We all remember, too, Atkinson's angry priest and Stephenson's exaggerated newsreader to go with her homage to TV presenter Janet Street-Porter's style and front teeth.

After watching on a Monday, when the programme was aired at the same time as the flagship *Nine O'Clock News*, we trotted out its punchlines for the rest of the week. There was even an honourable mention of football as hooliganism reached national consciousness, with Smith playing the role of a Cambridge University windbag. 'My team and I have really concerned ourselves fundamentally with a statistical analysis of soccer violence ... and behavioural analysis of over a thousand individual soccer hooligans and we have come to the inevitable conclusion that the one course of action the authorities must take is ... to cut off their goolies,' he said. In her role of Lambeth community worker – 'I know these kids, we are talking about their frustrations, the lack of community facilities' – there was forceful agreement from

Stephenson, who qualified as a clinical psychologist in real life in the 90s.

Other cultural heavyweights included David Attenborough's groundbreaking *Life on Earth*, Barry Norman's film reviews and the start of the BBC's long-running *Antiques Roadshow* and *Question Time*, while ESPN, CNN and *Late Night with David Letterman* made a first appearance in the USA. The music industry cashed in on the new CD player and Sony Walkman, the Rubik's Cube craze took on allcomers, Trivial Pursuit starred in a million social evenings and 'that's not what it says on the card' disagreements and Post-It notes spread like a rash after the accidental discovery of a temporary adhesive unsuitable for other practical purposes.

The names of inner-city Brixton, Toxteth and Moss Side gained national notoriety with dissatisfaction boiling over into rioting, joined in the headlines by CND and Greenham Common, Jeremy Thorpe and Norman Scott, 'Carlos the Jackal', Peter Sutcliffe and John Wayne Gacy Jr, Bobby Sands, the Queen's surprise visitor Michael Fagan, Port Stanley, Camp David and Three Mile Island.

Margaret Thatcher led a vote of no confidence in the Labour government and was elected on a 43 majority as the country's first female prime minister, with the Conservative government immediately starting the sell-off of national industry, beginning with BP, and introducing Right To Buy for council housing tenants. The UK faced a first steel works strike since 1926 and unemployment figures topped two million for the first time in nearly half a century and continued to rise. The National Coal Board announced widespread pit closures, British Leyland proposed cuts of 25,000 jobs to save the company and Consett steelworks in County Durham closed with the loss of 4,500 jobs, overnight making it the town with the highest unemployment rate in the country. Publication of *The Times* was suspended for a year as a result of labour disputes and was then sold to the Australian tycoon Rupert Murdoch.

Michael Foot was named Labour Party leader at the age of 67 and the National Front contested more parliamentary seats but lost more of its share of the vote. Ronald Reagan was sworn in as US president, Saddam Hussein rose to rule in Iraq and Ayatollah Khomeini returned from 15 years in exile to establish an Islamic Republic in Iran, forcing the Shah of Persia to leave, along with more than 1,000 US State Department workers.

Poland declared a state of emergency and martial law, arresting the leaders of the Solidarity trade union movement. The United States went into recession, the Soviet Union invaded Afghanistan and Israeli forces moved into Lebanon. Iran and Iraq went to war and Argentina's military government planned to take possession of the Falkland Islands in the South Atlantic. China instituted a one-child-per-family rule to control exploding population numbers and Bolivia experienced the 200th coup of its 160 years of independence. Dominica, the Solomon Islands, St Lucia, Kiribati, St Vincent & Grenadines and Antigua & Barbuda all gained independence from Britain, while Rhodesia installed its first black-led government in 90 years, changing its name to Zimbabwe.

The one-time Tyneside curate (All Saints Church, Gosforth) Robert Runcie was enthroned as Archbishop of Canterbury, performing the royal wedding of Charles, Prince of Wales, and Lady Diana Spencer. Their first-born son, William, became second in line after his birth in June 1982. Princess Margaret ended an often turbulent and intriguing marriage to the Etonian photographer Lord

Snowdon, who almost immediately married another blue-blooded bride.

Mother Teresa followed Israeli leader Menachem Begin and Egyptian president Anwar Sadat as winner of the Nobel Peace Prize. Sadat was assassinated during a Cairo parade in which another 11 people were killed and 30 wounded. The leader of the militants responsible was tried and executed. Anthony Blunt, known as 'the fourth man', was stripped of a knighthood after confessing to spying and the riddle of the forged *Hitler Diaries*, which would eventually reach the *Sunday Times* in a blaze of publicity, started to take shape in Germany.

Petrol prices topped £1.20 a gallon, putting an end to our two-pounds-worth trips to the local 'self-service' garage. The Vauxhall Astra, Morris Ital and Austin Metro were newcomers on the roads but the Belfast-made gull-wing DeLorean made more headlines under the weight of financial problems, receivership and legal action. The space shuttle *Columbia* was launched, France introduced the TGV high-speed train service and the Jubilee Line opened on the London Underground.

North-East lives were enriched by Geordie Jeans, Princess Margaret's visit to the Tuxedo Junction nightclub, the opening of the region's first Kentucky Fried Chicken and another bridge over the Tyne as part of the new Metro transport system. To try out the new urban service, I remember going with my mam to travel the one stop from Jesmond to the Haymarket and I still have the yellow ticket. The Kielder Water project also came to fruition, though my school had already gained a sneak preview after somehow winning a science contest the previous year. As a result, we visited an enormous building site in a wide expanse of open Northumberland countryside before it was fully flooded to provide the UK's biggest artificial reservoir and hydroelectric plant.

While events at our football club in the summer of 1982 would not guarantee success to follow, they certainly signalled a change of mood on Tyneside. For the first time in years, there was a genuine reason for newcomers to attach themselves to our fortunes and for any recent stayaways to count themselves back in.

Chapter Eight

Play the Game, Then it's Auf Wiedersehen

WHEN A newspaper back page reported that Newcastle United were interested in signing Kevin Keegan, I was on a family holiday and detached from the reaction closer to home. The England captain had apparently been told he could leave Southampton where, just a couple of months earlier, he had claimed the Golden Boot as the First Division's top goalscorer, netting 26 times in the most prolific season of his glittering career. In the previous year, his first on the south coast, they had finished sixth, the best in their entire history up to that point, and in 1981/82 they were just one place lower in a table again topped by Kevin's old mates at Liverpool.

Southampton had topped the table in March but won just twice in the last nine games when perhaps an outfit more used to glory would have remained relentlessly on course. There were stories that Keegan and other senior players at the awkward and outdated Dell felt they were just one or two quality signings away from being potential champions but nothing had happened. In his autobiography, he revealed that his situation took a turn for the worse when manager

Lawrie McMenemy questioned his workrate and called the players 'cheats' after a heavy defeat against Aston Villa, who had been champions in 1981. 'I'm sure Lawrie regretted it later, but the damage was done,' Keegan wrote. For a man who saw all of his achievements in terms of commitment and overcoming earlier rejection, he admitted: 'It was probably the worst thing he could ever have said.' We saw only too well later that Keegan lived by his principles and did not mess around if he felt they were being compromised by someone else.

As a player, he was happy to trade on the determination, strength of character and sheer workrate that took him to the top of the game after early rejections for being too small, notably by Coventry boss Jimmy Hill. But don't be fooled, Keegan's attitude was only part of the story. You do not become a European Cup winner, England captain, double European player of the year while playing in a foreign land, a football icon and a great success in the commercial world just by trying hard. If that was the case, we'd all do it.

He undoubtedly had a work ethic and developed a winning mentality once he'd got used to the feeling at Bill Shankly's Liverpool but, make no mistake, Kevin Keegan was also a special footballer. Influential as a goalscorer at the spearhead of attack, out wide in his early England days, as a supplementary striker or getting forward from a deeper midfield position, there was a quality and a precision to his game to go with the durability of his batteries. Remember the chip against Ireland off his wrong foot? The near-post header against Italy? The surge from his own half and one-two to net against Scotland? Or, yes, the flick and the volley for his first goal against Newcastle in the 1974 cup final immortalised by David Coleman's 'goals pay the rent' commentary? Keegan was also brave in thought and deed, had an appreciation of what was happening around him on the pitch, was a terrific team player and got on the end of a lot of that work with a vital goal. He was also just the kind of character whose infectious spirit could inspire a crowd and who could, in return, feed off their excitement. A story linking him with a move to Newcastle, therefore, was almost too much to take in. It couldn't possibly be true.

If the fans were excited, I couldn't even imagine how the likes of Steve Carney and Peter Cartwright, Kenny Wharton and Kevin Carr or Bruce Halliday and David Barton back at Benwell could absorb the news as they reported for pre-season training in their Ford Escorts, having finished the previous season ninth in the Second Division with average attendances touching half the capacity of a neglected home ground. Aside from that homegrown core of young men, the Magpies squad included Irish midfielder Mick Martin, a young Chris Waddle, with less than two years as a pro under his belt, and not much besides.

Keegan was on the front cover of the *Rothman's Football Yearbook* published in August and was a marketing man's dream, promoting products and putting his face or name to merchandise of all descriptions. Surely stories of a new home in the North-East were far fetched?

The board had long been accused of a lack of ambition, with the state of the stadium bearing testimony to their short-sightedness and precarious cash position. Sitting midway in the second flight told its own story. The city council, no less, had demanded changes at the club back in the mid-60s and the team's failing fortunes since qualifying for Europe in 1977 had concentrated the bile towards the men in charge. (Incidentally, I still recall the line in Roger Hutchinson's potted history entitled *The Toon* in which he says, I assume after giving it much thought, that '[Club chief] Lord

Westwood had an eye on the FA chairmanship'. Westwood, in charge when United won the Fairs Cup until stepping down in 1978, famously wore an eye patch as the result of injuries in a car crash.)

We were not alone in initially writing off the story as a cynical ploy to get the fans to stick with the club after the disappointment of a fourth successive season in the Second Division and to encourage a few more season ticket sales. There would have been grudging respect for the directors if that had been the idea, because at least it showed some creativity. It would have been a back-handed compliment to a board which would block any proposed investment from AC/DC's Brian Johnson (previously singer in a band called Geordie) just as they were reaching superstardom and also regularly resisted overtures from Malcolm Dix, the Newcastle Supporters' Association and Magpie Group until it was almost too late.

The newspapers also had Leeds in the frame for Keegan's famous flourish of a signature, which would have been an interesting switch after his clashes with their players during his Liverpool days. They'd just been relegated, losing their last game at West Brom three days after Sunderland clawed ahead of their fellow strugglers with a vital win over Manchester City. Personally, I just couldn't see him in the white or yellow of Leeds but that didn't mean it couldn't happen.

And then came the splash headlines to confirm the coup was real, Kevin Keegan had signed for Newcastle United. It was the summer that changed the club forever.

* * *

Even before the transfer, Keegan dominated the headlines that summer, though not for reasons he would have wanted. He had been captain of an England squad going to the World

Cup finals for the first time since 1970, a time before we'd even started school, let alone collected the stickers or Esso souvenir coins. This was the first chance fans of my age had to support England on the biggest stage, though sadly the skipper would play only a small part.

By the summer of '82, when Steve Carney was the closest thing I had to a favourite at St James', my other football hero was also North-East born but he hadn't been picked up by the any of the region's professional clubs. In Keegan's enforced absence, he also used the world stage in Spain to catapult himself to a new level.

Witton Gilbert is just a few miles from where Keegan's grandfather had been involved in rescue attempts during the Stanley pit disaster in the 20s and is not a name known well to anyone raised more than a few miles away. It is near Sacriston, next to Hartside, by Pity Me, up the road from Framwellgate Moor, none of them particularly well known, either. Okay, it's close to the city of Durham, which anyone could point to roughly on a map. Just over the main road from Langley Park, where Bobby Robson worked down the pit before beginning his career in professional football, Witton Gilbert is also usually listed as the hometown of an unrelated Robson who became my idol.

Like Keegan, he worried that he would fail to make the grade because he was deemed too lightweight for the man's game. His autobiography mentioned a bodybuilding breakfast of a raw egg in a glass of milk and, although the ship had already sailed as far as my own football aspirations went, I adopted it to start my day for a while as a teenager in an attempt to improve physique and, who knows, ability on the ball. The book also mentioned the benefits of a nutritional Guinness but it was too early in the morning for me. But Bryan Robson eventually made it at West Brom and overcame a series of leg breaks to blossom in an attractive Albion team alongside Cyrille Regis, Laurie Cunningham, Tony Brown and Len Cantello.

I'd previously had Aston Villa as a kind of 'second team' on the strength of admiration for strikers Brian Little and Andy Gray, plus the fact they wore the same kit as my local junior team, but they were overtaken on the fringes of my affection by these emerging rivals in the West Midlands. It was really little more than a passing interest – it didn't make or break a weekend if they won or lost – but I did enjoy watching them. There was still only one 'we' (a term one former work colleague struggled to comprehend whenever she asked about my plans for the weekend and I'd respond with 'we are home/away to …'). And when Robson followed boss Ron Atkinson to Manchester United as a British record signing, the allegiance disappeared.

The most expensive player in the country put pen to paper sitting at the side of the pitch at Old Trafford on matchday and, despite the brown suit and bubble perm, he became an icon. United were more than a decade on from their last league title win and were spending big again in an attempt to rectify that situation under the flamboyant Atkinson, a replacement for the vastly more stoic but highly regarded Dave Sexton. Robson became the fulcrum of his team as a competitor with an eye for goal, the all-round modern midfielder.

Robson had it all, from the underdog back story to becoming the golden boy of English football. He became the complete midfielder, the tigerish tackler who could trigger attacks from deep, exchange dangerous passes as a creative force and also finish as well as most strikers. There were few his equal in the ability to single-handedly drive a team onwards. At one stage after the 1982 World Cup, there was newspaper talk of what used to be called a 'moneybags move' to Italy and I responded by gathering signatures on a petition at school, which obviously made a difference because he continued to nail his colours to the Old Trafford mast for many years to come.

It seemed Robson rarely scored poor goals, they all had to be either important or spectacular, with my personal pick being an FA Cup semi-final screamer against United's old rivals Liverpool. Many of his goals were similar in style to Terry McDermott in his pomp. His character also flip-flopped between the snarling all-in snapper, the death stare for anyone who crossed him or the clenched fist to inspire team-mates in battle to the biggest smile imaginable when the ball hit the back of the net.

He was not yet 'Captain Marvel', the national team armband being worn by Keegan on the way to the World Cup and by veteran full-back Mick Mills in Spain. But he was essential to England in '82. It took Robson just 28 seconds to announce England's presence on the world stage after the failures of 1974 (missing out to Poland) and 1978 (to Italy), timing his run into the penalty area superbly to launch a volley home against France, and he added a second in an uplifting 3-1 win with a header that any centre-forward would have been proud of from another trademark run to support the attack.

With the perm long gone and resplendent in red shirt and sweatbands of red, white and blue, Robson was wearing No.16 in a squad named in alphabetical order. As captain when it was announced, Keegan was allowed to retain his No.7 but it was not long before the Manchester United man became the proud owner of both the shirt and the armband, though the torment of a shoulder injury would overshadow another World Cup in Mexico, which meant having to watch his team fall to the wiles and wits of Diego Maradona.

Robson received a curious reception at St James' when the Uniteds eventually shared the same league status. He was always seen as one of us but he was also captain of the opposition, with a battling countenance and overwhelming competitive spirit to go with it. Cheers were, therefore, mixed with jeers, praise with profanity, but no one ever underestimated his quality or his commitment. He was still a North-East hero for 40 games in a 42-game season.

Alongside the injuries, Robson was unfortunate that his club were still rebuilding around him and it was only at the tail end of his Old Trafford career under Alex Ferguson that he finally received the silverware his talents deserved, sharing in two title-winning seasons before joining Middlesbrough as player-manager. There, chairman Steve Gibson provided the financial backing to attract names like Fabrizio Ravanelli, Juninho and Emerson to rejuvenate Teesside and fill their new home at The Riverside.

* * *

Despite England's unimpressive record (a win in 1966 and a few quarter-finals were the high points in three decades of participation), they were controversially named among the seeded teams for 1982 and based in Bilbao. Following the opening victory there, they beat Czechoslovakia 2-0 and a Trevor Francis goal accounted for Kuwait, whose previous game had made the headlines only because their players, staff and federation president protested against a goal in their 4-1 loss to France.

In the second-round stage, also played in groups, England played out a goalless draw with West Germany and then faced the hosts, who had finished second in their pool to a Northern Ireland team featuring the teenage Norman Whiteside and indefatigable Gerry Armstrong, Billy Hamilton and David McCreery, who was then playing his club football in the United States with Tulsa.

Once the Germans beat Spain 2-1 in the second fixture, England had to win by two goals in Madrid to reach the semi-finals. Captain Keegan had not played a single minute of his only World Cup due to a back injury which had necessitated a top-secret trip to a specialist in West Germany but, with the game still goalless after an hour, Greenwood played what he hoped would be his trump card. Keegan was sent on, alongside old pal Trevor Brooking, so often the provider in a white shirt but also ruled out of action until that point by a groin injury. The West Ham midfielder almost scored, while Robson was narrowly wide with a header reminiscent of his strike against France and then created the best opportunity of the night, chipping across goal for the unmarked Keegan to write the headlines as he had done so many times in his career. Sadly, this time his header inexplicably drifted wide of the far post. His frustration as team-mate Paul Mariner lifted him to his feet was plain for all to see. 'If England are going to win the World Cup, that was the one,' said Jack Charlton on commentary as a man who knew what it took to lift the trophy.

England were unbeaten and had conceded just one goal in five games but they were still on their way home. As they landed, Greenwood handed over the so-called 'Most Difficult Job in the Country' to Bobby Robson, who quickly and controversially ended Keegan's international career and incurred the wrath of the same Geordie fans who would later hail him as a saviour back in the North-East.

* * *

Once the news broke that Newcastle had somehow managed to convince Kevin Keegan to take on a huge new challenge in black-and-white, what was left of the summer passed like an extended Christmas Eve. The excitement grew with every passing minute but the clock still appeared to be travelling backwards. Until finally, an almost unbelievable debut day arrived on 28 August 1982.

Two years earlier, attendances at the opening pair of home games had been 17,000 and 13,000. In September 1981 we'd started with a decent 19,000 but immediately dipped to 14,700 and 13,800 for the visits of Cambridge and Shrewsbury on the way to an average in the league of 17,250. In that same season, the hardy souls in a gate of 10,700 for the visit of QPR (who won 4-0) could hardly have imagined that their number would swell to 35,000 for the rematch a little over three months later. But then none of us could have imagined, either, that a double European player of the year and long-time England captain would be the big attraction.

Debut day dawned bright and sunny. I still recall it as stifling hot in the capacity crowd, though seeing the television coverage over the years since, 'King Kev' looks freezing as he runs out in shorts and white sweatshirt on a breezy afternoon ahead of kick-off.

We'd binned off our ritual of gathering in a group for *Football Focus* before heading to town. Just two of us had gone to get tickets in advance and, knowing the demand to be involved, we decided we had to get to St James' Park while everyone else was still having breakfast. We were there before nine o'clock in the morning. We were so early, among the very first arrivals, that we sat with our backs against the Gallowgate End wall next to our turnstile for several hours before it even started to get busy. Slowly but surely, more and more supporters arrived. A few police pottered around, passing the time of day with the early arrivals, and we stayed exactly where we had started for hour after hour.

As the numbers grew, the queue at first ran in an orderly fashion along the wall. Then the pavement filled up and the road started to fill, too. The police presence increased, with mounted officers trying to use their elevated position to organise the mass of bodies which, by now, had no real order. Getting close to a police horse in a big crowd is not a comfortable place to be but it was unavoidable as the whole area looked like it should have been on the other side of the turnstile wall, with the same unpredictable, sudden movements forward and back, left and right.

After hours sat and then stood against the wall, we somehow found ourselves in the middle of the road and started to fear not for our safety but whether we would ever get back towards the turnstiles. Then, with the queues merged into one mass as the gates finally opened, we just as mysteriously found our place in the queue again and got in. For all the tribulations and the stresses, we were finally on the inside. This was a special day in Newcastle United history and we were now guaranteed to be part of it.

We were nowhere near where we expected to be when we arrived with the best of intentions at breakfast time and there was now no chance of finding a place near where we normally stood in the centre section, so we aimed towards the right-hand corner and picked a spot somewhere around halfway, back where the elevation gave us a decent view. It was still very lively and all around got warmer and louder by the minute.

I'm not sure my feet touched the ground, figuratively or otherwise, when we saw our man run out in black-and-white for the first time, the chanting of his name rolling round and round the crowd. This was more exciting than being at a Wembley cup final because this was on our own ground. This was a day we didn't need to share with anyone else. It was all ours. All we had to do now was win.

There was barely breathing space or perhaps it was just the overwhelming excitement that did for me as, for the only time in my years of going to football, I had to momentarily give in to the heat and the claustrophobia and I ducked under our crash barrier to go and see if I could find a cold drink. Under the stand in the corner, there was a concrete bunker which passed as the refreshment area. Squeezing through, I got there to find it was just as rammed as the terrace and, when I finally got close to the counter, I could see a handful of staff and dozens of grown men pleading to be served. The cupboard was almost bare. I got a flimsy plastic cup of tap water. Mike, who I'd left on the concrete steps above, would have to go without because there was more chance of Arthur Cox calling us down to the dressing room than there was of me being able to keep another cup intact as I tried to retrace my steps to our part of the terrace.

I remember the details so well because I've replayed the day so thoroughly in my head and, thankfully, I got back to my place, or somewhere near it, in time to witness the greatest moment in the club's history during my lifetime, the fairytale moment when our hero netted the only goal of the game. I could see Mike just a bit further along from where I stood, though there was no way to get any closer and, when Keegan netted the winner with a finish into the bottom corner of the net, we celebrated a magic moment with anyone and everyone around us. We also described it in ever-increasing depth over and over as we finally met up again on the bus home, for all the 45 minutes until we got off at the other end and the extra quarter of an hour on the walk back to our street, too.

Since that day I have seen the goal hundreds of times from the angle of cameras located in the Old Stand above halfway, so it has now slightly clouded the recollection of my own line of vision, but the excitement of seeing the ball roll into the net remains undiluted by time.

The build-up to the goal started with full-back John Craggs, another of the summer signings. From near Annfield Plain on the south side of the river, Craggs was short of his 21st birthday when he played in the Fairs Cup win in 1969 but was better known for more than 400 appearances with Middlesbrough, where the broad band across their snappy kit made him look as barrel-chested as anyone in my dad's scrapbooks from the 50s. But in 1982, he returned on a free transfer for a second bite and he played his part in the historic goal.

After Craggs aimed a pass down the right flank, from in front of the dugouts, Keegan flicked on to Imre Varadi, whose immediate return provided the room for the newcomer to run on. With everyone in the ground holding their breath, the No.7 kept his nerve to thread the ball to goalkeeper Peter Hucker's left. Varadi, after leapfrogging one of the fallen defenders, was among the first to join the celebrations as Keegan threw himself into the crowd on those first five steps behind the goal.

The man who had seen everything in football was knocked sideways by the welcome he received from the three-and-a-bit sides of his new home. 'Fairytale stuff,' he told reporters afterwards. 'I tapped it and the crowd sucked it in.'

Life just does not happen like this, I thought. There is no divine script. Except, as we were to learn over time, if you are Kevin Keegan and dressed in black-and-white.

Team-mates Saunders, Haddock and Cartwright, like me, were not old enough to remember when the team had actually been in with a shout of winning something, so this was new to all of us. With the greatest of respect, none of the trio would figure in the club's best of the decade but they were the best of what was available at that moment in time, they came in to do a job and even if they had never played another game, that afternoon would have been enough.

Central defender Jeff Clarke joined Keegan and Craggs in making his debut in that opening game of the season and almost immediately impressed fans enough for us to forgive or forget that he had previously been a Mackem. He was great in the air, steady on the floor and went on to develop a fine partnership, if not an exactly watertight one, with Glenn Roeder, the only centre-half in Newcastle's rollcall with a 'stepover' until the arrival of the far more exotic Philippe Albert.

Keegan scored again in a win at Blackburn to make it maximum points from the opening two games and then Arthur Cox decided that having one England captain in the team was not enough, so he added another in the shape of Mick Channon, Keegan's old mate from Southampton. Two of Channon's 46 caps had been accompanied by the skipper's armband and he scored on his Magpies debut in a midweek game against Middlesbrough, celebrating with a trademark windmill salute as we watched from the new bench seats at the front of the East Stand.

Where once there had been a paddock, and before that the Popular Side, United installed wooden benches seemingly almost overnight that summer. Behind, they would add some executive boxes, though as they were an after-thought in a stand which was already a decade old, the development did resemble a flat-roof domestic extension and was quickly outdated, though not as rapidly replaced. The benches, we found on the handful of occasions we used them, were a boon for young supporters, the prices being only just more than the terrace but with an infinitely better opportunity to see all the action. A bit of arse-ache from the thin varnished planks was a small sacrifice. Also, you got the added bonus of being able to see all the swaying, the clapping and the chorus from the Gallowgate End, though it wasn't the same just watching it and we quickly returned to our own two feet over coming weeks.

It seems incredible that we got those bench places without any fuss for a game just ten days after Keegan's debut. Even with the euphoria of this promised new era and two wins out of three to kick off the season, we paid on the day as a midweek crowd of 28,000 saw the points shared from a 1-1 in the latest leg of Tyne-Tees rivalry.

Boro would have to play ten games before getting a first win under their belts, despite the presence of long-serving goalkeeper Jim Platt, the popular Dutch midfielder Heine Otto and livewire local Steve Bell alongside former Newcastle defenders John Brownlie and Irving Nattrass. They never climbed higher than 15th in the table under Malcolm Allison and would have to wait another couple of years to dodge the bailiffs and fashion a rebirth under new boss Bruce Rioch.

So far so good then for Newcastle after a number of tough years. But if a reminder was needed that the rest of the division would not just sit back and form a guard of honour for our hero, it was delivered as we then went five games without a win, dropping to 12th in the table.

Early in the season, I skipped a Wednesday afternoon at school – a decision I did not take lightly, as it was our weekly football session – and queued to meet Keegan in the city centre at Monument Sports, the company of Bill Gates, a former Boro defender whose name returned to the headlines 50 years after his retirement from the game during studies on potential connection between neuro-degenerative damage and heading a football. For his new store in Newcastle, I remained outside in the queue at twilight as many of the hundred or so people in front had been asking for multiple copies of Keegan's signature on items to pass to dads, mums, mates and sundry others. By the time I got anywhere near the front, security decreed Kevin could only sign what he had brought with him and, when my turn came, I nodded and quietly told him my name, receiving a signed poster of the man himself pictured making his Magpies debut. He also signed a postcard branded by sponsors Patrick and showing him in an England shirt and it sat on my desk for the first decade or so of my working life, put away only because I didn't want anyone to half-inch it when Newcastle became the country's 'second-favourite team'.

* * *

Gordon Lee, the man who had sent Malcolm Macdonald and Terry Hibbitt packing years earlier, was by now in charge at Preston North End and played a part in the arrival of another terrace favourite as the squad continued to evolve. When Lee decided he could do without defender John Anderson, the Irishman moved to Tyneside on a free, with Arthur Cox matching his headline-grabbing work in the transfer market with the sound acquisition of a man who would give a decade of service, playing at full-back, central defence and occasionally in midfield. For many, Anderson would be an automatic choice in any list of best value signings in Newcastle United's history.

It wasn't just the team on Tyneside that changed. The mood had lifted all-round, at the training ground, on the pitch, in the stands and in the wider region. Cox could also start looking at a different shelf for his shopping, away from the own brand bargains. A big pot of money hadn't just magically materialised – Keegan's arrival was supported by Newcastle Breweries and he was on a cut of revenue for attendances above a certain figure in a win-win for the club – and this was nothing like the later arrival of the ferociously rich Public Investment Fund but, between them, Cox and Keegan represented a change in attitude and the superstar could be used as a magnet to attract supporting talent. Of course, ten years later, he would be part of a repeat performance, this time as an accompaniment to Sir John Hall's cash as he presented players with a persuasive argument to join a team which came to be known as 'The Entertainers'.

As Keegan settled in, Cox brought Terry McDermott back to the club after sharing in sustained success with Liverpool. The Merseyside midfielder was 31 when he joined the revolution under way at St James' in the autumn of 1982 but his quality remained.

I had blamed schoolboy immaturity for many of my dark memories of the 1974 cup final (which I had ended in tears behind the door of the downstairs toilet) and decided I'd look for closure as an adult by watching it again. Another viewing also confirmed that Terry Mac was by some way the best player on the pitch outside of a red shirt and, after joining Liverpool, he developed into the country's best raiding midfielder, one of the best in Europe. He had a phenomenal workrate, playing box to box despite admitting less-than-perfect 'refuelling' habits, as Graham Taylor would have described them. He always showed immaculate timing in joining an attack and had a knack of scoring spectacular goals – a sort of Steven Gerrard with a naughty moustache. He had scored in a European Cup Final, too.

McDermott, always a straight talker, was under no illusions about what he was walking into, saying in his 1988 autobiography that in his opinion nothing had changed in the eight years he had been away from Newcastle. 'The club had, if anything, gone backwards,' he added. 'St James' Park was in decay ... the club was in desperate need of a lift.' But just three months after going to Spain alongside Keegan for a World Cup, his arrival took this United team up another couple of notches.

McDermott had been a winner as part of the best team in the country for so long at Liverpool and he had the vision, passing range and nous to know what Keegan wanted when he got possession of the ball. He communicated on and off the field and he helped the new messiah in pulling the rest of the team along. It was a relationship which would work wonders for the club beyond their two years as team-mates, too.

As Channon departed, joining Bristol Rovers and then Norwich before turning to a career in butchering the pronunciation of Gary Lineker's surname for television and then more successfully in training racehorses, McDermott made his debut in the unlikely surroundings of Rotherham's Millmoor. On a wave of emotion, he set up the first of Keegan's four goals in a 5-1 win over a home line-up which included their former team-mate Emlyn Hughes in the centre of defence.

Varadi was again in support mode, taking a hand in two of the goals. It is worth seeking out the highlights again just to see the McDermott pass and cool Keegan finish for the opener and for the bounce of fans in a packed away end when he smashes in his fourth. While we all remember Keegan's strikes, a few will also recall that Kevin Todd got the other (with a left-wing cross which drifted over the goalkeeper's head into the net) but how many also have memory of Kevin Carr saving a penalty on his return to the team or that the denied taker was Hughes himself? The outcome initiated a campaign on the terraces and sections of the media for an international recall for Keegan, though how hitting four against Rotherham, with all due respect, could fuel those particular flames escapes me still.

To see such a quick change in outlook after four dismal years was almost overwhelming for fans starved not just of success but of hope, too, for so long but it is impossible to know how the players felt behind closed doors. Varadi, for example, had been the team's prime source of goals, while also often playing a role as a selfless targetman in attack, but now he was sharing the burden with one of Europe's greatest players. Combined, they had cost the club less than £250,000 in transfer fees, with £125,000 going to Everton for Varadi and around £100,000 on his new senior partner.

Youth team graduate Chris Hedworth came into the squad and probably could not believe what was happening when he cast an eye around the changing room. He'd gone from the rustic benches of Benwell to a peg near internationals Keegan and McDermott. A versatile but rather lightweight defender, he was also the hairiest one on the books. Put it this way, Hedworth would never suffer from cold knees. His nine league appearances before spells with Barnsley, Halifax and Blackpool were spread over a four-year spell, ending between the sticks at West Ham in 1985/86 when he took the gloves from the injured Martin Thomas. The Wallsend-born Hedworth also suffered an injury in that game and handed over to Peter Beardsley. Typical of our star striker, he made one of the saves of the season. It didn't much matter, though; West Ham won 8-1.

Despite the fresh feelings of hope around the camp, it did not take long for McDermott to feel frustrated with life in the Second Division and he was twice sent off for dissent, while admitting to disappointment with his own form. He had come into a new-look team full of players he knew little about in a division he'd not experienced after a decade of outrageous success elsewhere. As he said himself, there was no Graeme Souness or Ray Kennedy at his side to control things in midfield or spot his runs forward while he played his own game. When he made his admission to Cox, the Merseysider was told to get on with it, which reflected the manager's strengthening position, as well as confidence in his plan coming together. The boss wanted to see the rest of the team move to match McDermott's standards, not see Terry drop his to Second Division levels.

The arrival of Northern Ireland international David McCreery would help with that process, making his debut just a week after the win at Rotherham. It is taken as read that everyone loved Keegan and the other headline makers – McDermott, Waddle and Varadi – but I will stick out my neck and say McCreery never had a bad game for Newcastle.

He was the fetcher and carrier in midfield, a thinking man's anchorman who viewed the opposition as a necessary evil. The bigger they came, the harder they fell. He usually won the ball cleanly and was not big enough or psychopathic enough to intimidate, though he didn't mind a timely trip or block as part of the armoury. He just went about his business, winning the ball and passing it to the likes of Keegan, Waddle and then Beardsley and, later, Paul Gascoigne to do something with it. Even his terrace chant was a simple 'David McCreery', which suited the lack of frills, airs and graces. It was fitting that he spent his time in America playing for a team called Tulsa Roughnecks. No other name could sum him up so beautifully but McCreery was more than a simple labourer. He had a touch of class about him, which in this case was directed towards bringing out the best in everyone around him rather than enhancing any personal spotlight.

McCreery was a dog in black-and-white stripes (or the fetching silver/grey away kit of the time) after a rabbit, with his scuttling stride all over the pitch, closing down opponents, winning tackles and shuffling possession along to colleagues. In a team with obvious skills in its forward line, there had to be a production line, too, and it was McCreery who led it, brought in at a cost of just £75,000 by a manager who exhibited a consistent strength in terms of finding transfer market value. Another key element of the team to finally end this spell in the Second Division had fallen into place.

McCreery already had plenty of experience with Manchester United and QPR before crossing the Atlantic and the midfield dynamo was named in the team of the tournament at the World Cup for his displays with Northern Ireland. He had left Belfast as a 15-year-old, aborting a move to Tottenham when Old Trafford beckoned, and was just a fortnight past his 17th birthday when he made his first-team debut there, given the opportunity as the fallen giants suffered the slap across the face of a season in the Second Division during 1974/75. McCreery also held the distinction of playing in two FA Cup finals as a teenager, on both occasions being used as a substitute for mercurial winger Gordon Hill. But by the time he came to St James' Park, the little man was a nailed-on starter.

Described in the native media as Northern Ireland's 'tormentor in chief' in midfield, McCreery was the archetypal workhorse in a holding role which would be more recognisable and highly prized after his own playing days were long over. But his value with the Magpies will never be underestimated by team-mates or fans who were there to watch him.

While his powers never seemed to wane during more than 270 appearances in seven years on Tyneside, McCreery's hairline did and, standing in the Gallowgate End, mate David and I used to count his tackles per game and multiply them by a random number – I think we settled on 150 – to calculate how many hairs had been lost during the 90 minutes. The number of tackles lost, however, was negligible.

It is unlikely that there are many in football with a bad word to say about McCreery, who went on to have an interesting, globe-trotting managerial career, including a spell in Myanmar (Burma). He'd been in charge, too, at Carlisle and Hartlepool, where I did get to speak to him in a professional capacity during my time at the *Northern Echo*. I could not have been more starstruck if 'King Kev' himself had answered the phone and asked me to hold for the gaffer. He was my last Magpies hero as a teenager, sitting alongside Bryan Robson as my favourite footballer of the time.

Replacing an international icon in the opening minutes of a European Cup semi-final on the back of just one top division appearance would be daunting enough for anyone. But gaining the total trust of team-mates in front of a 75,000 crowd at an Olympic stadium was not the only – or indeed the biggest – challenge faced by Howard Gayle in his fledgling career.

The Liverpool striker stripped off from the bench during the first ten minutes of the clash with Bayern Munich to swap places with Kenny Dalglish when the Reds legend hobbled towards the touchline with an ankle injury and, for the rest of the first half, the youngster looked raw and overawed on the right wing as his team searched for a breakthrough against the German champions, who had earned a goalless draw at Anfield in the first leg.

In the second half, though, after encouragement from the boys of the 'Boot Room' – Bob Paisley, Joe Fagan, Ronnie Moran and Roy Evans – he started to take on Bayern with much more confidence, using his pace from the left to stretch their defence.

He was eventually replaced by Jimmy Case in the final quarter, the sub subbed, shortly after receiving a harsh yellow card and with Paisley keen to bolster experience in a line-up already missing Phil Thompson and Alan Kennedy, but Gayle had made enough of an impression to be given the No.7 shirt during the run-in to the end of the season before Dalglish returned to start the final against Real Madrid. Gayle did still receive a winner's medal after being named among the substitutes, watching from the bench as full-back Kennedy supplied the decisive goal.

Only two black men, Viv Anderson and Laurie Cunningham, had been capped by England when Gayle picked up that treasured European Cup medal. Brendan Batson and Cyrille Regis had claimed international 'B' honours, with Justin Fashanu and Vince Hilaire leading a handful of others aiming to break through from the Under-21s, but there were few footsteps to follow as Gayle and his contemporaries, many of them the inner-city sons of immigrant parents, made their way in the game. His breakthrough also provided some good news for Toxteth, his home on Merseyside, where uglier headlines would be made just a couple of months later as racial tensions, high unemployment and the realities of a failing economy combined to inflame incidents around many of the country's inner cities.

Having already replaced one iconic striker, Gayle had to do it again when he was signed on loan by Newcastle when Keegan was injured. Already Liverpool's first black player, he was also the first to wear Magpies stripes.

Newcastle will not be proud of their reputation in the bad old days of the 70s and 80s, when terrace chants targeted black players from rival clubs, but fans were still excited to see if Gayle could turn that early promise seen on TV coverage into a statement of progress. He was already 24 years old but still understandably raw, with only a handful of Liverpool appearances to go with a loan spell at Fulham, which had ended in relegation to the Third Division. He had matured physically since the European Cup, though, adding a bit of timber to the bones, so he did not look quite so leggy, and he still had pace. When he was called in after Keegan's eye injury, picked up in a testimonial game for John Craggs at Ayresome Park, he looked like a threat in attack.

Gayle also had a bit of a temper and knew how to look after himself, a quality no doubt required in such intolerant times and, after celebrating his winning goal against Derby, we started to think about how he could fit in once 'King Kev' got back on the field. He probably should have scored more than twice in his eight games but the club decided not to turn the move into a permanent one. Instead, Gayle went to Birmingham in the division above for another loan spell before they parted with a fee of just £50,000 to make it more long term. In a squad also featuring Mark Dennis, Pat van den Hauwe, Noel Blake and Mick Harford, at least he was unlikely to be the first name in the referee's notebook there.

It would be another two years before Newcastle made Tony Cunningham the club's first black transfer. At a cost of £75,000, he did not have the skills or the pace of Gayle but he based his game on commitment and, like his groundbreaking predecessor, he received plenty of encouragement from fans, though the club would remain slow both in signing players of colour and providing those in visiting teams with anything close to a decent welcome.

Gayle, who titled his autobiography *61 Minutes in Munich*, spent just a year at Birmingham and won England Under-21 selection there as an over-age player (not an 'average player' as I once saw misprinted to describe Tommy Craig's inclusion in Scotland's Under-21s) but then enjoyed the best of his career in its second half when others thought he'd already missed out. After playing in a League Cup Final for Sunderland, he enjoyed great popularity in a long stay at Blackburn which, ironically for a history maker, ended when they opened a new chapter in their own story by spending big on signings like the young Geordie striker Alan Shearer.

In 2012, Gayle told a Liverpool website that during both spells in the North-East the fans had been great but as an opposition player at St James' Park he had been 'spat at, there were monkey noises and all sorts of racist abuse. It wasn't pleasant, but sadly it was something I had become used to.' Newcastle were by no means the only offenders but we saw right-wing groups outside the ground identifying a target audience among dissatisfied young men to raise their profile and recruitment while, inside, the racist abuse of opposition players was the era's most extreme extension of animosity. For all the good times and the treasured memories of my time on the terraces, I still feel ashamed that I heard and saw it, while also acknowledging the undoubted strength of the players who had to face it.

As one of the game's pioneers, Gayle developed into a prominent name with Show Racism the Red Card. With parents from Sierra Leone and Ghana, in 2016 he turned down an MBE in recognition of his work, saying: 'I had to decline the nomination for the reason that my ancestors would be turning in their graves after how Empire and colonialism had enslaved them. There will be others who may feel different and would enjoy the attraction of being a

Member of the British Empire and those three letters after their name but I feel that it would be a betrayal to all of the Africans who have lost their lives or who have suffered as a result of Empire.'

***

No sooner had Gayle gone, with Keegan back to fitness, than David McCreery found himself on the sidelines, recovering from a freak injury which had been inflicted by 'friendly fire', requiring more than 60 stitches in a wound along the length of one leg after being caught by the studs of a team-mate in a sliding tackle during a game against Bolton. Undaunted, he was soon back to what he did best, the epitome of the 'team man' in that line-up.

From the extreme of seeing international veterans Keegan and Channon in tandem with the experienced Craggs and Clarke, the canny Cox threw in 16-year-old Neil McDonald for his debut early in the season. The North Shields-born England Youth cap was promoted after just a handful of appearances at junior and reserve levels and, as a trainee, he was still responsible for cleaning Keegan's boots when he became the club's youngest-ever first-team debutant.

Progress, though, did not come immediately. The team remained resolutely mid-table and a run of three successive 2-2 draws around Christmas followed by defeat at QPR even pushed Keegan and co. down to 14th – also being dumped out of both cup competitions at the first hurdle – before finally going on a decent run of form.

John Trewick had been injured amid all the excitement of the opening-day win and was ruled out for the rest of the season, so when McCreery was also sidelined, McDonald returned and this time enjoyed an extended run, one which coincided with the team's best form of the campaign.

Physically, there was no doubt that McDonald was up to it and he made the most of his opportunity, gradually growing into an assured midfielder who would be talked about as one with a potential international future. While critics pointed to a lack of pace and a style which looked like a coaching textbook – head over the ball, knee over the ball, follow through the centre of the ball with the inside of the boot – he did not look short of much in this company. McDonald had good stamina and a good shot, too. After a time, there were stories of potentially converting him into a ball-playing sweeper from defence, which was in vogue for a while, with the same debate swirling around Bryan Robson and then the younger, unrelated Stewart Robson of Arsenal, without ever coming to fruition. McDonald got closer than the other two, settling into a right-back role later in a career away from his home.

In a momentous campaign under Keegan's influence, amid all the new faces and the fresh sense of optimism, I retain a personal highlight from a game which didn't even matter. It was a 'European Special' midweek friendly against Dynamo Kiev in November when I sat amid the antique wooden charm of the Old Stand, thus completing my tour of all four sides of the ground.

It is doubtful the Eastern Bloc powerhouses would have entertained a visit in any of the previous four years and an image burnt on to my brain was the warm-up where every member of the squad took turns to line up 30 to 35 yards out and cream a succession of accurate shots on goal. Even the extra keeper in the squad kept his shots low and true. Another memory of the day was a steady performance by a young defender named Ian Dawes, who seemed very assured to me. Sadly, I think it was the only time he appeared in the senior set-up before moving down the leagues to Northampton, though he subsequently climbed the ranks again when he left the game, getting as high as Detective Chief Superintendent in 30 years with the Northumbria Constabulary.

* * *

For the final months of an attention-grabbing season, Cox largely kept faith with a regular line-up, choosing Anderson, Clarke, Carney and Wharton in front of Carr; McCreery, McDonald and McDermott in midfield; with Keegan, Varadi and Waddle in attack.

Bouncing back from that loss at QPR, there were just three defeats in the final 18 games, starting with two goals from Wharton in thumping 4-0 win over Shrewsbury which had us bouncing in the stands. It's easy to slip into the 'it's only Shrewsbury' frame of mind, as I'm sure many did on the outside, but it is worth pointing out that they finished ninth that season, equalling Newcastle's record from a year earlier, and the fact we were still coming to terms with winning again.

By April 1983, we also had the novelty of watching international football on our home ground as England Under-21s hosted their Hungarian counterparts. Sunderland midfielder Nick Pickering was the only Geordie-born player in the team and, in the post-match interview with *Look North*, he commented on being booed by the crowd. Among his team-mates in a 1-0 win was John Ryan, who looked like a cross between Trewick and McDermott but played like neither when he later arrived on Tyneside from Oldham. He was joined in defence by Brian Kilcline, then at Notts County before an FA Cup win with Coventry and talismanic switch to United when Keegan returned as manager. The cover for keeper Alan Knight was Oldham youngster Andy Goram, whose 40-cap international future lay further north.

Back on league duty, a fistful of draws ended hope of a golden one-way ticket back to the First Division, though home games against Grimsby, Blackburn and Charlton yielded 11 goals, including five for Varadi while Keegan accounted for just one. Against Charlton, we raced into a two-goal lead, only to be pegged back before Varadi scored twice in the last 20 minutes, including a typical burst through on the goalkeeper to settle the points and send the terraces wild. While many football fans talking about drama will go to Manchester United's last-gasp win over Bayern in the Champions League Final, David Beckham's dramatic free kick against Greece or Martin Tyler's 'Agüerooooo!' moment describing a league title win for Manchester City, the closing stages of that win over Charlton remain near the top of my own chart in the context of taking the lead, throwing it away and then grabbing it back in a style which rocked the whole stadium, particularly as Varadi could be as unpredictable as he was quick. So, for him to race clear from the shadows of the great man himself and hit the winning double made it all the more memorable. If no one else had been watching, I might have even shed a tear or two.

Through the 23 home games I went to during that momentous season, Newcastle failed to score just once, in an FA Cup match against Brighton in January. Both Varadi and Keegan finished on 21 league goals, with the former adding one more in the cups. For Varadi, who had played in every game, there was also the satisfaction of topping the tally scored in front of home fans at St James' Park.

This was the team's best return since relegation five years earlier and it had been done to the backdrop of better crowds, home and away. But the club, backed by sponsors from the brewery, had not moved heaven and earth to sign Kevin Keegan to remain in the Second Division. The pressure was on to put that right and the ticking of the clock was getting louder.

* * *

Newcastle were installed as ante-post favourites for promotion in 1983/84 but then conceded what we saw as a dramatic own goal with the surprise sale of Varadi just before kick-off. Sending him to strengthen rivals Sheffield Wednesday merely added to the drama and to the shock.

A favourite with the fans, Varadi had top-scored in both of his seasons in the North-East and had missed just three of the 84 league games since his arrival. As part of the deal which took him to Yorkshire, David Mills became a Magpies player again and he wore No.9 when a rare John Anderson goal got us off to a winning start at Elland Road, Leeds, despite the loss of goalkeeper Kevin Carr to a broken arm.

But then, illustrating the point made years earlier by Malcolm Macdonald when he commented that the team's form often matched their contrasting colours of black-and-white, we suffered a single-goal home defeat to 'Just Shrewsbury' as the opening weeks brought a mixture of triumph and despair.

Martin Thomas resembled Carr in build, hairstyle and moustache, as well as in goalkeeping style, so he seamlessly fitted in as a replacement for the first half of the season but it was the arrival of a new striker with a unique skillset which transformed the campaign and provided the extra impetus that Keegan and McDermott had been looking for as keenly as boss Cox.

Taking the long way round from Wallsend, via Carlisle and Canada, with a one-game spell at Manchester United thrown in for good measure, Peter Beardsley nevertheless impressed everyone from day one and was destined to grow into one of the club's greatest-ever players. Football insiders were aware of his talent but he needed the right platform to nurture and fully appreciate his potential. That he found it just a few miles from his family's front door meant the world to the supporters.

Beardsley made his home debut in October in front of a 25,000 crowd in a 4-2 win over Portsmouth, with Waddle scoring twice. In light of what he produced from that point onwards, it was an 'I was there' moment to go alongside witnessing the debuts of Waddle and Keegan in the preceding couple of seasons. A week later, Keegan grabbed the 150th league goal of his career in the win over Charlton and we were on our way.

The Keegan-Beardsley-Waddle axis in attack finally gave us a team which could terrify or even bully the opposition, playing with a belief that we were now more skilful and more clinical than many others. It lifted confidence all-round, with colleagues knowing if they could get possession to the right people in the right areas, then good things would happen. After years of looking anywhere for a spark, Newcastle United's team now had more than a welder's bench.

***

Gates regularly topped the 25,000 mark, with the biggest visiting clubs occasionally given an extra section of the Leazes for fans who wanted a share of the mania, thereby creating the odd sensation of Newcastle being outnumbered in one part of their own ground. I was in that end, penned in one small corner, though I cannot recall why, in a crowd of 33,500 when Beardsley scored his hat-trick in a 5-0 win over second-placed Manchester City just a few weeks into his Magpies career. They were his first goals at St James' and, although I was there, I have only ever seen them on television because I had no clear view of the majority of the pitch through the fans packed into that corner.

As well as the numbers and the excitement, there was the added challenge of dodging incoming items thrown from the away pens. The ammunition was mainly loose change and occasionally something heavier, though not the spark plugs which lads next to us said they'd been peppered with at a previous game. Anything at hand came over the fence and most of it then headed back the other way while Beardsley got on with destroying the visiting defence. Cox described it as the best 90 minutes he'd seen from any team he had managed, which sounded good until you realised the state of the Newcastle team he had taken over and his only previous experience at Chesterfield.

The front three shared an uncanny understanding almost as soon as Beardsley joined the party. He had the dribbling skills of Waddle and the non-stop commitment of Keegan, but he had vision beyond either and enjoyed spraying passes to the wide channels as much as chasing back to win possession in midfield. He loved a one-two on the edge of the penalty area, had unique individual skills and scored all kinds of goals, though the special ones far outweighed the tap-ins.

As the goals rained in, though, there would be no repeat of the run Keegan made into the crowd following his debut goal as 1983 saw the introduction of fences around the perimeter of the pitch. Newcastle followed the example of three-quarters of clubs in the top divisions in using metalwork to help control supporter behaviour. The club had been on a warning after incidents during a cup game at Leeds a year earlier and there were reports of trouble at other games but this was a national response rather than an individual one.

The fences loomed high over supporters standing near the front of the terrace, though they also provided a great climbing frame for the same fans in response to a goal and could make quite a noise when slapped in time with the singing. The only difference they made to us was in adjusting our position a few steps further back so we weren't having to look through the criss-cross of wires and nets to see the pitch.

Keegan's unique pay deal included a slice of the gate money, which seemed only fair as he had inspired the upturn, but Cox still had a transfer kitty available, identifying this as the point of no return in trying to return to the promised land. While Beardsley had cost just £150,000 – putting him around the same mark as Varadi – Cox spent considerably more on England Under-21 left-back John Ryan and the experienced Malcolm Brown to play on the opposite flank. Brown had played 250 consecutive games at Huddersfield but then damaged an Achilles before we could even get a look at him and he spent the whole of his first season in the stands.

Clarke started the season in top form at the heart of defence but also spent lengthy spells on the sidelines and Cox identified Glenn Roeder as the man to solidify the rearguard in the push for promotion. A fee of £120,000 brought the England 'B' cap north from QPR. With Clarke injured, Steve Carney played more than 30 times in the season and Wes Saunders made way for Roeder, who had risen to prominence not least because television caught his double stepovers – what became known as 'the Roeder Shuffle' – on the 'plastic' pitch at Loftus Road in the build-up to one of the goals of the season. He was not afraid to use it, either, and an afternoon was not complete until we'd seen it at least once, accompanied by cheers and a series of wolf whistles from the crowd. It was like waiting for your favourite band to belt out their biggest hit during the encore – you knew it was coming but it was only going to come late on.

Wharton started the season in midfield but spent the second half of it at left-back, seeing off another challenge for his place as Ryan returned for only a handful of games before following the well-trodden transfer path out to Hillsborough.

In early February, the pace of the promotion charge clicked up another gear when Keegan and Beardsley shared the goals in a memorable 4-2 win at Portsmouth's Fratton Park, one of the stand-out performances in the Arthur Cox years. Though Pompey were sitting around tenth place in the table, they had quality in their ranks in the shape of midfielder Kevin Dillon and striker Mark Hateley, who would soon be wearing the shirt of AC Milan and England. They were also noted as a physical team but had no answer to the visitors' attacking trio that afternoon. Beardsley showed his full repertoire, famously putting two defenders on their backsides on the sandy pitch as he walked the ball into the net for the first of his pair. It became a key point in the battle to get out of the division at the sixth time of asking.

We were still celebrating the rise of 'Crown Prince Peter' when, a couple of days later, 'King Kev' announced it would be his final season before retirement. 'I've won a lot of things in the game but I can honestly say I've never wanted anything more than to leave Newcastle United knowing they are looking forward to the First Division football their marvellous supporters deserve,' he said in characteristically passionate fashion. The stakes to secure a promotion place had just gone up another notch.

The local media started to believe promotion was in the bag after completing a double over Manchester City in front of a Maine Road crowd of more than 41,000, a win which preceded a potential powderkeg game against top-of-the-table Chelsea. There were the usual rumours of trouble ahead, with legions of Blues fans heading this way. It also meant another early start to matchday for those of us trying to avoid them. It was McDermott – supplied by a cheeky backheel from his big mate – and the volatile David Speedie, formerly of Darlington, who got the goals for their respective teams as the points were shared. It may have been points dropped at home against a close rival but, as it came during a nine-game unbeaten run, adding another one to the total helped to tighten a grip on third place. We'd hoped for better but, by now, we also knew that it didn't really matter, so long as we slipped no lower.

Keegan, Beardsley and Waddle all scored in a big Easter win over Carlisle and promotion was confirmed with a victory over Derby when they did it again. Our usual group on the terrace was joined by a mate making his first matchday trip and he couldn't have picked a better introduction, though some other lads who knew he was actually a Leeds fan in disguise made our bus journey home more uncomfortable than the destruction of Derby. He'd already had to put up with us having a go at him for being the spitting image of a kid in a Boro scarf on the cover of the programme the previous season and, unsurprisingly, he stayed away in future.

Then came the final league game against Brighton when the holy trinity starred again. Strangely, as I'd barely missed a game in two years and had been a regular through each of the Second Division seasons before that, I made a conscious decision not to go for this one. It was the nervous, emotional gesture of a teenager trying to maintain memories of those years and hold it all together with a return to the First Division already in the bag. Still, I've seen the three goals over and over again – a Keegan tap-in, a Waddle header and a collectors' item from Beardsley featuring a sliding tackle and a delicious chip over man-mountain goalkeeper Joe Corrigan. I met Joe a few times in later years, through a friend who was also a golfing pal of the England international, and he still frightened the life out of me in retirement, which my mate thought was very funny. At least I could afford a smile of my own at the thought of that Beardsley finish. 'One of the best goals I've ever seen,' said Keegan and I agreed … but I didn't mention it to Joe.

Chelsea and Sheffield Wednesday were clear in the top two places but the Magpies reached the finish line ten points in front of fourth-placed City and surprise package Grimsby, for whom Nigel Batch always seemed to reserve his best goalkeeping form for games against us (see also Charlton's lanky Nicky Johns, who felt like he played us on his own more than once). But, after six long years working at an unforgiving coalface in the darkness, the cage was at last travelling upwards, back towards our loved ones. We could all finally blink into the light and breathe again.

Another 36,000 returned for the 'Auf Wiedersehen Kev' game and this time I had to be part of it, standing in the usual spot for a 2-2 draw with Liverpool which was billed as a testimonial for Kevin, though it was more a party for all of us, with the club having the added bonus of a game against the country's most successful team. 'We'll take more care of you, Craig Johnston,' we sang to the man in red that the media saw as Keegan's potential replacement in the United team before our hero theatrically disappeared into the night sky in a helicopter from the centre of the pitch. He had attempted to pass the No.7 shirt to his successor, Beardsley, the man he knew as 'Pedro', but legend has it that it never actually got that far.

Only one man could get away with such a dramatic finale. But now he'd flown and handed over the baton. He was gone, job done. We didn't know then, of course, was that he was only just getting started.

Chapter Nine

Today Went By So Fast

THE END of a journey provides time for reflection. The wilderness years still had their high spots (all things being relative), we still found our favourites and we still have warm memories around the team's struggles for identity and promotion. A huge number of players crossed our paths, some fleetingly, some making an impression on young minds, some even playing a prominent part in the seasons which followed back in the big time. One or two are still around.

After reliving those moments of being a fledgling fan, I have compiled a series of team selections, as all youngsters do, from the period following relegation in 1978 up to that memorable promotion at the end of the Keegan era (part one).

In line with the times, these teams feature four defenders (numbers 2,3,5,6), four in midfield (4,7,8,11) and two up front (9,10), though the Saviours XI obviously has to retain an unmatched attacking trinity.

Wish I'd seen them in their day XI

Chosen from the men I'd heard so much about from the decades before I was born or who disappeared before I was old enough to see them for real on matchday.

Simpson went on long enough to win a European title with Celtic, while Veitch is the grand old man of the team, one of the stars of the earliest successes on Tyneside and a true cultural all-rounder.

Eastham famously helped to change the system which tied players to their clubs even when they wanted to leave, taking United to court to obtain a transfer. He was also part of England's 1966 World Cup squad.

Green is listed in many greatest XIs selected by contemporaries, despite injury ending his career after fewer than 40 appearances for the club. Brennan and McNamee would frighten any attack individually, let alone as a pair.

1 Ronnie Simpson
2 Colin Veitch
3 Alf McMichael
4 George Eastham
5 Frank Brennan
6 John McNamee
7 Tony Green
8 Ivor Allchurch
9 Jackie Milburn
10 Len White
11 Bobby Mitchell

I wish I'd seen more XI

A selection of players I saw in my earliest visits to St James' Park but not as much as the men who followed. Many were into the final part of their careers, with only Kennedy finding greener grass on the other side of the fence in the long term.

Although Pat Howard was the main central defender in the first games I attended, I struggled to find a defensive pair that I had seen at work but still wanted to watch more frequently. A spare full-back, though, allows me to keep Craig on the right and move Nattrass into the middle, where he settled well later in his career after a switch to Boro.

The Macdonald-Tudor link up front was the toast of the Leazes End and, while I witnessed a lot of the 'second' Hibbitt after his return from a time at Birmingham, it is the Mark One version picked here, providing the ammunition for the goalscorers.

1 Mick Mahoney
2 David Craig
3 Alan Kennedy
4 Tommy Craig
5 John Blackley
6 Irving Nattrass
7 Stewart Barrowclough
8 Micky Burns
9 Malcolm Macdonald
10 John Tudor
11 Terry Hibbitt

Growing up in the wilderness XI

Selected mainly from those born locally in the mid-to-late 60s who joined the club when it was at a low ebb but turned professional around 1983 just as the promise of good times returned. Several inclusions were part of the FA Youth Cup-winning team in 1985 and one went on to a stellar career in England, Italy and Scotland.

Goalkeeper Kelly and central defender Scott gave lengthy service to United, while Carver's contribution was more as coach and then manager after injury ended his playing career early. Tinnion and Bogie moved on as young men but were then stalwarts at Bristol City and Port Vale, respectively, and

Allon was a noted goalscorer with Hartlepool before his big-time move to Chelsea.

Jackson, signed from Meadowbank Thistle as one for the future, joined Gascoigne as the group's other international player, capped by Scotland during later spells with Hibernian and Dundee United.

1 Gary Kelly
2 John Carver
3 Brian Tinnion
4 Ian Bogie
5 Kevin Scott
6 Jeff Wrightson
7 Paul Stephenson
8 Paul Gascoigne
9 Joe Allon
10 Darren Jackson
11 Scott Sloan

The discarded XI

A series of changes in management and players failing to fully find their feet in fleeting appearances are strong signs that a club is struggling to follow a definitive plan. In the relegation year, for instance, 35 players saw first-team action, a huge rise on the number used in qualifying for Europe just a season earlier. Young players were called up into a struggling team during the wilderness years and many would not be given another chance.

None of this line-up had a long spell in the senior squad at United and fewer than half carved out a full-time football career elsewhere. The group has just 30 Newcastle appearances between them, a third accounted for in Scott's one run in the team. There are others who missed this cut, too, including Keith Mulgrove (1 game) and Chris Withe (2), while Derek Bell (3) was forced into retirement by injury as a teenager. David MacLean (9) did add a few hundred more in the Football League with Darlington.

For context, a similar list covering the few years up to 1978, when United reached two Wembley finals, would feature goalkeepers Tony Bell (1 game), Eddie Edgar (1) and Roger Jones (5), plus David Crosson (5) and Dennis Laughton (7), while a sweep of the years immediately after the wilderness period would include Rob McKinnon (1), Tony Nesbit (4), Jeff Wrightson (4) and Anthony Lormor (8).

1 Keith Baldwin (0 appearances)
2 Martin Gorry (1 appearance)
3 Mel Owens (1 appearance)
4 Jamie Scott (10 appearances)
5 Tony Smith (2 appearances)
6 Phil Leaver (1 appearance)
7 Brian Ferguson (5 appearances)
8 Kevin Pugh (1 appearance)
9 Andrew Parkinson (3 appearances)
10 Alan Guy (4 appearances)
11 Peter Manners (2 appearances)

Wilderness part one XI

My pick from the first four seasons spent aimlessly in the middle reaches of the Second Division, where I started my life as diehard matchday fan. There are still some favourites and some undoubted quality, despite the surroundings. Looking at the list now, although they did not all play in the same team during their time at the club, you could be forgiven for thinking the team could have done more.

It can be argued that the way Carney and Shoulder adjusted to the professional game showed the standard not only of the former non-league duo but also of the Second Division at the time. Withe and Varadi were astute signings in an era not noted for such successful work in the open market. The latter gives up the No.9 jersey to Withe in my selection purely on account of the physical presence typically associated with wearing the centre-forward shirt at that time.

1 Kevin Carr
2 Peter Kelly
3 Kenny Wharton
4 John Trewick
5 Steve Carney
6 John Blackley
7 Nigel Walker
8 Alan Shoulder
9 Peter Withe
10 Imre Varadi
11 Terry Hibbitt

Best of the saviours XI

Inspired by the arrival of Keegan, the atmosphere changed in the summer of 1982, arguably never to be the same again. The forward line picks itself from the final two years of Keegan's playing career. His link with Waddle and Beardsley would have graced any United team through time and, after the dark days which went before them, finally brought Tyneside alive again.

Half of the team cost nothing or close to it, with the rest signed for under £200,000 a man. Even in the early 80s, this was very good business by manager Arthur Cox. Jeff Clarke made an immediate impact but he misses out to Carney here on the grounds that a) Steve is a personal favourite, and b) the former electrician played twice as many games in the promotion season. Perhaps not coincidentally, every single member of this team was also a leader in his own way.

1 Kevin Carr
2 John Anderson
3 Kenny Wharton
4 David McCreery
5 Steve Carney
6 Glenn Roeder
7 Kevin Keegan
8 Peter Beardsley
9 Chris Waddle
10 Terry McDermott
11 Neil McDonald

Appendix

Newcastle United 1978–84 – for the record

1978-79 – Second Division 8th

Pld 42	W 17	D 8	L 17	F 51	A 55	Pts 42
Promoted: Crystal Palace, Brighton, Stoke						
FA Cup 4th round				**League Cup** 2nd round		

1979-80 – Second Division 9th

Pld 42	W 15	D 14	L 13	F 53	A 49	Pts 44
Promoted: Leicester, Sunderland, Birmingham						
FA Cup 3rd round				**League Cup** 2nd round		

1980-81 – Second Division 11th

Pld 42	W 14	D 14	L 14	F 30	A 45	Pts 42
Promoted: West Ham, Notts County, Swansea						
FA Cup 5th round				**League Cup** 2nd round		

1981-82 – Second Division 9th

Pld 42	W 18	D 8	L 16	F 52	A 50	Pts 62*
Promoted: Luton, Watford, Norwich						
FA Cup 4th round				**League Cup** 2nd round		

*three points for a win from 1981-82

1982-83 – Second Division 5th

Pld 42	W 18	D 13	L 11	F 75	A 53	Pts 67
Promoted: QPR, Wolves, Leicester						
FA Cup 3rd round				**League Cup** 2nd round		

1983-84 – Second Division 3rd

Pld 42	W 24	D 8	L 10	F 85	A 53	Pts 80
Promoted: Chelsea, Sheffield Wednesday, Newcastle						
FA Cup 4th round				**League Cup** 2nd round		

Acknowledgements

Thank you to Paul, Duncan, Ian and the team at Pitch Publishing for their encouragement and professionalism. I am deeply grateful for the permission granted by the writers to use lyrics from *Whatever Happened To the Likely Lads* and *Auf Wiedersehen Pet* theme tunes in these pages. Thank you for that gesture and also for the memories.

'Breakin' Away' – lyrics by David Mackay and Ian La Frenais

'That's Living Alright' – lyrics by David Mackay and Ken Ashby

'Whatever Happened To You' – lyrics by Mike Hugg and Ian La Frenais

Thanks to my former colleague, Paul Jones, for his keen eye in the editing of a first proof.

And a massive thank you to Ian La Frenais for the 'best wishes' note. You have no idea how much those words meant as my book started to take shape.

Selected Bibliography

Clark, Frank *Black & White and Red All Over* (Bowles Clark, 2018)

Freddi, Cris *England Football Fact Book* (Guinness Publishing, 1991)

Galeano, Eduardo *Football in Sun and Shadow* (Penguin Random House, 2013)

Haigh, Gavin *Black-and-white Stripes: The Greatest Collection of Newcastle United Matchworn Shirts* (Conker Editions Ltd, 2022)

Inglis, Simon *Football Grounds of England and Wales* (Willow Books, 1984)

Joannou, Paul *Newcastle United: A Complete Record* (Breedon Books Sport, 1986)

Joannou, Paul *The Black & White Alphabet* (Polar Print Group, 1996)

Joannou, Paul *United: The First 100 Years* (Polar Print Group Ltd, 1995)

Keegan, Kevin *Keegan: My Life in Football* (Macmillan, 2018)

Kurt, Richard & Nikeas, Chris *The Red Army Years: Manchester United in the 1970s* (Headline Book Publishing, 1997)

Macdonald, Malcolm *Never Afraid to Miss* (Cassell Ltd, 1980)

McDermott, Terry *Terry Mac: Living for the Moment* (Sport Media, 2018)

Moncur, Bob *United We Stand* (Pelham Books, 1971)

Motson, John *Match of the Day* (BBC Books, 1992)

Moynihan, John *The Soccer Syndrome* (Simon & Schuster, 1989)

Potter, David *Newcastle United: The Great Days 1904-1911* (Pitch Publishing, 2022)

Robson, Bobby *Farewell But Not Goodbye* (Hodder & Stoughton, 2005)

Thomas, Dave *Guiding Me Home and Away* (Hornet Books, 2019)

Tully Paul, *Evening Chronicle All-Time Greats* (Newcastle Evening Chronicle)

Wells, Andy *Get Shirty: The Rise and Fall of Admiral Sportswear* (Conker Editions Ltd, 2022)

Rothman's Football Yearbooks (Queen Anne Press)

Newcastle United programmes

Evening Chronicle and *Sunday Sun (DC Thomson)*